BENEATH ARCHERS TREE

H K NICHOLSON

authorHOUSE®

AuthorHouse™
1663 Liberty Drive
Bloomington, IN 47403
www.authorhouse.com
Phone: 1-800-839-8640

First published by AuthorHouse 9/15/2010

ISBN: 978-1-4520-4650-1 (hc)
ISBN: 978-1-4520-4651-8 (sc)
ISBN: 978-1-4520-4652-5 (e)

Library of Congress Control Number: 2010911303

Printed in the United States of America

This book is printed on acid-free paper.

Special Thanks to
Dallas and Eletha Cole
And Family

This book is dedicated to
Mentors, Teachers and Heroes

TO: _____

_____

FROM: _____

Today, Ryan was a divorced man in his forties, looking over what remained of his past, now scattered in the dust on the floor of the old barn. There was the broken remains of a B.B. gun. It was his first. He was given the gun on his eighth birthday, along with instructions on how to use it safely. His grandmother had asked him not to shoot any animals, this included his little brother Shawn, Ryan promised. He never did shoot his brother, even though he was tempted at times.

The other end of that promise lasted four days, until Sunday after church. Ryan rushed home, changed his clothes, grabbed his gun, and headed for his grandmother's house. Standing in her front yard, he looked up into one of the three big cottonwood trees. He could hear the birds, but couldn't see them among leafs. Walking around the base of the tree he stared into the foliage until he saw the small silhouette of a bird. Raising the gun, he aimed, and then he pulled the trigger. Ryan watched the B.B. slowly arc on its way to its target. Then he heard a hollow thump. The bird fell from the branch and hit hard on the tin roof of the patio. It spun and thumped around on the corrugated metal. Ryan could hear its claws and wings scratch and beat against the roof. Finally, the bird fell at his feet, it was an English sparrow. Ryan picked it up. There was no hole nor blood that he could see at first, but then a bright crimson bead slowly started to appear on top of its head and ran down onto Ryan's fingers. Ryan then remembered something that Reverend Richards had said during his sermon that day; something about God knowing when the sparrow falls. Ryan panicked. He thought what should I do? God knows! What was going to happen?

Ryan waited, no lightning, no thunder, nothing happened; maybe it just didn't matter anyway? Maybe, just maybe knowing God knew, was enough. Then he made a deal with God, saying, "God, if you don't want me to shoot anymore birds, then don't let me hit anymore of them." This was Ryan's first negotiation with God. This verbal contract gave God control over the shot, leaving Ryan with a clear conscious. Soon he was shooting every bird he saw. This was killing just for fun.

His grandmother again pleaded with Ryan, "Why shoot these birds? If you're not going to eat them, why kill them?"

Ryan was deaf to her words; and besides, God was a willing participant. It would be five years before he would understand her words. Only then it was with the help of a few responsible hunters, and one that was totally irresponsible. These hunters traded at the station. The most responsible was Sam Bird, and the most irresponsible was Charlie Whitehorse. They were extreme opposites. All other hunters fell somewhere in between these two, but sadly; all hunters are judged by only the one example, the bad example.

Samuel Bird was the hunter who only a few lucky hunters would ever come in contact with. Even these lucky few would often leave somewhat bewildered and wondering if he was serious, or just pulling their legs, or perhaps he was just plain crazy - crazy because who in his right mind went hunting for bear with a slingshot? Those who took the time to learn more about Sam and not to just merely pass him off as just another crazy Indian, found an old spirit. They also learned not only that he was quite sane but he knew more about hunting and grandmother earth as he called it than anybody in the area. Then there was an even smaller group, the ones who really knew Sam, truly knew him. He was a teacher, a teacher revealing the ways of nature, and of the underlying hidden nature in man. The nature that is hidden under the guises and trappings we call civilized man. Sam knew the darkness and the light. When asked a question, he often would answer with a story that was seasoned with his incredible sense of humor. Frequently the listener left, wondering if his question had been answered. Sometimes they would walk away, only to get a few yards, stop, and then turn back around to Sam and say, "Now I get it." Sam was like all great teachers. He was not there to give them the answers but to point them toward the direction in which the answers could be found. Ryan was to become one of Sam's students. Like all of his memories this day, they became fresh in his mind, and refreshing to his soul. He remembered the first day he discovered just how special Sam really was.

Ryan had finished filling a one-gallon gas can for old man Clark and was waiting to be paid. A long moment passed, then Mr. Clark became angry, demanding that Ryan check the oil, the air pressure in the tires and the water in the radiator and battery. Ryan didn't say anything, but just did what he was told. Mr. Clark was watching Ryan's every move and reminding Ryan what the tire pressure of each tire should be. After he had finished, Ryan stood there again waiting for payment. Clark's face became bright red to match his already red nose, and then he thrust his clenched

CONTENTS

1. A SHORT RIDE DOWN A LONG ROAD 1

2. THINGS THAT GO BUMP IN A BARREL............................ 21

3. STAINED-GLASS SKY 39

4. MAGIC AND MENDED WINGS.................................... 55

5. FOR THE LOVE OF GRACE, A MOCKINGBIRD SANG....... 69

6. BENEATH ARCHERS TREE... 83

7. BONES AND BRIGHT PLACES: THE DAY HE KILLED
   GRANNY... 111

8. SPIRIT DANCE... 131

9. RINGS RISING 171

CHAPTER ONE

A SHORT RIDE DOWN A LONG ROAD

It was four-thirty in the afternoon. The check list was complete everything was accounted for and loaded into the bed of the truck. Soon Ryan would be on the road. He would travel the eighty-two miles in an hour and a half to reach the ranch, but a lifetime would pass before he was through. Ryan had waited for this day with all the anticipation of a child counting down the days before Christmas. Maybe tomorrow there would be a present under a tree?

It had been many years since Ryan had made this trip and memories made the time pass quickly. Soon he was standing in front of the cable blocking the dirt road that lead into the ranch. Ryan took the lock in his hand. It felt warm from the sun and was inviting to the touch. Turning it up he inserted the key and twisted it. The master lock opened as easily as it had the first day at the service station and for the thirty-plus years since. For twenty years it was the lone sentry hanging from this rusty post. Ryan looked in the dust for signs of trespassers. Footprints showed that someone had crossed the cable. When he reached the barn he saw more evidence. Boxes were open and things appeared to be missing and others items lay scattered about on the dirt floor of the barn. Ryan's feelings went through the whole emotional scale starting with rage and ending a sickening numbness. He sat down at the old picnic table that once had been in his grandmother's patio. As he sat looking at what was left, the memories attached to these things started to gather at his feet like leaves at the foot of a great tree.

The table where he now sat was taken into his grandmother's small cottage during the holidays, where a tablecloth was laid over it to become the kids' table. In the summer time, it stayed on the patio for the large family get togethers. When Ryan's great- uncle Walter and his family showed up, a gathering was guaranteed. Uncle Walter always brought some sort of wild game with him, usually wild pig or bear meat. After-dinner stories of the hunt became Ryan's dessert. He listened to every word and savored each as much as he had the meal. Permanently stored in his head, where nothing else seemed to stick, these stories made him want to become a hunter when he grew up.

When these random family gatherings happened there was lots of work to do. Chickens or rabbits had to be butchered and prepared for meals. Ryan helped with the killing. He learned early that things die so others can live. It became a natural, if not easy thing to do. After the killing came, the responsibility of cleaning and plucking, he also had to lend a hand with this unpleasant chore. Only that which was inedible would be discarded. Nothing was wasted, this was Grandma's rules. This was the dirty work it was nothing like Uncle Walter's stories of hunting and stalking big game.

Grandmother's house was the gravitational pull that held the family together. It was a very special place. The house itself wasn't planned. It was as though it had evolved from a porch attached to a trailer house. What was a screened-in porch, which was comfortable in the summer, would become too cold in the winter, so it was closed in to become a room. Then in the summer, a new screened in porch was added on, and when winter came again the process was repeated.

All the material came from scraps left over from construction jobs that Ryan's grandfather, Howard, had brought home from work. One day the trailer house burned down to the ground, leaving only the closed in porches standing. Soon where the trailer once stood, a small bedroom was added. The house was almost complete by the time Ryan was born. A garage was added, then a covered patio. Next, minnow tanks and pigeon and pheasant pens were built. Later in life, Ryan would remember all the great times he had there, where sometimes thirty or more relatives congregated. He was amazed that so many people could be in such a small place at one time. It was as if this vine-covered patchwork cottage had wrapped its arms around itself and had given all who had gathered there a hug. How had it held so much family, so much love?

In those early years, Ryan's father had a problem with authority and drink. This meant unemployment and time spent in jail. It didn't mean that Mr. Olson was lazy or that he was unskilled. The problem was that there were lots of places for him to work with the skills he had. One week, he might work as a mechanic, and the next week he might help build a hospital but sometimes a drink was more important. When times were slow and work was hard to find, Mr. Olson would earn enough money to get by, by junking cars or raising night crawlers and trapping minnows to sell for fishing bait at bait stores. This became a family project with everybody involved. When it was time to gather the minnows and re-bait the traps, they would have wonderful picnics along the creeks and streams where the traps were set.

Then, when Ryan was four, his brother Shawn came along, and that same year a new law was passed prohibiting the sale of shiner minnows in California- another mouth to feed and one less way to make a little money. Things were tough and getting tougher for Ryan's parents, but like most children on the west side of town, Ryan didn't know what the meaning of being poor was. There were times when dinner was whatever was in the pens or what could be caught from the river, which meant many hours were spent along it's banks. This was a wonderful time to be alive. Ryan learned to love the river and was taught to respect its power and its spirit. He thought that as long as the river ran, a person could never starve. In the innocence of his youth he believed that the river would never change, it would always remain clean and safe for any river-wise kid.

One evening, Ryan's mother packed a bag and left his father. For the next year, she would move many times to hide from his father. Ryan was six years old when this happen, and because his birthday fell in January, he had just started school. Teachers knew there was a problem. Ryan seemed slow to comprehend, and he couldn't read at all. Just when a teacher was about to get a handle on his problem, it was time to move again, this time to a small cottage in an alley in the airport district. One afternoon, Ryan walked to the end of the alley where the road began, as if he had been drawn for some unknown reason. Then his father passed by in a car. Ryan ran after the car yelling for his father to stop, but Ryan's calls were unheard and the car continued. Ryan walked forlornly back into the alley. Tears streaked down his cheeks. He missed his father and his grandparents. His mind was full of anger, and the sound of his shouts were still echoing in his head that he didn't hear the car back up to the alley or hear his father calling him. Turning, Ryan saw his dad standing there next to the car. He was dressed in a white tee-shirt and blue jeans with the cuffs of his pants rolled. Ryan ran and jumped into his father's arms. To Ryan his dad was the tallest, strongest man in the world, instead of the five-foot-five man that he really was. Now many years later, Ryan could still almost feel that hug and see his dad standing there, young and strong.

Within six months, the family was whole again, but this time they moved into a house of their own just four houses down the street from Grandmother's. Mr. Olson had given up drinking; now his family came first. Two years later, Mr. Olson had saved enough money to buy an old service- station, Don's Hancock was born, it stood at the corner of Paradise Road and Vernon Avenue. Ryan's grandfather, Howard Stout, had retired and would be helping out by opening up the station in the mornings. After school, Ryan would work the gas pumps. He was now nine years old, and his father figured, since Ryan was more than a little slow in school, he could learn a few skills that might help him earn a living when he grew up. Ryan would wait on customers and do his homework each afternoon behind the counter. Mr. Olson was right, Ryan would learn many life skills here.

Soon Mr. Olson had eight businesses that he operated from the gas station, and now there wasn't any time for him to go fishing or hunting. So Mr. Olson would pay one of his employees to take Ryan to do these things. Ivan Hudson would take Ryan deer hunting and fishing, and Bruce Hamby would take him dove hunting. Ben Hays, their barber would take him to the delta to hunt for raccoons or to the Sierras for bear. They didn't have much luck, but it sure was lots fun chasing them. It was during this time that the family bought a piece of property in the Sierras, above the town of Mountain Ranch, off the Jesus Maria Road in Calaveras County, where Ryan now sat.

fist in Ryan's direction. Ryan ducked. No blow landed, but Clark's arm remained extended past Ryan's head. There at the end of his arm, the fist remained. Only a single digit protruded-Clark's index finger pointing to the "full service sign."

"What about the brake fluid?" Clark demanded.

Ryan stuttered out a reply, "I, I, I didn't think."

"That's the whole problem! People like you don't, or can't think. All you kids are the same, lazy and stupid, oh hell!"

By the time Clark finished, everything wrong with the human race was Ryan's fault. Ryan stood there unblinking. He had been taught that the customer was always right. Clark's last words stung the most. Clark reached into his pocket, pulled out his folding knife, exposed its blade and said, "Idiots like you should be neutered so you can't reproduce." This was a lot nicer and shorter than what Clark had actually said. The thought of having that part of his anatomy removed shook Ryan out of his blank stare and into a defensive mode. Clark realized he had gone too far and put his knife back into his pocket. When his hand came back out of his pocket, there was a quarter in it. He tossed it to Ryan, telling him to keep the change for the twenty-one cents he owed for the gas, a four-cent tip. Then Clark climbed back into his truck, and drove off into the darkness.

Ryan stood there shaking with anger. He wondered whether he should have hit the old man or if he did the right thing? Ryan's shoulders rounded and slumped forward; he stared at the ground by his feet. The little confidence he had gained was now shattered, he felt vulnerable and alone. His father and grandfather were working inside; unaware of what had just happened. Suddenly, somebody cleared their throat.

Startling Ryan from his deep thoughts, he turned around to see Sam standing next to the outside pumps. Sam had a way of showing up out of nowhere. He had heard and seen everything that had just taken place. Sam had pulled his truck into the darker outside isle at the same time that Clark had pulled into the well lit center isle. Sam was pumping his own gas when the row began. He stopped pumping and prepared to intervene, if he had to, but let Ryan take care of Clark on his own. It looked to Sam as though Ryan had handled it quite well. Ryan looked like a whipped pup, and Sam told him so, adding that he hadn't seen Ryan look like this since Ryan was in the special-reading class at the Lincoln Elementary School.

"What did you mean, at the Lincoln school, and when did you see me there?" asked Ryan. He was a little embarrassed, self-conscious that Sam or anyone else might know that he was in the "special class," and that embarrassment showed on Ryan's face.

Sam could see this and said to Ryan, "That's okay; I had a problem reading when I was your age. How old are you anyway?"

"Eleven," answered Ryan.

"Eleven, Eleven! My God, boy, I thought you were in your teens! You're big enough to go bear hunting with a willow switch." A smile crossed Ryan's face. "How tall are you, and what's your weight anyway?" asked Sam. The smile left as quickly as it had come. This was another area in Ryan's life in which he was teased and chided by the other kids. "Boy, kid! I'm not doing too good a job at trying to cheer you up am I? You see, I had a hell of a time learning to read. It wasn't until I was in my twenties that I learned how," said Sam. Ryan seemed to relax now.

Answering the first question, Ryan said, "Five foot nine and two hundred seven pounds." Ryan had tried to insulate himself from those who berated him, calling him "stupid" and "lazy" and "fat." He did this by trying to grow bigger and stronger than anyone in his school. Since he was held back a year, he had a year's growth on the rest of his class, but this still couldn't explain Ryan's growth in size and strength. it was as if Ryan had willed this change. He was determined to be good at something.

He chose sports and excelled, causing him to gain a small portion of self-esteem, but even this was, at times, not enough to keep the old wounds from being opened. Ryan then asked a question of his own, "How did you know that I was at Lincoln, anyway?"

"Well, I was the janitor there, and you, like everybody else, probably looked at me but never saw me. Most people think of janitors as glorified garbage men who are there only to pickup after them. But you, you were different. You picked up after yourself and after those around you also. There was something familiar about you, something special, something rare. You showed respect. Your body language said a lot about you. I had been there once, myself. While you were at recess, I would go to your desk and leave clippings out of my Outdoor Life magazine."

Ryan remembered those clippings. He had always thought that his teacher, Mrs. Cochrane had left them. Until this moment he hadn't known that it was Sam. The clippings were called, "This Happened to Me!" They were like cartoons, depicting the high adventures and mishaps of hunters and fishermen who fought against wild animals and nature's elements, sometimes to the death. This captivated his eight-year-old imagination, like the stories after dinner. It was hard at first for Ryan to read these clippings. He eventually learned to think of his eyes as a camera taking snapshots capturing each word. This kept the letters from jumping around. Now, as an eleven-year-old, Ryan learned that Sam was more than a crazy old-man who hunted bear with a slingshot. He was a true teacher.

Sam then said something that brought Ryan back to the moment. "Why didn't you thank Clark for the compliment?"

Ryan looked puzzled. "Why should I thank that drunk? What compliment did he give me? What he said and what he wanted to do to me didn't sound like any compliment. I thought about putting him on his butt." Ryan spoke before thinking, unlike his normal self, where he would have thought awhile before saying anything. Adrenalin probably was the reason for this.

"Well, kid, if you had hit old-man Clark, you probably hurt him bad, and that wouldn't be good business, now, would it? You're eleven years old and outweigh Clark by twenty pounds, and you've got two inches in height on him. Heck, you're taller even than your parents. You did right, son. There is a time to fight but only as a last resort." Ryan nodded his head. Sam waited a few seconds, and then started telling Ryan one of his stories. He started by asking Ryan if he knew the difference between good lazy and bad lazy? Ryan shrugged his shoulders, indicating that he was unsure or didn't know.

"Well I think you're the good lazy." Ryan shrugged again. "I've watched you so you can believe me you're the good type. You see there are those people who make work hard, and those who make it look easy. Just think, where we would be if it weren't for the good lazy people. Well, here's an example of what I'm talking about."

"One summer day, this good old boy was sitting on his front porch when an idea hit him. His lemonade was getting warm. He looked out into his front yard where his wife was mowing the lawn with one of those motor less push mowers. That's the only type of mowers they had back then. He then said to her, 'Babe my lemonade is getting warm. Could you be a good wife and get me some ice?' She went to the kitchen; then something else struck him, besides the thought of his warming lemonade. When he came to, it became painfully clear that something had gone terribly wrong in the kitchen. How else could you explain the frying pan lying next to him and the large knot on his head? There also was the note, it was safety pinned to his chest, equally as painful. Of course, it wouldn't have been all that painful had he been wearing a shirt at the time. Written by his loving wife, the note said that she had gone to her mother's house to calm her nerves. He could understand why she had gone. An explosion strong enough to throw a frying pan out of the kitchen, through the screen door and hit him in the head. Well, naturally would have been unnerving to a delicate lady such as his wife. He went into the house to survey the damage. To his surprise, she must have cleaned up the mess before she left. Well, the grass still needed to be mowed, so he headed back outside to finish the job. He had pushed the mower maybe about twelve feet, when another thought struck him, this was hard work. Before he could duck another idea hit him, he mounted a motor on the mower. Now, this was something great!

"After that frying pan, and all that thinking, his head hurt, so he rested a-bit. When he got up, well, he pushed that thing around the front yard like a proud father. In a way he was, because this is as close as a man gets to giving birth. He and his mower became quite an attraction, the talk of the town. Soon he was posing for pictures with his new baby. It's like this; somebody invented the wheel. Then, the wheel was attached to an axle, the axle to a cart, the cart attached to a horse. Then somebody got rid of the horse, added a motor, called it a car. Then somebody else said, 'If I put wings on this sucker, and get it going fast enough, I bet it could fly,' all to get someplace easer and faster, all to leave more time to relax, and rest. Heck, son, laziness is an oft maligned and underrated skill. Hell, it's a national resource. Where would we be without it? The real lazy ones are still working hard, because they haven't a clue as to how to make work easer, or they have just plain given up. I've watched you and your dad build things together, and your guys are the good kind of lazy." Sam's animated story, his movements, and all his facial expressions-made Ryan laugh.

"Now that you're in a better mood, I'm going to tell you something about Clark. He and I went to school together, and he was quite the ladies man and the life of the party. He never left the party. He was voted most likely to succeed, then never succeeded at much of anything. He ended up marrying one of the prettiest girls in school. The drinking and abuse became heavier, and more frequent, so his wife left him, taking their son with her. The son, now a young man, has climbed into his father's shoes and is going to prison for murdering his own wife. You see, what a parent can't put down, the child will pick up. Now the son is leaving a child to be raised by the state because old man Clark was found to be unfit to raise it.

"So, this is Clark's reason for drink today, and like every other addict, any reason is a good enough -excuse to get screwed up. It helps when you hate in others what you can no longer find in yourself, whether that be your lost youth, or opportunity or sobriety. It's easy to hate others, because you can't love yourself. Humans aren't the smartest animals on this rock. As a friend says, 'sicker cats than that got well,'" Sam paused, watching Ryan's body language. By the look on Ryan's face Sam could tell that Ryan had another question, and he was figuring out how to ask it.

Breaking the silence, Ryan asked Sam, "If you and old-man Clark went to school together then why does he look so much older than you?"

Sam started laughing. "Thanks for the complement, I think, anyway. It's not the years, it's the miles. Clark took the easy road, to be accepted by friends, and this made his life hard. It's hard to say no to that first drink, or drug, but down the road it's easier on the body if you do say no."

Another long pause. Ryan was biting his lower lip; he was deep in thought. He had a question but, again, didn't know how to ask it. "Well! There is something else bouncing around inside there. If it's a question spit it out, boy," said Sam.

"Well, well", Ryan's stammered his voice breaking a little. He cleared his throat. "Some of the others, like Charlie Whitehorse, think your crazy."

"Why?"

"You go hunting, you have some of the best dogs and you never kill any of the bears you tree. And that slingshot! Don't you know that they laugh at you?" Laughter had been one of the weapons that used to hurt Ryan, and now that he could see Sam for who he really was, Ryan was ashamed that he too had laughed.

"They're right. What man in his right mind goes hunting bear with a slingshot? But, you see, at one time I was just like the rest of them when it came to killing. Then one day things changed, and it was no longer important to kill, but I still love to run with the dogs. Occasionally, I harvest an animal, and on those occasions, I do it with respect, using the old ways. Yes, I've stopped killing bears. It's because I've killed enough bears in my lifetime. There's a time when enough is enough. The slingshot, I use it to jump a bear out of a tree, but only after it's rested a bit. I shoot it in the butt, stinging it with marbles, making it mad enough to come down out of the tree. The bear isn't hurt- just pissed. That way I can run him again. You see I haven't really lost my marbles; I just use them differently than most people."

It all started to make a little more sense to Ryan. Charlie Whitehorse, he was on the other end of the spectrum. He was the hunter, that all other hunters are judged by in the court of public opinion. Because few would ever know those hunters like Sam, and hunters like Charlie make the headlines. Charlie, being a hunting guide should have had a greater interest in preserving wildlife, after all, this was his livelihood, but such was not the case. His only concern was how much money he could make, and how many people he could impress. He didn't tolerate kids or those who criticized his way of doing things. Sam and Charlie, both with Native American ancestry, yet they were as different as night and day.

Sam, because of his ancestry, felt a deeper responsibility for his actions. Where, according to Charlie, he felt that he had the God given right to do whatever he wanted. Charlie even bragged about taking clients into Yosemite National Park. This was no idle boast, indeed he had. He even once climbed a tree to kill two orphaned bear cubs. His client offered him a little extra cash to kill the cubs without leaving any holes. He bludgeoned the cubs to death with a baseball bat he kept behind his seat in his truck. They knew the cubs were orphans because his client had just killed their mother. Today, the cubs are mounted to appear as they had in the tree. They're mounted clutching a tree trunk, close to each other, and now sit above a fire place mantle. They look down to the floor in front of the clients fireplace, to where their mother is now a rug. What a family portrait. It's one hell of a statement about what is worst in a very small percentage of hunters and is held against all hunters.

Ryan's understanding of things started to change; he started thinking more about his own actions. He would still go to the river to shoot his

B.B. and pellet guns with his friends, but as time went by his friends began to have less of an influence on him. He eventually stopped going there to shoot altogether.

Sam was a little less a mystery to Ryan than he had been before, although Ryan still didn't understand what Sam had meant by killing an animal and doing it with respect. Then one day, Sam drove into the station. When Ryan walked up to the truck, Sam had already got out of it and was standing alongside of it, looking into its bed. Ryan also looked into the pickup bed. There was a nice buck, all field dressed and ready to be cut and wrapped. Then Ryan saw something else. "What's that?" he asked, pointing to the corner of the bed at a small ice chest and a semi-clear plastic bag with what appeared to be intestines inside.

"What's it look like?"

"Guts?" asked Ryan.

"It sure is." Looking at Ryan's shocked expression, Sam laughed. He loved doing this to the youngster. "So, what do you think?"

"It's a beautiful buck." Again, Ryan pointed to the plastic bag, "But that's sick! And why did you bring them home with you anyway?"

Sam's expression became somber, almost reverent. "Remember when I told you that when I take game, I do so with respect?" Ryan nodded his head. "There was a time in my youth when I was a lot like our friend Charlie. A time when I didn't understand things, like balance in myself or in nature and my part in keeping that balance. Then, with the help of older, wiser hunters, they showed me how to find my center. This led to a greater understanding of myself and human nature. The old ones speak of visions and enlightenment. They said that by listening to nature, I would find the true nature within me, and nature would become my teacher. They also showed me how to respect the animals that one takes. When you take an animal for food, you kneel down next to it, and, in a low voice talk to it. Saying, brother thank you for giving up your body to feed me and my family. You next offer it fresh grass and give it a symbolic drink of clear water. Then you ask it to tell its ancestors that you treated it with respect, that you gave it food and water, promising not to waste anything that could be used. That way the animal's spirit is happy, and others of its kind will happily give their bodies to feed you and your kin."

"But what are you going to do with those?" Again, Ryan pointed to the bag. He was kind of afraid of the answer he might get.

"Eat them," Sam said.

"What? That's the sickest thing I've ever heard!" Ryan expression was that of total disgust and disbelief.

"Nah, I was just pulling your leg, son. I twist them together into thick twine and dry them, and use them to make ceremonial drums. I'll tan the hide and stretch it over a spruce hoop, using the dried strips of intestine to tie the skin to the hoop. Sometimes, I'll also use rawhide or sinew. The important thing is not to waste anything, if you can help it. Here's a little history for you. Cat gut was used for everything from stitching up wounds to making violin strings, or was it bows, no bows were horse hair? Anyway, they have been used for years."

"What do you do with the drums?"

"I give them away to be used in traditional ceremonies or to old friends. If you want, I'll show you one someday. How about that?"

"That would be great!" Ryan's voice reflected his excitement.

A week later, on Saturday, Ryan was helping a customer out in the aisles. Sam pulled his truck alongside the station, went into the office, and was talking to Ryan's father. When Ryan finished helping his customer and entered the office his dad asked him if he would like to take the rest of the day off and help Sam a little. Ryan nodded his head and said enthusiastically, "Yes!" "Well then, you can go with Mr. Bird, but you have to listen to him and mind what he says. Do you think you can do this?"

"Yes," replied Ryan.

Climbing into the truck, Ryan noticed a large black iron pot with a wire handle and a heavy-looking lid at his feet. Sam saw him staring at the pot, "It's a Dutch oven," he said "We're taking it to a friend of mine. Your dad and I thought that you might like to meet him." Ryan's curiosity kicked in to overdrive and he started asking who, what, where and why. Sam would only say that Ryan would find out in a little bit and to sit back and enjoy the ride.

They were drove south on Carpenter road, Ryan knew that Clark lived on this road, but they surely wouldn't be going to his house. As they approached Clark's house, Ryan became nervous, and his breathing slowed. Then he stopped breathing altogether for a moment. Sam was watching Ryan out of the corner of his eye and could clearly see Ryan's distress. When they got to Clark's driveway, Sam put on his turn signal as though he were going to turn in, but then he turned off the signal and continued south.

"What the heck was that, and where are we going?" Ryan now demanded an answer, but Sam couldn't hear anything, he was laughing too hard. Ryan crossed his arms and waited for Sam to stop laughing then repeated his question, this time in a less demanding tone.

Sam apologized and said, "We're going to Mr. Jordan's. He lives out off of Monte Vista Avenue in an area called Sand Hill by the locals or also known as Monterey Track."

This community was made up of mostly black folks. They were very independent people who wanted only to be left alone. Sam explained his connection to these people, "Mr. Jordan was my first boss when I became a city school janitor. We became friends and both of us enjoyed hunting and fishing. We spent many hours talking, telling hunting stories and talking about the hunters we had known. Mr. Jordan's smart, he spent his breaks and lunches in the school library, reading. He helped me get over my resistance to learn about our shared Native American Indian heritage. There was a time in my life when I was torn between cultures, and was an out-of-balance spirit. Jordan himself was a descendant of the buffalo soldiers. They were the black cavalry men who were sent out west to help subdue the hostile tribes. These men knew prejudice and persecution first hand. They found that they had more in common with those they had came to hold down than they did with the people that sent them. Many of these solders had taken Native American wives, and Mr. Jordan's Grandfather and Grandmother were offspring of two of these unions."

"It was a slow process. Mr. Jordan was subtle, showing me a little bit of the culture connecting us to a common ancestor. He helped teach me responsibility for my actions, our responsibility to preserve and protect the sport we both loved for future hunters, and to educate other hunters, even hunters like Charlie. Then again, some people just don't catch on very fast, or at all, for that matter."

What Sam had learned, he was now obligated to teach Ryan, only Ryan didn't know this. He was just along for the ride, as far as he knew, and to give Sam a hand with something.

Twenty-five minutes had passed since they left the gas station. Sam was preparing to turn onto a road that Ryan had never been down, to a place he had never been. Ryan looked around at the homes; they reminded him of those where Ivan Hudson lived in River Dale Track back at Carpenter Bridge. Somewhere between Monte Vista and West Main lay Sand Hill also known as Monterey Track, Sam parked along a wood fence. When leaving the truck, he asked Ryan to bring the Dutch oven with him. Before they reached the door of the house, a dog inside barked, announcing their presence. A voice called out to them, "Who's there."

Sam called back, saying, "Hey kid, it's me."

"Pup is that you?" the voice reflected the recognition that a welcome friend was at the door. "Come in, the doors open. Come on, it's been a while, and it's good not to see you."

What a strange greeting, thought Ryan. Upon entering the house, the air was heavy and humid from the swamp cooler. Heavy drapes darkened the room. The red-and-white cane made the greeting make a little more sense, Mr. Jordan was blind. He had lost his vision and a leg to diabetes.

Sam took the oven from Ryan and then, introducing Ryan to the old man, he said "Ryan here is Don's boy." Then he excused himself, saying, "I'll just put this on the stove. You'll have to guess what's in the pot."

"Well, it's a pleasure to meet you, young squire. Your father is well thought of in these parts. He has always been fair and even with the folks around here. He's given folks here credit and helped lots of people here during hard times. Sam's told me a lot about you."

Ryan thanked Mr. Jordan for the compliment.

The old man began removing things from the top of the table, small stacks of papers and envelopes. Ryan started to help him. Mr. Jordan stopped Ryan and thanked him, then added, "Son, sit down and relax. My granddaughter came by here the other day and organized my mail." He laughed and said, "Heck, there are times we sort it by weighing it on the bathroom scale to decide which pile gets priority. The bills with the most ink weigh more, you know." Then he acted like he was going to drop the stack into the waste paper basket, letting out another hearty laugh. After the table was cleared, the old man went about setting three place settings on it, all the while he was doing this, he was talking to Sam. Sam hadn't said a word since the introduction but went straight to the stove, lit it, and began heating what was in the pot. Ryan listened while the old man started describing what was in the pot. The meal was already cooked and only needed reheating.

"I'm glad that you're using that Old Dutch oven instead of that new Teflon one you brought last time." As each ingredient warmed and released it's essence into the steam, the old man announced its arrival, "Good, garlic and Stockton reds" (a sweet onion grown in Stockton California, almost sweet enough to eat like an apple.) "Bay leaves, ooh! What a meal! There, is that a venison roast in that big black pot of yours?" Sam smiled, "I just heard you smile; there is a haunch of venison in there. Sam, you lucky dog; how'd you get so lucky? Did you hit it with that old Dodge of yours?"

Sam laughed. "No, this is prime road kill, hit by a Cadillac. Heck, the sun had it half cooked when I came across it. It may have a little pea gravel and road base in it, but an old bird like you needs a little gravel in his craw to help with the digestion." Both men laughed, Ryan laughed along with them, but his face showed that he wasn't sure that Sam was really just joking, especially after seeing the bag of intestines just days before.

Sam placed the oven in the middle of the table, and he served up a large portion into each plate. Mr. Jordan and Sam had savored a few bites when the old man said, "Pup, what's wrong with the young squire? Did I forget his fork and spoon?"

"Nope, it's all there, but by the look on his face, he's never had road kill before." Both men started laughing hard. They laughed so hard that tears streamed down their cheeks.

Mr. Jordan was the first to stop and said to Ryan, "Son, do you think that Sam or I would be eating this if were old road kill, its fresh road kill." Then he winked, and smiled. "Your feet are under my table, and your plate is full. Now eat up, or there will be no dessert."

Ryan started eating. "This is great!"

"Yeah, fresh road kill is a lot tastier than old," quipped Sam. Ryan shot a confused look at Sam. "Nah, I shot this buck near Early Intake over by Cherry Valley, when I was looking for bear sign. You know, the buck that you saw in the back of my pickup last week, this is it."

This was the beginning of the story telling session. The first story was about the deer that was the center of this meal. The spell of the storytellers was being spun, to hang in the ether of the evening. The only pause was when Mr. Jordan reached over to the window ledge to retrieve a candle and a box of wooden matches. Opening the box and lighting a match, he held the lit match to the wick of the candle as easily as a any sighted man.

Using the break in conversation Ryan asked Mr. Jordan, "Do you still hunt?"

"Heck, I hunt more now than I ever did. Every time one of my kids or grandkids come over, I have to hunt where they have misplaced all my stuff. Do ya think somebody's going to take me to the woods and give me a gun?" Then he started to laugh and swing his arms around as if he were aiming a rifle. Everyone was now laughing.

Ryan realized how dumb his question sounded and became embarrassed, then he started to stammer through an apology. "I didn't think," "well you know," "I watched you move around in the house, and you knew it was getting dark, and you lit the candle so easily."

Mr. Jordan said to Ryan, "Don't be embarrassed; those were all good observations. Your question was based on what you saw. In this house, I've memorized where everything is." The old man paused. "Even a blind man who has never seen the Son knows from which direction he shines. But it's still not the best idea to hand him a loaded gun and set him out in the woods. I now rely on family and friends to take me to the river or over to the aqueduct to see if I can still catch old Mr. Whiskers (cat fish)." Later Ryan would ponder what Mr. Jordan's meant about the sun and the direction he shines?

The stories began to flow again. Soon the air was painted with all the sights and sounds of past times and better times. Too soon it was time to leave.

Sam and Ryan were on the road again. When they came to Clark's place, Ryan asked Sam, "What did you mean when you said, 'sicker cats than that got well.' My Grandma says the same thing, and I've been trying to figure it out without asking her."

Sam said, "It's a saying of a good friend of mine, Sadie. It's something she always says in such cases as Clark. You know Sadie, don't you?" Ryan shook his head. "She's the lady out off of Paradise where people get help for their animals." Ryan didn't know her name, but he had been there a few times. Sam said, "With time, Clark might change. Who knows?"

Sicker cats than that got well. True to those words, within the year,

Clark had sobered up, straightened up, and eventually would help raise his grandson. With the help of a few good people, he made amends to those he had hurt. Clark still had his moments, but they became fewer with time. Charlie, on the other hand, was a different story. Within that same year, this would prove itself out in a most unusual way.

CHAPTER TWO

THINGS THAT GO BUMP IN A BARREL

The first arrivals started showing up around four -thirty in the afternoon. For most of the year, they had hibernated, awakening slowly to wander around hollowed eyed until this day. Now bright eyed and awake, some would scurry around, getting what they needed and rushing off again. Others lingered as though still groggy from there long hibernation, watching and waiting and wondering if Charlie would show up again. These men were hunters, they spent most of the year thinking about or talking about hunting. When the season rolled around, it was always the same they'd go to work Friday morning before the opening day. After work, they'd load the truck, pat the wife on the head put the dogs in the box and plant a big kiss on their favorite pup before shutting the tailgate. Or maybe it was the other way around? Perhaps it was kiss the wife, well, some of them must have gotten it right.

After the first weekend, those who had held back seldom were disappointed. Charlie Whitehorse ran the Big Boar Guide Service. His clients were wealthy. They had to be with Charlie charging up to five hundred dollars for a large bear or wild pig. They also had to be free to go hunting in the middle of the week, usually on Wednesday or Thursday. Going hog or bear hunting on Thursday would give Charlie the opportunity to show off to the other hunters, maybe just rub it in their faces. He would show up at the gas station on Friday afternoon with some dead critter tied to the top of his dog box.

Charlie would cruise through the pumps and around to the back of the station and wait for the curious to come around and stare while Charlie spun his tale.

There would be lots of questions, leaving Charlie the center of the known universe, just where he wanted to be. To say Charlie had a bit of ego would be quite an understatement, he was a one-man parade. Where the other hunters existed through the week to hunt on the weekend, Charlie lived for the crowd. Ryan was often present when Charlie put on his show. Who could resist this man with his piercing stare and high cheek bones? His short cropped hair gave him more of a hawk than human appearance. He was always the hero in all of his stories. Ryan noticed that there was one thing missing, however. Where were the old hunters? Occasionally they would stop and listen, but they would only stay for a couple of minutes, and they walk away shaking their heads.

One day Ryan was working the pumps. He was trying to hurry through his customers so he could run back to where Charlie was putting on his show. Ryan finally finished with the last customer and had just walked around the corner of the building when the hose bell rang again. Somebody needed gas, dammit! Ryan thought who now? Walking back around the corner, Ryan saw Sam. Ryan's mood quickly changed, Sam was always a pleasure to see. After a bit of talk, Ryan started to service Sam's truck .While doing so, one of the old-timers came from behind the service station where Charlie was and started talking to Sam. Ryan listened in. Ryan caught bits and pieces of the conversation, something about the liars-club meeting around back. Liars' club? Ryan thought. His young, impressionable mind had never considered Charlie a liar, just a highly successful hunter and a businessman. Charlie did have the biggest rig, the biggest gun, the biggest baddest dogs, not to mention large ego. Liar? Well probably. Ryan never considered until that moment that there was more to Charlie than what was on the surface. Soon there would be an event that would change many other people's perception as well.

A large group had gathered that day. Charlie was bragging about his new dog. Listening to Charlie, one would think that this new dog was created in hell, part chainsaw, part alligator covered in dog hair, able to latch onto a bears butt and not let go until the bear had climbed fifty feet up a tree. Then after the dog had let go of the bear and hit the ground, the dog would gnaw its way through even a giant redwood to get another chance at the bear, perhaps a bit of a exaggeration.

One of the old-timers standing in the back of the crowd spoke up. "I bet that a dog like that could take a coon in water." Everybody knew that there wasn't a dog alive that could do that, a raccoon in water will climb on top of a dog's head and drown any dog that tried. Charlie smiled, not his usual crowd pleaser, this one was scary, temperature suddenly dropped. Was this a challenge? Charlie laughed. "I bet he could," he said. Then another voice arose from the back once more Ryan recognized it immediately as that of Sam

"Hey Charlie, how about a badger in a barrel?" was all that Sam said.

Charlie's new smile returned, with a lot more teeth than the first time. His cold stare focused solidly on Sam. "I bet you a hundred bucks," Charlie shot back at Sam. The way he said this, with his lips peeling back over his clinched teeth, now made the thermometer bottom out. The gauntlet had been tossed. Yes it had become a challenge. Ryan thought, could Sam be serious?

"Ok! How about next Saturday afternoon, say around two-thirty at my house? It's the first weekend after bear season-that's if you're not busy." Challenged, Sam and Charlie agreed. Ryan could only wonder, this wasn't at all like Sam. Would Sam really go through with this? Had Sam gone mad?

No, Sam was mad, as a matter of fact, he was so mad that he not merely wanted to teach Charlie a lesson but also to destroy him. Everybody thought Sam was staring down Charlie, but Sam focused on the animal on the top of Charlie's dog box. It was an old boar bear. Leaves and dirt were stuck to the dried blood in its matted hair. Then there was the notch in its ear.

Sam had named this bear by its identifying mark. Sam had run into this bear to tree many times over the years. Earlier in the season, Sam and Charlie had a run-in about this bear. On that day, Charlie was hard set to fill a client's tag, and, while driving down a dirt logging road, he came across Sam's truck. Stopping, he could hear Sam's dogs on a hot track, they were moving and not to tree yet. Charlie figured about where they might cross at the bottom of the canyon. If he could get there before Sam's dogs and put his dogs on the bear as it crossed the road, Charlie would claim the bear for his client. When he reached the place at the bottom of the canyon where the bear should have crossed, he turned off the truck and listened. Nothing just silence. Strange, he thought. Charlie decided to walk up the canyon to look for signs. He had covered a couple hundred yards when he came across Sam's dogs at the bottom of a large oak tree. The dogs weren't baying or barking, they were just sitting looking up into the tree. Then Charlie looked up into the tree and saw the bear. Now something even stranger happened the bear spoke. Taken aback by this, it took a few moments before Charlie realized that it was Sam's voice. Sam was sitting in the tree laughing and holding on for dear life.

"I wish you could see the look on your face, Charlie Horse. Did you think that bears had started talking? Kinda make you wonder what a bear would have to say about you, doesn't it? What the hell are you doing out in the daylight? Anyway shouldn't you be off the hill and home by now?" Sam was only joking, but he could tell that he hit a sour spot in Charlie.

Charlie pushed his hat off his brow and wiped the sweat from his forehead. He then explained that he was living a little bad luck and that he had a very big important client in his truck. The client had even offered a bonus if he could fill his tag so he could get the hell out of the hills. After saying this, he offered to split everything down the middle if Sam would pull his dogs off and let Charlie bring his dogs up. Charlie pointed to the bear. "Look, he is old and long in the tooth, and probably wouldn't make it through another winter anyway."

Sam pointed to the bear. "Charlie, this is Notch; he's a friend of mine and brother, no, your client can't shoot him. You don't shoot friends. Well maybe you do, but I don't!" Then Sam pointed to Charlie. "Notch, this is Charlie. See now you're introduced. Notch you stay away from this man, and, Charlie, Damn you, stay from my brother, Notch."

Charlie was silent. His poker face gave no clue as what his next move would be. Then he did speak, his voice was strong and forceful. "Sam, I could bring my man up here and shoot your bear out of the tree, and there ain't a thing you can do to stop me except shoot me with that sling shot of yours."

"Well! I guess we have a problem," Sam said as he brought a pistol up and into view. Everybody knew that Sam never carried a firearm, but for some reason, today he had. "You know, Charlie, that I could maybe shoot you with this, or maybe just wing ya in the leg and let Notch eat you. Nah, that would be inhumane; Notch could get a case of food poisoning or terminal indigestion for that mater."

"Hey! You said you didn't shoot friends!" said Charlie, his voice cracking with fear. Sam smiled. "Charlie, when did we become friends? Two minutes ago, you were going to shoot my friend Notch, here, whether I wanted you to or not. Why don't you go back to the dump and shoot one of the garbage bears? That's right; the warden's been hanging around the dump at nights, catching poachers. How did he miss you, Charlie? When the lights come on, I thought guys like you ran back under your rocks to hide. Now why don't you head back to where you came from? Oh, and leave Notch alone!"

Sam didn't know just how close he had come to the truth. Charlie had been chased and almost caught the night the night before. Charlie had his partner Skeeter riding up in front of the truck in the mother-in-law seat. The mother-in-law was an old motor cycle seat, the type of seat that looked like an over-sized bicycle seat, which was attached to a piece of pipe and mounted to the front bumper. The seat was used on dirt roads, especially at night, to spot animals on or alongside the road. Fresh tracks in the dirt or deep dust could easily be seen this way.

The alternative was to road a dog, that is to let a dog run in front of the vehicle until it crossed a warm track. Because running a dog like this would tire it out. Charlie considered Skeeter riding on the bumper to be the better choice, because a rested dog could run harder and longer. Skeeter never questioned Charlie when asked to do this type of thing. Skeeter had spent a lot of time in his younger days riding in rodeos on the backs of animals that didn't want to be ridden. This, and a little to much partying after the rodeo, made Skeeter seem to be a little slow mentally. This was reflected in the way he spoke like an old prize fighter who didn't know when to quit. He spoke little. He, however, could read the faces of people as he fumbled for the right words. He knew what he must have sounded like to them, and what they must thought of him. Just another stupid red neck rodeo bum. This embarrassed Skeeter, so he would often tell people he met that he was hit in the butt by a bull until his brains fell out. Everybody would laugh, and that would be the end of it. It was kind of a apology.

Charlie stopped the truck about a mile from Mather dump. He and Skeeter stood in the headlights and talked for a moment. They walked a little father and then stop to look for signs of animals or tire tracks-not just any tire tracks, just those that might be the game warden's. Everything appeared to be normal except, that Charlie seamed disturbed about something. Something was definitely eating at him. He had heard rumors that the game warden might be in the area looking for spot-lighters. There was something else pushing him-to what would have been an unacceptable risk any other day. What was it?

Charlie had Skeeter climb up into the seat again. With his hooked nose, which had been broken more than a dozen times, and his ears cauliflowered from too many fights, Skeeter looked as if he had been to one too many Mexican hat dances and had forgotten to take his head out of the hat. Combine this with skinny legs and arms, Skeeter looked like an under-nourished gargoyle or some weird alien. Like he was some creature, a creature setting under a cowboy hat that somebody was using as a hood ornament. They came into the dump slowly, quiet and with the headlights out. They were trying not to scare any bears that might be feeding. Charlie turned on the spotlight on the roof of the truck and played the beam across the piles of garbage. Little points of light reflected back to them, from hundreds of pairs of eyes of rats and mice. A large dark form could be seen at the east end of the dump. It moved, turning to look directly into the spotlight, its eyes shining like roadside reflectors. Then another set of eyes appeared. It was a sow with a yearling cub. Charlie thought quickly. They could shoot her now or let the dogs run her and the cub to tree and then shoot them at first light. Before he had a chance to do anything, a spotlight from the west end of the dump hit the truck. It's the warden, Charlie thought, and he was right, it was. Charlie killed his spotlight and his headlights still drove toward the only way out of the dump. He had to get out before his escape would be blocked by the warden. They made it. Charlie had a lot of knowledge of these roads, with this knowledge and the help of a little moonlight, and a little luck, they just might get away. Luck was not on Skeeter's mind, life was. He was still on his perch.

With the speed at which Charlie was driving the truck, Skeeter now looked more like one of those pilots the ones you see in pictures, testing rocket sleds. The noise coming from him would have stopped cows from giving milk and chickens from laying eggs. Any Sasquatch within hearing distance would have either fallen in love, or ran deeper into the woods. They made it to the asphalt, now there wouldn't be any dust to follow. Charlie knew this and used it to his advantage. When shadows blocked the moonlight and the road was hard to see, Charlie turned on the headlights just long enough to get his bearings. This gave anyone in the area looking into Skeeter's direction, such as small children, furry woodland creatures, and of course oncoming traffic an unforgettable snapshot of Skeeter's many facial expressions and bodily contortions. When the ride, was over Skeeter still had his hat. Skeeter's looks would never be the same, but this might, in some ways, be considered an improvement in the way he looked before this ride.

They had made their getaway. When the truck came to a stop, Skeeter climbed down an got back into the truck without saying a word. On the other hand, the client had lots to say, such as what the hell was going on to start with, then another string of cuss words followed by a question or two. He then threatened to withhold his fee. Charlie had to think fast, so he lied. He said something about animal activist and such. By the time he had finished, he was a hero, saving everybody's life and the client was so impressed that even offered Charlie a bonus, if they could get a bear, and get the hell out of the woods. Charlie needed the money desperately. Only he knew why.

Three weeks later, Notch lay on top of Charlie's dog box and nothing would change this fact. Dead is dead. At the same time, Charlie went from man in need of money to a man who seemed to have more money then he could ever spend. Even if he had doubled up his clients, this couldn't explain the amount of cash he was now throwing around. What had changed?

Nobody could have guessed what would transpire on the day of the challenge. Nothing like this had been seen in the West Modesto neighborhood before, nor since, nor was there anyway to prepare for what took place that day. Word had spread. It was now apparent that hunters from all over had shown up to watch what was going to happen. Pickups were everywhere. There wasn't a place to park for five or six blocks. It looked like a mountain-man's rendezvous. Everybody was here except Charlie. Then the crowd started to part and Charlie walked through, leading a large dog on a leash. Maybe Charlie wasn't exaggerating. This dog, with its coarse black and brown hair, looked as thought he had been signed by fire. Perhaps it was Ryan's imagination running over, but maybe there was faint smell of brimstone, perhaps it really had come from hell? Charlie looked up on the porch. Sam sat there staring straight into Charlie. There seemed to be a look of distaste on both men's faces, this had become something more than a bet. Ryan watched and wondered how far this would really go. Would Sam put Bump in a barrel? This wasn't like Sam. Why would he place Bump where he could be injured or maybe even killed? Charlie had his crowd and he couldn't resist the opportunity to play to it.

Charlie was the first to speak, "Okay old man, are we going to do this nor not? Or are you going to give me a hundred bucks?"

Because of a argument between Sam and his son, Jim he had refused to be there that day, so Sam asked that Ryan give him a hand. Sam didn't respond to Charlie's words, he just asked Ryan to get the Barrel from around the corner of the house. Sam had been sitting in the overstuffed chair with Bump lying across his lap. He slowly scratched the top of Bumps head.

The barrel was placed on the sidewalk in the front porch, with the opening facing Sam. Sam stood up and walked off the porch with Bump in his arms and placed Bump into the barrel. Looking at the men in front of him, Sam smiled and spun the barrel opening toward Charlie. The dog now went nuts trying to get at Bump. Bump, on the other hand, seemed to be relaxed, lying down in the back of the barrel. Sam looked at Charlie then at the barrel, then brought his arm down and across with palm open, indicating to Charlie that he could start anytime.

Charlie let go of his leash. The dog lunged at the barrel but could only get his head and one shoulder inside. The crowd pressed in a first, until the noise coming out of the barrel sounded as if it would explode and one or both of the animals would be catapulted from the barrel. Leaving it at somewhere around mach three. The struggle didn't last long. Charlie's dog gave up, and ran from the barrel with his tail between his legs. One of the spectators caught the dog before he could get out gate. Charlie protested loudly, saying, "No dog can get a badger out of the barrel!"

"I got one. How about double or nothing?" These were the first words that Sam had spoken to Charlie.

Before Charlie could answer, somebody else spoke up. "How about Ten thousand dollars?" It was a new guy who had come with Charlie. Nobody knew his name or who he was.

Sam ignored the stranger. "Well, what is it, yes or no? Are we going to do this or not, Charlie Horse?" Sam directed this question straight at Charlie, knowing that he hated to be called Charlie Horse. This had the desired effect. Charlie's face became red, and a vein throbbed across his forehead.

"Yes, lets do it!" Charlie shot back.

The stranger stepped between the two men, demanding that Sam acknowledge his bet. Sam's response was very direct and firm. "Mister, I don't know you, and this is between Horse's ass and me. I don't want your money." The stranger again insisted. "Okay, damn it, you're on too!" Sam now told everyone to move back and away from the barrel, because his dog wasn't used to crowds and he didn't want anyone hurt.

When Sam turned to go into the house, he almost ran over Ryan, who was standing behind him. In low voice, Ryan asked Sam where he was gong to get a thousand bucks. Sam just winked and walked past.

Sam disappeared into the house for a moment, and then he soon stuck his head out of the door. "Is everybody back?"

Ryan answered, "Yes." With his back to the crowd Sam came out. All eyes were now focused on Sam's back and trying to get a glimpse of what monster would soon appear. Sam turned to face the gathering, cradling in his arms was a mass of trembling fur. It was Precious his wife Maggie's poodle. When Maggie had first seen the pup, she said "Isn't she precious!" so this became the dogs name. Precious was fresh from the Poodle Palace, her hair neatly cut and wearing little pink ribbons in her ears. She was quite a sight. The laughter could be heard for blocks. This scared her ever more, she tried to hide deeper into Sam's arms. Sam brought his index finger to his lips, gesturing for everyone to be quite. When the crowed became quiet, Sam raised Precious up to his face, cupping one hand over her left ear, and whispering softly to her. Before he put her down in front of the opening of the barrel, Sam said in a loud voice "Let's go babe! Get that nasty old Bump out of the barrel!" When her feet hit the concrete sidewalk, she began spinning, jumping, and barking. Her painted toenails clicking wildly on the sidewalk. She stopped, tilted her head from side to side, and ran from the porch. A roar of laughter rose up that was almost deafening. The little dog paid no attention; she was on a mission, looking frantically for something.

She jumped up on the overstuffed chair, then off again and ran around behind it to emerging with an old towel that was bigger that she was. Racing back down off the porch, she tripped and stumbled head over hills over the towel before rolling to a stop at the barrel opening. She stared into the darkness and started to growl. Then, with great ferocity, Precious began shaking the towel from side to side. Bump came out, and both animals played tug of war with the towel. The laughter stopped, mouths were agape. Disbelief could been seen of some of the onlookers faces, while other's were all smiles, Charlie had been had. All was quite, except for the noises coming from the two playing animals and they were oblivious to the crowd.

Sam broke the animals apart, picked them up, and carried both back into the house. When he came back out of the house, Sam strode up to Charlie and stared into his face. He could see that he wounded Charlie where it hurt him the most, in his ego. A long moment passed before Charlie tried to hand Sam two new one-hundred-dollar bills. Sam shook his head. Charlie then tried to place the bills into Sam's shirt pocket, but Sam pulled away. Sam said, "The bet was double or nothing, I choose nothing." He turned to the stranger. "You owe me something a little more, don't you? This is going to be an expensive lesson."

The stranger laughed and said, "It was a good dog and pony show, but it's not worth ten grand." He had just exposed himself for what he was, as one without honor.

Sam turned his attention back to Charlie, "Well, Chuck, This is the kind of people you choose to hang around. I now see where you're getting your money. What are you doing to earn it?" Charlie raised his fist to strike Sam. Sam stood his ground, not even blinking, solid and unwavering.

Charlie's anger turned to blind rage and instead of hitting Sam, he brought his fist down with great force, striking himself in the upper thigh. Charlie looked like a two-year-old getting ready to throw a temper tantrum. He then threw the crumpled bills in Sam's face. Turning, Charlie and the stranger stomped their way past the silent onlookers. Charlie stopped only long enough to take the dog leash away from the guy holding it. The poor dog was now even more scared than he had been in the barrel with Bump, he was frozen in his tracks. Charlie pulled hard on the leash and the dog flinched but couldn't move. The animal cowered in the shadow of Charlie's rage, which now overflowed, and Charlie began to kick and stomp the dog unmercifully. Recoiling from the attack, the dog managed to slip its collar and took off running down the street, almost into a path of a car. Charlie never said a word. He and the stranger left in a hurry, leaving those closest to his vehicle in a huge cloud of dirt, flying rocks and smoke.

Ryan looked at Sam. Sam had the look on his face that comes from great satisfaction, as well he should, after all, he had shown everyone Charlie's true self. Sam bent down and retrieved the money at his feet. When Sam looked over at Ryan, Ryan asked, "What you going to do frame it?" Sam grinned like a possum up a paw-paw tree.

Speaking to the crowd almost in a boastful manner, Sam laughed and bantered back and forth with different individuals, he was having fun. Then Sam said, "I guess Charlie was absent that day at school when we learned that the best way to defeat an enemy is to make him a friend." At that instant, Sam's expression changed, his own words had stung him. His shoulders now dropped, the air was let out of his sails. He realized at that moment that he had become what Charlie was - a man seduced by ego and need to have approval of the group. He had made an enemy not a friend. Charlie had lost face and was humiliated in front of his friends and Sam knew that things would never be the same between him and Charlie.

Yes, things were never the same again. Charlie started buying gas at Barbours gas station in Ceres, a town just south of Modesto. There would be the occasional story here and there about Charlie's exploits. He rebuilt the legend elsewhere but legend and truth seldom shake hands. Strange how connections link everything and everybody at different times. The future owner of Barbours, Dennis Barbour, would someday be one of Ryan's best friends and benefactors.

That day of the challenge, Sam turned his back to the crowd, lowered his head, and solemnly walked back into his house. He had lost something; there were no winners that day. The bystanders were leaving, Ryan stood in the front yard watching them go. Most of them had the look of confusion and bewilderment. None of them understood what had just happened, especially Ryan. In ten minutes, there would be only Ryan and Skeeter left.

Walking over to Skeeter, Ryan said. "I thought you would be riding with Charlie and the other guy. Who is he, anyway?"

Skeeter looked down the street in the direction that Charlie had headed and said that he and Charlie wouldn't be hunting together anymore. It seems that Charlie's new benefactor liked the way Charlie made his getaway at Mather dump and was now using Charlie to deliver product to his people in the surrounding areas. What the product was, Skeeter wouldn't say. What he did say was, " I'm not the sharpest tool in the shed, but I'm smart enough to not get into what Charlie has gotten himself into." It seems that Charlie still took hunters out, but now they were the same people he delivered during the week, and Skeeter didn't like any of them. Skeeter then left, shutting the gate behind him. Ryan watched him limp his way down the street, and that was the last time Ryan or anyone else in Modesto would ever see Skeeter.

Skeeter packed his things and moved to Nevada to work as a real cowboy. Steers and wild mustangs, plus the bonus of having the world's largest living-room ceiling, all this and fourteen dollars a week to boot, made Skeeter a happy man. Either it was the wide open spaces or change of friends, or it might have been the solitude of his new lifestyle, because, in time he changed. He became confident and seemed to have gained wisdom. Skeeter became one of those people called cowboy poets. He was best known for a poem about graffiti not the inner city type or the unreadable scrawl of the taggers, but that of the desert. His poem described the graffiti he saw in the evening sky, where colors are wet and fresh, running down, and covering all below. It went something like this.

I've never seen him.
But he seems to be everywhere.
He paints the rocks, he paints the trees-heck,
he even paints the air.
Morning and evening skies,
his best works are always there for all to see.
Wet and fresh, it flows from the sky to ground,
filling puddles all round.
I've watched it happen every day for all these many years.
Its beauty sometimes can be seen inverted in a lonely cowboy tear.
People ask me if I'm lonely out here under the painted skies.
They don't understand the relationship between me and the artist that
paints on air.
No matter where I travel,
I always find he's beat me there.
On the day I met him,
his face seem familiar,
as familiar as my own.

He introduced himself and said, **good work cowboy, welcome** home.

It seems that Skeeter had found success and a happiness not connected to money or fame. On Sunday, Sam cut a bunch of flowers from the yard to take to Maggie. When he opened the back gate where his truck was parked, something dark moved beneath the vehicle. Looking under it, Sam saw Charlie's dog. Sam coaxed the animal out and gave him a look over. The dog appeared to have a broken rib or two and knows what others injuries that couldn't be seen. Sam was now in a spot that he didn't really want to be in. Hunter's etiquette dictated that Sam would have to return the dog to Charlie, and Charlie more than likely would just shoot the animal anyway. That's the way Charlie was, mean. There was a place, however, where Sam could take the dog and not violate this rule, yet still protect it from Charlie, that was Sister Sadie's place. She ran a shelter for lost or injured animals. Charlie and Sadie had a couple of run-ins in the past and she put him in check each time. Charlie always referred to Sadie as the witch woman. Sam could take the dog there for medical help and still tell Charlie where the dog was. Then it would be Charlie's choice to go and retrieve the dog. Charlie wouldn't even try to get the dog back from her.

Sam opened the door to the truck and helped the dog up into the front seat. Even Sam's gentlest touch caused it to whimper. The pain must have been terrible. Usually, an injured dog tries to bite when being picked up, but this one never even tried to bite Sam. Driving to Sadie's house wouldn't take long; she lived on Paradise Road just past the turn after Grimes Avenue, in a house made out of cinder block. Pulling into the driveway and then around behind the house, Sam saw Sadie. Her hands were on her hips and a look of disapproval was on her face. She had heard about what happened the day before and didn't like it one damn bit. She let Sam know so as soon as he got out of the truck. She peppered him with strong language, backing him clear back to the tailgate, and threatening to beat him like a red headed stepchild. She would never hit Sam; they had been friends too long.

Sam kept saying, "I know, I know. Sadie looked in the truck."

Sadie stopped, looked inside, and called the dog to the edge of the seat where she could get a good at him. As she examined the animal, she interspersed her analysis about its health with comments about Sam, how he had disappointed her and let her down. She said that, of all the hunters she had dealings with, Sam was one of the few she respected with the highest regard, and now this stupid stunt. Sam was ashamed. He listened, saying nothing Sadie turned to face Sam and saw tears pooling in the corners of his eyes. Seeing this, Sadie apologized; she had never thought that her words would ever have that effect on Sam. Sam admired Sadie, and she was right, what he had done was stupid and irresponsible, and he missed his Maggie. Emotionally, it all washed over and overwhelmed him, threatening to drown him.

Sadie placed her wrinkled hand on top of Sam's head and swished her fingers around, messing up his freshly combed hair, then she gave him a motherly pinch on the cheek. "Come on, little brother. Give me a hand getting this pup into the shed where I can get a better look at him."

Sam gently cradled the dog in his arms and carried it into the shed, placing it on the bench under the light. This caused the dog a great deal of pain, but again, it never attempted to bite. Instead, he gratefully licked Sam's face. Sam laughed as he tried to duck the canines wet gratitude.

Sam scratched dog behind the ear. "You'll be okay. Sadie's going to fix you up fine-good as new," Sam said. Taking from his wallet the money that Charlie had thrown at him, Sam handed it to Sadie and told her to use it in good health.

Sadie accepted the money and told Sam, "Go out and see your little brother. He's pacing the wire ever since you got here. Now go, and give me a minute with his pup, and we'll have a cup of tea when I am done." Sam left and Sadie concentrate on the dog. Sadie knew more about treating animals than most veterinarians, especially wild animals. This was because; by law veterinarians were required to report and destroy injured wild animals. It would be many years before this law would change. The only exception at the time concerned endangered species. Sadie on the other hand, and in her own words, "I don't give a rat's ass. I'm not turning anyone or any animal away that I can help." To most people Sadie was an enigma, a local legend. There were stories about her early life as a hell raiser, and some said she liked women was well as men in the most intimate of ways. Some, such as Charlie, said that she was a witch in league with the devil. Nobody knew for sure because, like most legends, the stories were added to over the years, and depending on who the story teller was and what they wished to prove, the stories would change. She always seemed somewhere between Satan and Saint. This made little difference when people needed help, especially those with little or no money. Again, no one was ever turned away. She gave treatment and advice freely. Sadie had overheard some of these stories and had seen those who talked so poorly about her. Some of the things said were outlandish, hurtful and others were just plain disturbing. But when she would treat an animal of these people who talked about her, she was always courteous and pleasant. More than once while doing this one of her friends had dropped by, they had also heard the stories and had seen was telling them. Once, after the animal and owner had left, this friend asked why Sadie would help somebody who had said such terrible things about her. Then tried to tell her even more of the gossip this person had spread. Sadie just said, "Sicker cats than that got well." She was referring to the people, not their animals. She also said that "you can't judge a child by the parents or a parent by the child." These were also Ryan's grandmother's favorite sayings. This was the way Sadie lived, without judgment. There was too little time in life to be mad or to hold a grudge. Few things raised

Sadie hackles faster than disrespect for life, whether it be animal or human, and in that order. Her house was accessible by all, she had bird feeders in every tree and bush plus feeding bowls for the different critters that would come up from the river bottom below the house. A family of kit foxes and a family of raccoons showed up every night to eat, even the skunks had a bowl of their own. They all took turns coming at different times so there was never a confrontation. Even if there had been, Sadie was always there watching and ready. There seemed to be an unspoken rule that this was a place of peace and quiet.

Maybe she was a witch after all, because there seemed to be magic here, but to the animals it must have seemed more like heaven than hell. Sadie was a woman who was self-empowered and fiercely independent, a force of nature. Soon she finished with the dog and went over to the open door, where she watched Sam. and Samson.

Samson was a one-eyed half starved bear that hated men when he came to Sadie after his owner had died in an auto accident west of town on highway 132, near the Old Fisherman's Club. Samson was used in a carnival side show by his late owner. When he was just a yearling cub, Samson had his eye poked out during one of the owner's many drunken rages. There was no wondering why Samson hated men, that is all except Sam. Sadie always said that Sam was endowed with a spirit of great bear and that's why Samson and Sam were great friends and brothers.

The bear leaned into the chain link fence while Sam scratched him behind his ears and on his forehead. Sam talked to Samson, softly telling him about Notch and what had happened to him. Sam had some jelly beans that he retrieved from the pickup on his way to see Samson, and he was giving the bear a few at a time. Samson always seemed to look forward to these visit, as did Sam. The bear liked Sam a lot but he loved jelly beans more and Sam knew this, so he never came without sweet treats. Sam even gave Samson the nickname of the Jelly Belly Bear.

Sadie called Sam, she needed help placing Charlie's dog in one of the holding cages. There it would remain warm and quiet, soon to mend under Sadie's healing touch. When they finished with the task, it was time for a little tea. Sadie always seemed to have a pot of hot water going in case company stopped by.

Sam was the first to speak, apologizing again, and explaining that he never thought that the dog would have been able injured by Bump, because it wasn't in Bumps nature to be vicious, and Bump would be protected by his thick hair and loose skin. A badger's skin is so loose that some say that they can almost turn around inside it, making you think that they have teeth at both ends. Badgers earn a living by digging ground squirrels and other below ground dwellers from their dens. Sam always kept Bump's claws trimmed close to prevent injury to himself and others because, even in play they could do a lot of damage. As for the dog, he could only get his head and one shoulder into the barrel, so Bump would be safe. This made Sam confident that both animals would be safe from injury, but he had not counted on Charlie's reaction. Sam continued talking while Sadie listened, not saying a word. She was just letting Sam get it all off his chest. When the cups were empty, she offered Sam another cup, which he declined.

Sadie placed her hand atop Sam's and gave it a squeeze, she then told him to stop worrying, adding, "The pup's going to live. It had a few broken ribs and its spirit was broken. It will probably never hunt again." She promised that she would see to it that it got a good home and plenty of love.

She had also seen the flowers in the truck and knew where he was going. She gave his other hand a squeeze and said, "Maggie's waiting." Sam nodded and arose; he walked to the sink, rinsed his cup and thanked Sadie one more time. Yes, Maggie was waiting.

CHAPTER THREE

STAINED-GLASS SKY

On a clear fall evening, Ryan set his telescope up near the west wall of the upholstery shop. This allowed him a good view of the coastal mountains. He chose the middle-power eyepiece, this optic would be more than powerful enough to see trees and radio antennas silhouetted atop Mount Oso Spanish for (Bear Mountain) as the sun passed behind it. Near this mountain is Corral Hollow where the man and legion Grizzly Adams Ryan carefully cleaned the telescope's optics with lens paper, paying extra attention to the twelve-millimeter eyepiece. He placed it into the receiver then lowered and locked the telescope's barrel in place. Ryan bent his head down and focused the telescope on the top of the mountain. The image shimmered because of the heat rising from the valley floor, but he could still make out details of trees on its peak. The shoulders of the mountain were covered with fog that had moved inland from the ocean. It was held back by the same warm air that distorted the view. In two places, the fog had managed to clear the ridge. This created the illusion of two hands, with cold mist moving down ravines giving the appearance of fingers. Ryan thought that the fog looked like a prowler waiting at the garden wall, waiting for the darkness so that he could cross over and walk silently through the garden.

The evening air was cooling fast, this would help calm the atmospheric distortions and the shimmering would decrease, making Ryan's view clear, or at least it should have. But things now started to became hazy. Ryan raised his head, across the street in the vacant lot behind the Richland service station was a large pile of leaves burning. Leaf burning was one of the things that Ryan really liked about fall, unfortunately it made for poor viewing. The pile consisted of leaves of all shades and hues of red, yellow, and orange. Ryan looked back into the telescope; the mountain was all but hidden in the haze. Ryan started to take the scope down when he saw a patch of clear sky above the orchards along Grimes Avenue, beyond Mape's Ranch.

Unlocking the barrel, Ryan swung the telescope to this clear piece of sky and refocused, his view was filled with the sight of thousands of birds. They were too far away to be seen by the naked eye. Through the telescope he could recognized the different species by their silhouettes and the way they flew. Large flocks of blackbirds looked like feathered balls rising and falling, folding and expanding. Crows were crossing back and forth with the younger ones, playing a game of aerial tag. They would chase each other, tumbling through space like fighter pilots in a dog fight, eventually falling behind and having to catch up with the flock.

By changing focus, Ryan could now see large numbers of ducks and geese in the background. They seemed to be heading both north and south at the same time, looking for a place to settle down for the night. This was becoming interesting. Ryan changed the focus again, the foreground and background condensed and merged. The light was also changing, bringing his hand up to his brow to block the side light from streaming in. Ryan could smell the gas and oil that permeated his flesh. He could not remember a time in his life where this odor wasn't part of his being, tainting body and perhaps his even his soul. Colors were changing; the sky was going through the transition where day passes into night

Ryan had become so engrossed that he no longer could hear the near by traffic or feel the cooling air flowing around him. The colors were so vivid, and they seemed to run together like watercolors on wet paper. The blue-gray haze from the smoke gave way and now seemed to carry the essence of all the burning piles of leaves into the sky, and was now declaring, "This is who I was. Look at me one last time." Yellows and oranges with reds deepened in the denser stratified formations of smoke.

The birds took on the appearance of a giant mobile, hung from the ceiling of God's nursery, with the golden edges of the fog bank below them. They started to rise higher and flew in tighter circles stirring the air. It was as though they were caught in some invisible vortex, a vortex of their own making.

They flew higher into the evening sky, there to dance into last days light. Now, Ryan seemed to be pulled by that same whirlwind. His eyes filled with colors, his fifteen-year-old mind opened and his soul took a deep breath. He felt cleansed, lost in a cinnabar sky among a million beating wings, he felt at home and comfortable.

"Hey! What the hell do ya think you're doing?" The voice was forceful and commanding. It yanked Ryan's spirit from the air through the telescope, and slammed him back into this shoes. His hair stood on end, and gooseflesh covered his body. He had heard this voice only once before, when he was eleven-years-old.

That day, he and his friends, Terry and Philip, were shooting their pellet guns along the river. They were competing to see who could kill the most. Everything was fair game; birds, lizards, rats, anything except humans. This gave them a lot of latitude. Ryan excelled at this game; it became easy to take life. They thought it was good practice for when the nation might call them to go to war; at least it was their excuse for the game. Mostly it was just their justification for their actions. If the country ever needed eleven-year-olds in war, they were ready.

On this particular day, Ryan shot a young magpie. It was wounded and was hanging from a limb, upside down by one leg, at the bottom of a cottonwood tree. The poor bird was terrified and was crying out. Ryan knew that its calling would bring other magpies to the tree, trying to help their wounded brother. That's just what Ryan was counting on. In a matter of minutes, he had shot three more. Then a voice yelled up from the base of the tree, "What the hell do ya think you're doing? Leave my birds alone!" That day, Ryan had seen only the faceless human form at the base of the tree. Now that man stood behind him.

Spinning around, Ryan stared into the gentle, smiling face of his friend, Sam Bird. The vision at the base of the cottonwood tree was still frozen in Ryan's mind, his eyes were open, but the image of Sam was not registering. Sam's mouth was moving, but Ryan couldn't hear the sound coming out. He was caught in the electric silence that now enveloped him. His ears were buzzing and crackling and his heart seemed to race around his rib cage like a hyperactive hamster. Within twenty seconds, Ryan regained his composure. His look of shock was now replaced with that of shame for what he had done four years earlier.

Sam apologized for startling Ryan. Now over the shock, Ryan listened to what Sam was saying. Ryan's father had mentioned to Sam that Ryan raised pheasants and pigeons, and Sam's son, Jim, wanted to buy some barnies. Barnies are pigeons that show up and hang around pigeon breeders' coops, trying to attract mates. They're usually single, wild males, born in the lofts of barns. That's why they're called barnies, but any wild pigeon is considered the same by breeders. Most breeders who raise pigeons would merely wring the necks of these unwanted suitors. Ryan was the exception to the rule. In four years of listening to the older, responsible hunters, Ryan no longer killed just to be killing. One of the most respected of these hunters was Sam, which was why Ryan was so ashamed earlier when he realized that it was Sam that day beneath the cottonwood. But why didn't Sam ever mention it? Ryan wondered.

Ryan told Sam that he had a few barnies and that he normally sold them to the feed store but he would be happy to sell Jim whatever he had on hand. They shook hands on it.

Then Sam commented on how beautiful the colors of the night sky were, especially the blues and purples. What purples, Ryan thought? Then, looking above his head, he could see these colors that before were hidden through the myopic view of the telescope. The entire sky now opened up to him - it was glorious. The dance in the distance was now gone, fading with the light.

"When does Jim want to get together?" inquired Ryan.

"How about dropping by the house on Saturday?" Sam asked.

Saturday rolled around, and Ryan rode his bicycle over to Sam's house on John Street. This wasn't far from the sewage treatment ponds. At times, the whole west side of town smelled of this place and the Union Hide Company, also called the tallow works.

Ryan opened the front gate slowly, pushed his bike in, and closed the gate behind him. He moved quietly across the yard and laid his bike against the porch. Ryan had heard stories about the old man's other wild, wandering pets and had seen Bump on that one occasion when Sam challenged Charlie. Stepping up on the porch, Ryan was getting ready to knock on the door when he noticed a black snout appear from under the skirt of the overstuffed chair beside the door. The whole body soon followed, it was Speed Bump.

Speed Bump was given his name after being found near the Delta Mendota Canal. His mother and sister had been run over on the road. If it hadn't been for Sam and Jim, Speed Bump would have been next. Now he was a full-grown badger. He burrowed his nose up Ryan's pant leg and licked Ryan's salty shin. Frozen in place, Ryan's first reaction normally would have been to do the bumblebee dance. The first time this dance was performed was when Ryan, Phil and Terry were shooting birds along the river. A bumblebee flew up Terry's pant leg, sending him leaping, spinning, running, and rolling. Ryan and Phil watched Terry do all these things and a few others, for which that there are no words to describe. Terry was a lightning rod for such accidents. If something was going to happen, it would happen to Terry, sparing everyone else nearby. After that day, the boys added this new game to their repertoire to break up the boredom when there was nothing to kill but time. You never knew when one of these friends suddenly would break into the bumblebee dance. Of course, the dancer, or victim, had some help from his buddies, who had stuffed some critter down his back or down the waistband of his pants. The critter chosen had to want out of victim's clothes as much as the victim/dancer wanted them out. The dancer was always critiqued at the end of his performance. He was scored on his air time, body motions, and bodily functions, plus the longest sustained cuss word. Hell, this was performance art at its finest. Ryan had done this dance many times but never with an adult badger attached to his leg.

"Hello!" someone called from around the corner of the house. It was Jim, Sam's son. He walked up on the porch, shook Ryan's hand, and said, "Follow me." Ryan just stood there as Jim disappeared back around the corner. Jim returned and said, "Come on." Ryan looked down at this right pant leg, which was now pushed up around his knee. Jim said, "It's okay. Bump seems to like you, and, who knows, it might just be love." Ryan slowly moved his leg, and Speed Bump dropped down on all four legs and followed Ryan to the edge of the porch where he lay on his stomach and watched until Ryan and Jim entered the back yard. Ryan had been to Sam's house only that one time but hadn't been in the back yard.

Jim opened the vine-covered gate to reveal a large, enclosed back yard. The vines covered the fence and the tops of bird pens to provide both shade and cover. They also made it nearly impossible to see into the back yard from the outside. Ryan could see many different birds in the shadows varying from doves to hawks. In one of the pens was a magpie all by himself. Ryan got closer and could see that the magpie had a bad wing. The bird glared back at Ryan. Ryan wondered if this could be the same bird that he had shot four years earlier. Jim asked Ryan if he was ready for the nickel tour.

"Yeah," was Ryan's reply.

Jim gave a running commentary about each bird, especially the more exotic ones, and their countries of origin. Jim had bought from various bird breeders from around the country. One of the names that came up was old man Ichenberry. Like Sam, he was a retired janitor for the Modesto City Schools. Ryan had bought many birds from this same breeder.

Looking around, Ryan asked Jim, "With all these great birds, what do you need with barnies?" Using his index finger, Jim gave the "follow me" gesture. Ryan followed him over to two pens that were separated from the others. They only could be seen from the back yard. There, sitting on a manzanit branch, was a large red-tailed hawk.

"This is Reeek, its short for Eric the Red." Ryan would later find that this word and a whistle was how Jim called his hawks to return to the lure when he was training. In the next pen was another proud bird. Jim asked Ryan if he knew what type of bird it was.

With hesitation, Ryan replied in an unsure tone "Peregrine falcon?"

"Good guess, but are you sure? You sound a little unsure."

Ryan didn't answer. He was captured by the piercing stare of the falcon.

Jim noticed this and said, "It's like they see right through you, and in one glance, they know everything about you. It's like they take an x-ray of your soul."

Ryan came out of his trance and asked, "What's its name?"

Jim said, "Care-if-val, but when calling her to the lure, it's Carieee."

What a strange name, thought Ryan. Care-if-val now started to bob her head and body up and down and was making a sound that could only be described as clucking and mewing.

"She likes you. That's the sound she makes when she sees a friend," Jim said.

"Wow. With all these great birds, what do you need with some dumb pigeons?" Ryan asked. This kind of embarrassed Ryan when he remembered that he had already asked that same question.

"To train with," was the reply. Jim then tapped Ryan on the shoulder and said, "Let's grab a cage and see how many barnies we can get." As they crossed the back yard, Ryan could feel the magpie's stare following him. His mouth went dry as he spit out his next question. "Where did you get the magpie?"

Jim stopped to look over at the magpie and said, "That's Maggie. Dad came home with her four years ago." Jim paused and then explained in a low, almost apologetic fashion. "On the day of my mother's funeral, my uncle talked Dad into having a drink. It was Dad's first drink and it didn't take much to get him drunk. No one noticed when Dad left or when he returned. We found him later that evening sitting in the corner of that pen holding the wounded magpie. He sat there in his best suit and cried silently, rocking that bird. It was Dad's first and last drink. He doesn't even know where or how he found the bird. Dad gave it the name of Maggie, which also was my mother's name."

Ryan thought to himself, so that's why Sam's never said anything.

As they walked back through the gate toward the front yard, Ryan asked Jim, "How did you know that I was on the porch?"

Jim's answer was a strange one, "The animals told me, telling me someone was here. When you're in tune with the animals, they'll let you know when something is wrong or somebody is around."

"What animals let you know?"

"The dogs. Dad's two hounds and my Labrador."

"I didn't see any dogs and there wasn't any barking," said Ryan.

"They've been trained to bark only when Dad or I am in the house. By the time we made it into the back yard, I had already sent then back under the back porch in the shade. You should've noticed their tracks in the dirt."

Ryan felt a little dumb for not noticing the signs right under his feet and said so.

"No, don't feel that way. Dad taught me how to listen and watch animals, to read their signs and the signals they make when something has their attention. If you want, I'll teach you. It's easy when you know what you're looking for. Dad likes you. He told me that he had taken you to visit Mr. Jordan a couple of times. He even thought he might introduce you to some more of his friends. He would like to show you some of the things that he had taught me. We both can teach you, if you want."

"Yes, thanks, and any pigeons you get from me are free." Still, Ryan thought to himself that he should have known about the dogs, especially since Sam had two of the best bear hounds in the country. Sam could do with two dogs what other hunters could do only with a pack of hounds. So why wouldn't they be in the back yard? Another piece of evidence showed up when Ryan got into Jim's old station wagon. It was located on the bottom of Ryan's shoe. After cleaning his shoe, Ryan climbed back into the station wagon. The inside of the wagon was as weathered as the outside, but it was neat and uncluttered. They had gone only a couple of blocks when Ryan remembered that his bike was on the porch, unlocked. He asked Jim to go back so he could lock it.

Jim looked over at Ryan and said, "with Bump on the porch, who's going to bother your bike?"

"Right," replied Ryan. Riding along, Ryan gave directions and told Jim what to expect, plus what to watch out for with one of the tricks his friends enjoyed playing on the unwitting. He told Jim that he had worked out a deal with the owner of the feed store on H Street to buy all the barnie he could get. This arrangement worked well for them both because kids usually bought these birds. They were always given instructions not to release the pigeons to fly for a couple of weeks. Kids would get impatient and release them too early, and in a day or two, the barnies would end up back with Ryan's flock to be caught and again resold to the feed store.

What Ryan warned Jim to look out for from his two friends, Bill and Keith, was a trick that they always tried on new guys. One or the other of them would distract the victim while the other would remove a squab from a nest. Then they would turn the squab upside down and shake it. The shaking would cause the squab to empty its bowels when righted and placed into the victim's hands. This sometimes could be repeated several times with those who were slow to catch on. Bill or Keith would keep bringing out birds, asking questions or making comments about genetic qualities of each squab that the victim was holding. When the new guy was gone, they would almost hurt themselves laughing at the trick that they had played. One guy had been tricked six times in a row. That was the record.

The two boys arrived at Ryan's grandparent house on Avalon Avenue, and Ryan gave Jim a quick tour. When they reached the pigeon coop, Ryan opened the door and they entered. All kinds of pigeons where here, from tumblers to fantails and racers. Looking around the coop, they could only find three barnies. As Ryan had thought, they would need to go to Bill's house on the next street. They went back out to the car, where Ryan again warned Jim to watch out for the trick and not to pay more than a buck apiece for the birds. They got there just as Bill was heading into his coop, with Keith following close behind. Ryan and Jim walked up to the coop and talked to Bill through the wire. Ryan made the introductions and explained what they needed. Bill usually destroyed barnies as soon as he found them, but he had been away camping for two weeks and was just getting ready to check his birds. Sure enough, four barnies had made it in through the one-way door. Barnies could be distinguished from the other birds by the metal band on the legs of coop - raised birds.

Keith quickly caught the barnies. He invited Jim into the coop, and the birds were placed into the carrying cage. Ryan watched as Keith reached into a nesting box. He grabbed a squab and shook it while Bill and Jim discussed the price of the birds he was going to take. Keith leaned over and tapped Jim on the shoulder. Jim turned and placed both hands in his pants pockets. Jim then bent over to look closely at the squab, but he kept his hands in his pockets. This made the squab a pin-feathered time bomb in Keith's hand. Even if not righted, it would go off in a few moments, which it did before Keith could put it back. Keith gave Ryan a knowing look. The deal was struck and everyone left the coop. As Keith passed Ryan, he placed his soiled hand on Ryan's shoulder and said, "Have a nice day!"

On the way home, Ryan asked Jim how he trained the birds of prey. Jim asked Ryan if he wanted to go along on Sunday and watch how it was done. This was something Ryan had always wanted to do. He could hardly believe his ears.

"Yes!" he said. Soon they were back at Jim's house and the pigeons were placed into a pen. Then Sam came out and told Jim that he had a phone call.

Jim went inside the house, while Sam stayed outside and kept Ryan company. They chit-chatted for a while, Ryan occasionally glancing over at the magpie when Sam wasn't looking.

Ryan told Sam that he and Jim were going to train the falcon and the hawk the next day.

"Good. I'll go with you," Sam said. Jim finished his phone call and rejoined his father and Ryan outside. They talked and agreed on what time to leave the next day. Jim told Ryan that he would pick him up at his house around eleven in the morning. They talked a little longer, then Ryan excused himself saying good bye, and adding that he would see them in the morning. Really, he wanted to stay longer, but he feared getting caught looking at the magpie, which might have given away his secret and expose his shame.

The next morning, Ryan was waiting, it seemed as though the time would never come. Eleven o'clock finally arrived and so did Sam and Jim. Ryan got into the back seat and then turned to look at the birds in the back of the station wagon. There they sat on perches attached to plywood, sand bags were used to keep the perched from sliding around. Both birds were hooded and leather straps and bells were attached to their legs. This was all new and strange to Ryan. As they rode, Sam, Jim, and Ryan tried to converse back and forth, but, for the most part, Ryan could make out only a few words now and again because of all the noise that the vehicle was making.

After a while, Jim, Sam, and Ryan reached Del Puerto Canyon. Care-if-val and Eric were unloaded onto the fold-down gate of the station wagon. Jim brought out the different equipment needed for a training session and as he did so, he described the function of each one. There was a long cord that was used in the early stages of training. One end was attached to the leather straps on the legs of the bird, and the other end was held by the trainer. The trainer would call the bird to his gloved fist, then give the cord a light tug. When the bird flew to the glove, it was given a small piece of meat as a reward. Jim had attached heavy fishing-type snap swivels plus a rubber shock cord to the end of the main cord to act as a cushion. This was to prevent injury to an excited bird that was trying to get away. Because both birds were well beyond this level of training, the cord was used to swing or fly the lure around the trainer's head. The leather lure was filled with old cloth and had pheasant wings attached. In flight, it looked much like a bird. There were two sets of gloves, one for Jim and one for Sam. Normally, they flew the birds on different days, but since his dad and Ryan were there to help, Jim decided to fly them on the same day, but separately.

Jim placed one glove on his left hand and handed glove to his father. They each picked up a bird by placing the gloved fist under and against each bird's breast. The bird then climbed onto the glove by itself. Jim asked Ryan to hand him the pouch that was next to him, Ryan did so, and Jim placed the shoulder strap over this head so that the bag hung at his side. Jim put the cord and some meat into the bag, along with a whistle and other odds and ends that were already in it. Everything seemed ready and in order when Jim asked Ryan to grab the pigeons. Ryan had a confused look on his face as if to say, what pigeons? Jim pointed to a gunnysack in the back of the station wagon, where the barnies that Jim had gotten the day before lay motionless. They had not moved nor had they made a single sound. It was as though they knew the close proximity of the birds of prey and what fate was in store for them. They were being held in silent prayer of the condemned, their fate sealed.

As Ryan grabbed the gunnysack, the pigeons panicked, beating their wings against the fabric and making noises of distress. Ryan felt sorry for them, but at least they had some kind of chance this way. As they walked, Jim talked about the purpose of all the gear that was attached to the falcon and the hawk. The hoods were to keep the birds calm. The leather straps at their legs, called jesses, carried a name tag. If a bird flew off and was found, it could be identified and returned. The other purpose for the jesses, was that they were to be held tight in the gloved hand to keep the birds from flying off until the falconer cast the bird. The bell on the jesses would help the falconer locate his bird in tall grass or brush after a kill was made.

When the men reached the bottom of the canyon, the brush opened up, and a couple hundred yards of dry grass stretched in all directions.

The trees consisted mostly of scrub oaks and digger pines, with California buckeyes here and there. The brush was western white thorns and sagebrush. Ryan knew this place, this is where his father used to set the minnow traps in the creek below.

Jim stopped and carefully removed the hood from the falcon, while talking quietly and calmly to the bird. Care-if-val shook and fluffed her feathers, and then preened herself. Jim pointed out the small hair-like feathers near her eyes at the base of her beak. He explained that these feathers enabled the bird to detect changes in wind direction, even in flight. Jim then left Sam and Ryan at the edge of the clearing and walked to its center, where he cast the falcon into the wind. She rose and circled every now and again, calling to her master with a "klee, klee" kind of sound. While she circled, Jim readied the lure to the snap-swivel end of the cord. Jim started swinging the lure around his head and yelling, "Carieee. Carieee." Care-if-val tucked her wings tight to her body and dived. She was a feathered blur at more than a hundred miles an hour, and this was only half the speed that she could attain. As she closed in on the lure, Jim gave the lure a jerk, causing Care-if-val to miss. She pulled her body into a swooping turn and gained altitude. Jim repeated this process many more times before the falconer allowed her to catch the lure. When she hit the ground with it, she quickly mantled the lure. "This is called mantling," Jim explained. While mantling, she would alternate raising and lowering her legs while kneading her talons into the lure. Jim had attached a small piece of meat to the lure that she eagerly dined on. He slowly walked over to where she was on the ground. She turned her back to Jim, remantled the lure, and spread her tail feathers. As Jim got closer, she began making a new sound, similar to a hissing noise. Jim slowly placed her back on his gloved fist. Next would be the real thing.

Jim asked Ryan to get a pigeon ready. Ryan untied the sack, reached into its darkness and retrieved one of the barnies. Ryan could feel the bird's heart beating against its chest in the palm of his hand as the bird struggled to break free. Ryan thought to himself that, if the pigeon could understand that, upon its release, the falcon would be sent in pursuit, sealing its fate, it might not be so eager to get away. Jim turned to face Ryan and made sure that Care-if-val had seen the pigeon in Ryan's hand. Jim said, "to release the pigeon." Giving the pigeon a toss, Ryan watched as the bird began to climb, its wings beating a fast retreat. Care-if-val waited without challenging Jim's grip on the jesses, yet totally intent on her prey. Jim cast the falcon, and she broke to the air with wings moving so fast that they were just a blur.

Ryan watched as the falcon quickly closed the gap. It looked like a quick kill, but the pigeon had other plans for the rest of the day and being lunch wasn't one of them. The falcon flying for a meal and the pigeon flying for its life. The pigeon dived into the cover of the trees and brush along the clearing. Here, the falcon lost much of her advantage, and it became a new game. Feathered flashes were seen darting here and there through the thickets and tree branches. Then came a sound, a strange whistling noise, not like a modern metal whistle but a haunting single tone. Jim had placed the whistle around his neck while the others were watching the pursuit and was now calling Care-if-val back to the glove. Ryan heard Sam clearing his throat as if he was choking back something. Looking over at him, Ryan could see tears running down Sam's cheeks. "I'll be damned." Sam said. You see, Sam and Jimmy hadn't worked the birds together in years, not for any particular reason, just because they were doing other things apart from one another. Now Jimmy was standing with his arm stretched out at his side, blowing through a whistle that had been his great-grandfather's. The whistle was made from a bone of an eagle. The image of an eagle feather was etched into it, a piece of leather was tied to it, and an eagle feather once hung from it. It was used during the sun dance ceremony in which a boy became a man and a man to understand something of the pain of birth and purification, to reaffirmed his belief in the great mystery. Sam took in a big breath, held it, and exhaled slowly. To Ryan, the air about them seemed to become dense, like a gathering was taking place. Sam's face softened, and his expression took on the look of a man who has just come home to loving relatives who had long awaited his arrival - a circle coming closed.

In two hours, all the pigeons had been released and both great birds had flown. The score: Care-if-val, two, Eric one. Jim explained that even in the wild, a bird of prey usually connects once in every sixteen tries, cast from the glove; the pigeon had a little advantage, so Carrie was above average. "This is also why I use barnies," Jim said. "Because they have had to evade hawks and other predators all their lives. This is why they work out best in training." Jim and Ryan would become good friends and fly and hunt the hawks many times during the next year.

They returned to the station wagon as the light was fading. Ryan watched intently as Jim fed each bird some meat from the pigeons that were killed. Sam knelt down in the dust and called Ryan over. He pointed to the ground in front of him and asked Ryan what he saw. Ryan could make out faint animal tracks that Sam had drawn in the dust. Ryan pointed to the different tracks and named the ones he knew. Sam quickly corrected Ryan when he was wrong. When the light was almost gone, Ryan said, "I can't see the tracks any more."

"You're sure?" asked Sam.

"Yes," answered Ryan.

Then Sam told Ryan, "Don't look directly at the tracks - just use your peripheral vision." To Ryan's amazement, the tracks now seemed to stand out even more then they had before. From that day on, every time Sam stopped by the station, he showed Ryan something about hunting or fishing or some plant used in Indian medicine. These lessons were not lost on Ryan, everything that Sam said seemed quite important and urgent for some reason. Ryan remembered everything.

One winter day, Sam didn't come back from bear hunting. He was found by Ben Hays and Eddy Hardy. They had came across Sam's truck in the woods and stopped to see if he had any luck. When they got out of their truck, they could tell that something was wrong. They could hear Sam's hounds; the dogs weren't baying at tree but were making what could only be called a sorrowful sound. The men had followed the trail only a few yards when they saw something hanging from a bush, it was Sam's medicine bag. Ryan had once asked Sam about it, and Sam poured out its contents. There among small stones and bundles of leaves there was a small bottle with little white pills in it. Sam said that it was heart medicine. Why had he hung it from the bush? Maybe it was a good day to die, as Sam had joked about so many times before they'd go into some greasy-spoon diner for breakfast with his friends. Only this time it was no joke, it was for real. Maybe Maggie needed him? Sam would be missed to all who knew him. A great void opened up, and to Jim and Ryan it threatened to swallow them as well.

Two weeks after the funeral, Jim asked Ryan if he wanted to go along to fly Care-if-val on Saturday. Saturday came and Jim and Ryan headed out of town toward the table-top mountain area near Jamestown. Ryan asked why they were going there instead of to the Del Puerto Canyon where they had always flown the bird before. No answer came to this question, so Ryan changed the subject, but Jim seemed preoccupied and lost in thought. After awhile, Jim loosened up and started talking about his plans for moving and where he was going to go. Ryan felt bad about this, but he also knew that Sam's death had hit Jim hard, as it had himself. Jim wasn't his normal happy-go-lucky self any more. Who could blame him?

Pulling off the road, they found a nice area not far from Melonies Reservoir where they could fly the falcon. Ryan noticed that Jim was giving Care-if-val larger pieces of meat each time he rewarded her for coming to the lure. Ryan remembered Jim's warnings about overfeeding, because a full bird might not come back to the lure. It was now close to dark, the sun would be set in forty-five minutes. When Jim called Care-if-val back to the glove, he slowly removed the jesses and bell, looked her over, and cast her into the air. "She's free," is all he said.

After a long silence, Jim told Ryan why he had released her. Jim had caught her as a young adult, and it was now time to send her back to find a mate.

"What does Care-if-val mean anyway?" asked Ryan.

"Nothing," said Jim. "It's just letters from girls' names - girls I loved and could not have in my life for one reason or another. The letters made into a name that would remind me that I could never own anyone body or spirit, especially this bird's body or spirit. If she wanted to, she could have flown away at any time and I knew that one day I would have to release her. As for the girls, most didn't even know that I existed." Ryan realized that both he and Jim were more like barnies than falcons when it came to the opposite sex.

Car-if-val was released into a stained glass sky, free forever, but she still continued to fly in circles above them. Jim and Ryan watched her and the way the light played off her feathers. As night fell, she settled onto the top of the oak tree above them. Jim and Ryan sat on a rocky outcropping, silently waiting for something, although neither knew what. Then Jim removed the whistle from beneath his shirt, he had tied one of Care-if-val's primary flight feathers to it. He placed it to his lips and blew one long note that faded into the night. Care-if-val had been making mewing sounds before this, now she made the klee sound as the tone of the whistle echoed back form the darkness where it had gone. Coyotes started to sing all around them, from every direction that the wind blows, they sang; north, south, east, and west. Jim and Ryan sat in the center of the great circle and listened to the songs for hours. When they left, it was early morning.

Most people wake up one day to the realization that almost everything in their life has changed, a slow gradual change. They have no way of knowing at what point in their life the changes had occurred, it just somehow happened. But on that night, Ryan and Jim realized that something special had just happened. For Ryan, this event would become a most significant moment, a moment of clarity and insight, a new understanding of what Sam had been trying to teach him. As for Jim, his life and his plans were also to change.

As they traveled home, Ryan noticed that Jim had the same look on his face that Sam had when they had first flown the birds together on that warm afternoon. Jim seemed at peace and totally content. Ryan was first to speak. "What just happened?"

Jim paused and scratched his head. "It was the weirdest thing. As the Coyotes were singing, I thought I could hear voices in the Coyotes song, singing songs from my childhood, songs from when Dad and Mom would take me to gatherings of kinfolks, the songs of the old ones."

Jim didn't move away from the neighborhood for many years, instead, he stayed and taught as Sam had taught. He took his animals to school classrooms and to wherever there was interest. His awakening was almost in the blink of an eye. Ryan's awareness was a bit slower. He used what his father and Sam and all the others had taught him to become the foundation and the beginning of a new understanding. For most of his life, Ryan was like parched earth, where the first rain would bead up and run off without soaking in. Now the cloudiness of his past had condensed into the rain that would become a flood. He was grateful to all those who had shown him so much, and to his father, who had the wisdom to know that he didn't know everything and that he didn't have all the answers. Instead, he had guided Ryan to those who that had the knowledge to help his son. The rest was dumb luck.

CHAPTER FOUR

MAGIC AND MENDED WINGS

Ryan was guided to Sam and the others by his father, where his venture into the public school system turned out to be the luck of the draw. There wasn't any testing of these waters for Ryan, it was jump in and sink or learn to swim. A third option was to flounder. On the river and in the wild, he was confident and little surprised him. His parents had taught him well, with respect and common sense, little here would harm him. He learned that the water was a living thing, as alive as anything can be, as was all of nature. It had a pulse; it was a barometer of the health of the valley. This was a place of wonderment and magic. The possibilities were unlimited. It was a place where an invisible tongue of wind licked the surface of the water, causing a wake to race across the surface. In his imagination, this could be a fairy skating or dancing on the water, or maybe it was the invisible finger of God pointing to where the fish waited to be caught. If this was a high point in Ryan's early life, then the lowest point was his first steps into "higher education?"

Ryan was almost six years old when he entered kindergarten at James Marshall Elementary School. He was a half-a-year older than the other kids and ill-prepared. He was behind even before he got started. The first day at school, he suffered separation anxiety, these strangers scared Ryan.

He would soon learn to have fun finger painting, playing with the giant blocks, going outside for recess. After all this fun, there was the milk, cheese, crackers, and a brisk nap later this would be called a power nap by those that thought they had power in position. The latter done without a towel brought from home. All and all the day flew by. This school thing wasn't half bad, he thought, at least for the first week or so anyway. Then the finger paintings and random scribbling needed to have structure in the form of letters and numbers. No matter how hard he tried, Ryan couldn't seem to get it right. Half of his letters and numbers were printed backwards. So much for his first year of school. He left kindergarten much the same as he entered it.

First grade, "SEE DICK, SEE DICK RUN!" What Ryan saw when he tried to read this book was Se, Deckr Un. Letters had merged, some overlapped and others were backwards, or they just disappeared altogether. No matter how hard he tried, Ryan couldn't make heads or tails of this book. This thing called reading was totally alien to him. His world was a tactile world; a touching, feeling, a visual world, where hearing and sight was what kept him out of danger. In the classroom with its four walls and four corners, there was no place to hide when they started to laugh at him for his inability to read this simple book about Dick and Jane. His fear-or-flight instinct, was telling him to run, but two things held him back. The fear of being punished by the teacher and then again by his parents when he got home, because that is what his father had told him would happen if he was bad in school. His parents told him that they had given the school permission to punish him if he acted up or was bad. Things went from bad to worse.

Ryan's parents separated, and, for almost a year, he went to a couple of different schools. There was no improvement in his school work, if anything; he slid backwards into a dark place. What else could happen? But something else did happen, his father and mother reconciled, and the family was together again. Things were looking up. Now it was back to James Marshall and the second grade. Ryan's new teacher looked like everybody's favorite aunt or grandmother, at first impression anyway. She was an artist. You might call her an impressionists, because she was there to make an impression. Usually it was an impression on Ryan's knuckles or his backside with a ruler or a yardstick. She would whack his knuckles with a ruler for not holding a pencil her way. Then when his bottom stuck out beyond the back of his chair, she would hit him with a yardstick or one of her round, oak pointers. This usually would happen when Ryan was deep in thought, trying to figure out some word or math problem, then surprise! The sound of the wood striking him would get everybody's attention. The other kids would giggle and laugh, "The dumb kid got hit again." These words stung Ryan, more than the smack of the ruler. One problem was that his desk was too short. Ryan was larger and almost a year older than the rest of the class, so he had to bend over to see his work and then, his bottom stuck out the back of his chair. This was a minor thing though, compared to the other things this teacher did. SEE DICK, SEE DICK RUN!!!!

Ryan's teacher would ask the class to form a circle with their chairs for reading, not quietly to themselves but aloud. The book was the same one that Ryan had tried to read in first grade. Ryan would start to panic. He would sit in his seat and the only thing he could hear was the rushing sound of the blood pumping past his eardrums, muffling the sounds of his classmates reading. When it became time for Ryan to read, he had no idea where the other reader had stopped and he was supposed to start. He started to speak; he stammered and stuttered what the words sounded like to him. The other kids would again start laughing at him, and the shame would well up inside. He was embarrassed. The teacher bent over him. She took her index finger and pointed to a word and said, "What's this word?" Ryan's stuttering increased. The more he stuttered, the more insistent she became, her finger tapping the word faster and faster, like a woodpecker on pulp. The room began to close in, becoming even more of a cage, a cage without air. His mind was like a butterfly in a jar, beating against the invisible barrier that prevented him from the freedom of the air. Next came the terror, it was suffocating him. No air, no air! Things were spinning, the letters on the paper started to move around like ants running around on a white background. He desperately tried to make sense of it all. There wasn't any structure to it.

" What's this word?" She demanded.

"I,I,I don't know."

"Read it, what's it say? Spell it out - sound it out!"

" I can't, *I wont!"*

Her free hand came up amazingly fast to cover Ryan's face. Her palm covered the bridge of his nose. With her thumb on one side just under his cheekbone and the rest of her fingers on the other side, she began to squeeze his face. The skin stretched tight over his cheek bones. She then brought her face down close to his. The smell of cigarettes was on her fingers and when she spoke, he smelled the combination of coffee and cigarettes on her breath. A spray of spit sprinkled across his face. She took the same index finger that she had used to point at the word and began thumping Ryan on his cheekbone. She was saying over and over again, "Mister, you will learn to read." Ryan felt the sting of her assault and every time she opened her mouth, he felt the spray of her spit on his skin, almost making him sick to his stomach. He could hear her loose dentures clacking together. Then all of a sudden, she stopped and spun Ryan's chair around to face the window.

Ryan stared out the window to where the magic used to be, but it was gone, replaced by the nothingness of an empty blue sky. Ryan didn't question what had just happened. He must have done something wrong. After all, they had the right to punish him for any infraction. In a few minutes, Ryan's teacher spun his chair around and it all repeated again. Ryan's eyes were full of tears, but few crossed his cheeks. This scene would happen many times that year but after the first time, there would be no tears, just strong defiance on Ryan's part.

At one point, there was the parent-teacher conference where Ryan heard his teacher recommended to his parents that he be held back in her class. She said that she could give him extra help in the area of reading and comprehension that he so desperately needed. Ryan was numb, not a sound came from him, but in his head there was only one sound - that of one long silent scream. His parents protested but later agreed. Ryan's head hung from his shoulders and he stared at the floor. He was lost and another year behind. Fate would have it that the next year, he would have a new teacher. She was nice but she had inherited what the other teacher had made of Ryan, in the written world, he was a cripple. She tried to help him but soon gave up. Later she found a program in the city schools that was designed to help kids like Ryan, but this move would only further stigmatized him.

A short bus ride across town to a reading lab at another school. Kids at both schools called the bus the M.R. bus, which stood for "mentally retarded," and those who rode that bus were the "M.R's." The bright side of this was the teacher, Mrs. Cockrun. She was patient and honestly tried to help Ryan and the others in the class the best she could, but, for all her efforts, Ryan remained unchanged. The only good thing about the bus ride was Thelma, the bus driver. Thelma had heard what the other kids were calling the bus and the kids who rode it. She tried to insulate her kids from those who would hurt them in word or deed. She treated her kids with respect, almost as if they were really her own kids and they treated her in kind, some even called her Mom. She would tell them stories about her own children. She let it slip one day that she was also a hunter. This impressed Ryan, a girl who hunted, wow! Ryan knew that his grandmother used to hunt, but somehow, another woman hunter surprised him.

One day, when Thelma picked them up, she was quiet. Something was wrong, Ryan couldn't help but ask her what was wrong. She started crying as she drove. The only words she spoke that afternoon was, "Kennedy's dead." Ryan felt responsible in some way.

Because the reading lab took up the first half of the school day, Thelma made sure that everyone made it back to their schools before lunch time each day. After lunch, there was recess. The playgrounds were separated; the kindergartners and first graders had the southeast playground. The second and third graders had the southwest playground next to the cafeteria, and the fourth, fifth and sixth graders had the larger playground on the north side. Buildings and the basketball court separated the playgrounds. Then there was Miss Foret. She scared Ryan, but he wasn't the only one. Almost all the other boys felt the same way. He soon found out that she was the third barrier to cross if a second or third grader wanted to play with the bigger kids. Ryan would have to get past her if he wanted to see some of the kids went ahead of him after he was held back that year. He would try this only once. Ryan thought he was sly and slick, but he had made it across and into the big kid's playground. Then, "Where do you think you're going, mister?" She was behind him, Ryan turned around and headed back to where he belonged. He thought she must have eyes in the back of her head because she was looking the other way when he made the attempt.

Miss Foret could stop any rough-housing with four words, "Hey. Stop that-NOW!!" It was not the words but the way she said them. She could have been a drill sergeant. She was very forceful and commanding. If a ball was over thrown or kicked into the big kid's area, she was always the one who would retrieve it. She would then throw or kick it back to where it belonged. Miss Foret could out-throw and out-kick anybody in the school. She could kick a ball so high that it seemed as though it was never coming down and when it did, few would attempt to catch it. When she threw a baseball back, it would sting your hand when it hit your mitt.

Ryan felt threatened. He had to out-throw and out-kick Miss Foret. It just wasn't right that a girl could do anything better than a boy. He would practice and practice, making improvement, but he still couldn't outdo her. In order to improve any more, he would have to get closer to her and learn how she did it. Ryan would get as close to her as he dared. The truth was that she still scared him, so he devised a plan. He talked a couple of his buddies into engaging Miss Foret in a game of catch or have her kick them a football. While she was preoccupied, Ryan would move in close enough to watch how she did it. She held the baseball across the stitches when she threw it, giving the ball a lot of spin. She used her whole body when she threw a ball, transferring her momentum into energy and putting power into her throw. Ryan later learned how she was able to kick a football so far. The trick was that she would hold the lacing of the football down and at a slight angle, but the ball was still parallel to the ground. When kicked, the lacings on the ball would make contact with the top of her shoe. The lacings and shoe would meet as her leg swung up in a sloping arc, sending the ball away spinning in a perfect spiral. One day, he challenged her to a contest to see who could kick or throw the farthest. For Ryan, the contest was to prove male superiority and to confront the thing that scared them the most-failure. He had to prove himself. He had to be better at something, to be better than anybody else, even if it was a woman. The contest was a tie.

Summer came and so did summer school and baseball. Then after summer school ended came freedom. Ryan tried to forget about school and hung out on the river with his friends. All too soon, summer was over, and Ryan hoped that he wouldn't have Miss Foret for a teacher. After all, there were two third-grade teachers, so there was a fifty-fifty chance of getting the other one. Ryan's luck took a turn for the better. Of course it would take awhile before he would realize it. Miss Foret would be his third grade teacher.

On the first day of school Miss Foret laid down the rules, "Rule number one, we are going to learn to have fun learning and that just about covers the rules." Miss Foret knew that most of the kids she taught were from single-parent or lower-income families. Because of this, she often would bring something to class from a country that they were studying. The item might be a toy, or a game, or a traditional garment. Sometimes she even brought delicacies - some sort of exotic food from one of these far off lands and cultures. Some of it was mighty gross, so gross that only the brave might give it a try. She never forced anybody to eat what she brought to class; she always took the first bite. There was caviar from Russia and candied ants from somewhere else. Most of these things were gathered by Miss Foret during her travels. Her summers were spent seeing the world, a world that most of her students would never get to see except through the pages of a book. Her experiences, her way of teaching - tactile and tangible - breathed life into otherwise dead text, she made the lessons live because she made school interesting.

The rumor was that Miss Foret had inherited a lot of money and property, which made it possible for her to travel as she did. Supposedly, she did need to work another day in her life if she didn't want to. When Ryan heard these rumors, he was dumbstruck. Why on earth would anybody work, especially as a school teacher, if she didn't need to? He still didn't want to be in school. Why would she choose to stay in school teaching when she could be seeing the world? Maybe the rumors were true. She was the only teacher who drove a Mercedes Benz convertible. This was the only thing that hinted of her wealth, but for the most part, she dressed modestly. She would either eat in the cafeteria with the kids or eat a sack lunch on the playground. Maybe she had inherited wealth, but this still left a puzzle that Ryan needed to solve. It didn't matter to him if she was rich or not, but why did she continue to teach?

Ryan watched Miss Foret closely. For some reason, he needed answers to his questions about her. He would watch and listen. He had overheard other teachers talking about her. Some were jealous, while others admired her. It seems that she rarely went to the teacher's lounge; instead, she preferred to be with the children. While at school, they were her responsibility and she was there to see that they played safe and that no harm would come to them. She was ever vigilant. Besides, the kids were more fun than the teachers in the lounge. It would take some time before the pieces came together, but Ryan picked up a piece here and a bit there. The picture was coming into focus. It wasn't until later in the year, that Ryan understood that she cared. Like Thelma, Miss Foret looked on her students as her kids, but, unlike Thelma, she would never have children of her own, this was it. This fact was what made all the difference in the way he would eventually look on this teacher and all others to come.

The school year had hardly begun when Miss Foret asked the class for volunteers to help out with a couple of special projects that she had planned. She asked the class to gather praying mantis eggs. She wanted mantis eggs to be taken from the limbs of trees or bushes. The eggs needed to have an inch or so of the limb at both ends when they are removed from the plants. This was so that they could be tied to the tree branches that were inside a round cage of fine screen which she had made. The eggs remained in the cage at the back of the classroom to incubate until spring. There was also another cage of the same construction. The only difference was that the branches had many white, elongated sacks hanging from them. To Ryan, these sacks looked like black widow eggs. These actually were silkworm eggs that would hatch soon.

Ryan was still required to go to the reading lab every day and he wasn't doing too well in his other subjects so it came as a total surprise when Miss Foret asked if he would do her a favor. The favor was to take the responsibility of picking mulberry leaves to feed the newly hatched silkworms. Miss Foret explained each cycle in the life of the silkworms as they transformed from worms into chrysalides to rest and wait and later to become moths. She said that this was what was called metamorphosis, the ability to change - to change from a crawling worm to a beautiful creature that could fly. To Ryan, it was like magic. It was a small shaft of light shining into that dark place where he had gone. It was the first drop of water on a patch of parched earth, beading up to slowly soak in and making it easier for the next drop. This wasn't like school at all; it was more like being outside. It was alive, no longer the lifeless letters on dead trees. Ryan opened up. He started listening and learning about other places in the world. Then something strange happened to Ryan, he started linking information together.

One afternoon, his older cousin, Sandy, who was staying with his family for awhile, was sitting at the table doing her high school homework. She asked Ryan's mother to help her with a couple of subjects that she was having problems with, biology and astronomy. Ryan was sitting quietly at the table, eating a sandwich and drinking a glass of milk. He listened as Sandy and his mother discussed Sandy's questions. At some point, they both were stumped for answers. Then it happened, Ryan started to answer the questions for them. They didn't, or couldn't, believe that he could possibly have known the right answers. When his mother and Sandy looked up the answers, they were amazed that he was right. How could this be? Ryan had no idea where the answers had come from, but they were right. He couldn't spell cat twice the same way, but somehow he could answer questions well beyond the level at which he was functioning in school. This was bizarre!

The school year was passing fast, and for the first time, Ryan was enjoying being in class. It was now spring and the praying mantis eggs started hatching. Some of the kids were disturbed when they learned that as soon as the mantises hatched, they started eating each other. Miss Foret explained that predation was natural and played an important part in nature's cycle. She released as many of the young mantis she could, to live or die as nature had intended. After a while, only a few mantises were left to grow into adults. Now volunteers were needed to catch flies and other insects to satisfy the growing appetites of their little wards. Ryan and Gerry Bernette proved themselves to be the best in the class at this task and they began a friendly competition to see who could catch the most insects. The only winners were the mantises - they were well fed.

Spring also meant that baseball season was here and Ryan was a pitcher on the Little League team. He loved the game and ended up on two championship teams. Ryan was more than a little surprised when Miss Foret started going to his games after school. She even brought girls to the games with her. The girls she took were the ones Ryan had crushes on but he was way too shy to even talk to them. How did she know that he liked these girls? Miss Foret showed great interest in Ryan's ball playing and continued going to the games even after school let out for the summer.

She was the first teacher to show any real interest in Ryan. With a little water, light, and attention Ryan started to blossom. The healing had begun, time would tell.

The next two years, Ryan's progress was slow but steady. The other two teachers he had were average, nothing special. Then in sixth grade, he was fortunate to have drawn an exceptional teacher. Mr. Dailey was his name. Unlike Miss Foret, he spent his summers working in the canneries. He had sons of his own, and one reason he worked through the summer was to support a hobby that he and his sons loved, waterfowl hunting. They spent their weekends in the fall and winter in the wetlands pursuing their sport. When Ryan learned about their love of this sport, he never missed an opportunity to ask Mr. Dailey questions about hunting.

At the beginning of the school year, Mr. Dailey asked the class how many wanted to be astronaut. Hands shot up in the air. Then he asked how many wanted to be a scientist. More hands went up. Mr Dailey noticed that Ryan never raised his hand. The next question was how many of them had straight A's on their report cards from last year. Two hands went up, Ken Mackey's and Nathan Northup's. Next Mr Dailey asked how many of their parents worked in the many food processing plants in the area. Then how many worked as mechanics or were construction workers. After each question hands went up. Then the last question, how many of your parents are astronauts or scientists? Not a single hand went up this time. He explained that the reality of life was that not everybody could be rocket scientists or astronauts and there actually is a greater need for those people who can make things. "If somebody hadn't designed and built the rocket and capsule to get the astronauts into space, the astronauts would be as grounded as a rock. It takes thousands of workers to build just one rocket and that rocket carries three lucky individuals into space. That doesn't mean that some of you won't end up in space." He paused, then explained that he had worked alongside some of their parents during the summer. "There isn't any shame in this kind of work as long as you take pride in what you're doing and you do the best you can. That's all that I ask of you - just do your best." This was Mr. Dailey's way of teaching, reality based and filled with personal experience. He embraced diversity, which created an atmosphere where all of the students had a sense of pride in themselves and their fellow classmates.

Ryan wasn't the only one with reading problems, Mr. Dailey understood this. Even those who were prolific readers were, at best, technical readers. They understood the words and sentence structure, but the words were little more than pigment and pulp. The spirit of the word was lost. Mr. Dailey would read to the class, choosing books that dealt with issues of the day. In the sixties there was racial unrest. The blacks were marching and rioting, the Hispanics also were marching. Then there were the war protesters. They all were trying to make a statement - to create change. These were issues but not the only ones Ryan would deal with that year. Physical differences also would be addressed. For the first time, Ryan heard the term "physically challenged" used instead of "handicapped." Mr. Dailey defined "handicapped" as a term used in sports such as horse racing and explained that it never applied to people.

The first book that Mr Dailey read was about slavery titled, Amos Fortune Free Man, which was about Amos's hard-won freedom for himself and his family. Mr. Dailey started to read, as he did so, his voice changed in tone and inflection. To his listeners the story became visual. Pictures of a black slave's life unfolded and feelings were aroused. Feelings of helplessness, rage, love of family, purchased freedom, loss of family, burden of long hours of labor, fatigue of the body and soul, all of which Amos felt as he labored to buy his family's freedom. One could hear the slave speak through this wonderful teacher. His words rang true even over more than ninety years after this former slave's death. His words were loud and clear. They were clear enough to create change in a classroom of kids that always knew freedom and who recognized prejudice in themselves and others. Their minds opened up and they were able to see that we were still dealing with equal rights and were still shuffling along in the shackles of ignorance. Mr. Dailey had shown that change starts with the individual and ends there if it is not shared. The saying of the time was, "free your mind and your ass will follow." Ryan would add to that saying later in life, "Bring along a friend because the road is lonely."

The last book that Mr. Dailey read was The Snow Goose. He read this book as he had read the others, with all the emotion and inflection of an actor. This story was about a lighthouse and its keeper, somewhere off the British coast during a time of war. The keeper was physically grotesque, he was so deformed that he was shunned by other people, but he was befriended by a lost, injured snow goose. The lighthouse keeper didn't have any human contact. Monthly provisions were dropped off on his dock and those who left the provisions would speed away so as not to see or be required to speak to the keeper. The keeper knew the sea better than most sailors or their captains and he knew all of the sea life in the area, finned or feathered. He was surprised when he found the snow goose; it was a lost traveler from another shore, blown off course by a storm. After the goose had rested and mended its body, it was free to fly away but instead, it stayed. He was a welcomed companion to a man who had no other living thing to call a friend.

The lighthouse keeper had heard over the radio that the British Army had been pushed back to a French beach and that their ranks were being decimated by the German guns. A call was put out for all able-bodied sailors with shallow draft boats, to come to the aid of their stranded, retreating army. The keeper had a small boat that could be used in case of an emergency, such as a ship running aground. He and the goose set out to cross the channel to try to help these brave men on the red beaches. They did reach the other side and helped to save many young men that day. Not one of these soldiers saw a monster that day, only a smiling face and a helping hand into his boat. To the keeper, who saw the smiling faces of the soldiers and heard their words of thanks, this was their acceptance, he was human after all. After many trips hauling soldiers to safety, he was on his way back to the beach to pick up another load when his boat was hit by a shell. All that was left were splinters of wood. Some of the men who had been saved by the lighthouse keeper witnessed the shell hit the small boat, destroying it. The keeper was gone. Only the snow goose remained. It had taken to the air. Rising higher and higher, as it circled over the spot where the shell had hit the boat. It was as though the tortured soul of the keeper was being carried away on the wings of his only friend. The goose finally disappeared into the sky.

Ryan noticed the effect that this story had on his teacher, as tears streaked Mr. Dailey's cheeks. Then silence as Mr. Dailey wiped the tears from his face. This was a turning point for Ryan. He saw the power of the written word, he had to learn how to read, not just the words but also the feelings. Ryan thought he heard something like a cracking sound in his ears, kind of like the sound when ice first cracks before the thaw.

Ryan was now well on the mend. These teachers were never voted Outstanding Teacher of the Year, but to Ryan they were the ones who made all the difference in his education. One brought the magic back, the other healed the wound. He didn't know when or how, but some day he would have to somehow find these teachers to say "thank you." Just to let them know what an important role they played and letting them know that they made a difference. Ryan was an honor student from that day on. There is an Indian saying that, "When the student is ready the teacher will appear".

CHAPTER FIVE

FOR THE LOVE OF GRACE, A MOCKINGBIRD SANG

Ryan sat there staring into his past, in the grip of memories lying there in the dust. Then a Steller's jay flew in the other end of the barn and landed in the rafters. Ryan's thoughts went back to Sam and what he had said about animals, both domestic and wild. They knew more about what was happening in the world than any man could ever know, and a smart man watches and listens to what they have to say. The Steller's jay was one of the early warning system of the woods, he was the watcher. More hunters have been screwed up by one of these feathered noise makers flying from a bush or tree, squawking and scattering game as they go. Ryan sat stock still and watched the jay hopping from rafter to rafter, looking for a meal in the spider-web buffet. The bird found little here to keep its interest and soon flew out the end of the barn where Ryan sat. Ryan thought it odd that the jay left without sounding an alarm. Maybe it was too absorbed in what it was doing and hadn't notice, or maybe Ryan had sat so still that the jay hadn't seen him? Never the less, it was strange. These jays normally never miss anything or anyone out of the ordinary. Ryan's thoughts turned to a cousin of this jay, a mockingbird and the memory of a blind man. Ryan hadn't made the connection yet, but birds were playing a big part in his life and one bird in particular would figure greatly in bringing life's loose ends together for him.

Ryan and other kids in the neighborhood made a game out of borrowing fruit from anybody's yard especially any that hung over their back fence into the alley. One of their favorite fences was in the alley behind Larry's house. The alley separated Avalon and Faustina. An Old Italian couple lived behind Larry, and they had a great garden. At the back of their property was a four-foot high wire fence, along its length there grew two types of grapes, huge round muscats and lady fingers that grew over an inch long. The grapevines hung over the fence and draped to the ground. Ryan and his friends would sometimes hide under the vines, eat grapes, and listen to the music that came from the blind man's house next door. The blind man earned a living tuning pianos and other instruments.

To Ryan, it was wonderful to sit under the canopy of vines on a summer evening, eating grapes and listening to music that was popular long before Ryan's birth or even that of his parents. This was music from a time when this couple was young and their world was new. Some of the other kids thought their music was funky and made fun of them. To Ryan, this was something special. It wasn't the songs or the piano playing, it was the way the blind man and his wife expressed their feelings and emotions for each other through the music they played. Ryan wasn't the only one who enjoyed the music. Many of the neighbors spent their evenings in their backyards or on their front porches listening to the music.

This one evening, the blind man was playing the piano by himself while his wife made dinner. Then the music stopped. Ryan hadn't heard the Italian come out his back door, but now he was cutting grapes for the dinner table right behind Ryan. Ryan froze. He was like a rabbit holding tight to the bush. He turned his body to the right and through the fence he could see a huge pair of boots. Then he heard a male voice coming from his left, it came from the blind man's yard. The men spoke briefly. After a bit, the Italian's wife shouted something out the back door and her husband shouted something back at her. Ryan didn't know if these two were always mad at each other or if shouting was the way they always talked to each other. At any rate, they sure were loud. Ryan held tight to the cover, waiting for the blind man to leave. Then he heard the soft voice of the blind man. "Hey, kid, you should come out now, Manuel's gone but he could come back."

Ryan crawled out from the shade of the vines. His eyes hurt from the sunlight. Squinting, he looked at the blind man, who was leaning up against the fence. His right arm was extended over it into the alley in the direction where Ryan stood rubbing his eyes. "My name's Bob and my wife's name is Grace. Now to whom do I have the pleasure?"

Ryan stuttered out his name, taking the blind man's hand and shaking it. Then he said, "How did you know, I, I, I was under there, sir?" "Bob-call me Bob. I have heard you and your buddies out here many nights. Where's your buddies anyway?"

"Bob. We were, well, kinda been borrowing the grapes out here in the alley." The old man started laughing.

"Borrowing? Borrowing? Taking something that's not yours isn't borrowing, now, is it?"

" No, I guess not." Answered Ryan.

"Good. Then you know the difference. How do you think you should repay Manuel for the grapes you've borrowed?"

"I don't know," was Ryan's response.

"Well how about paying him for his grapes? What about that?"

"How? I don't have any money."

"Let's see, what do ya got going for you? You're young and Manuel could maybe use a hand around his house mowing the lawn or weeding the garden and such. How's that sound to you?"

Ryan didn't want to even hear about weeding the garden. He hated weeding his mom's flowerbed, but he said "Okay," anyway.

"Good! Come by tomorrow, and I'll explain to Manuel what's happening and that you want to do what's right. Okay?"

"Okay." Ryan answered. He was feeling very small; his family had taught him better than this. He was only eight years old and he felt like public enemy number one.

"Now, where are your partners in crime?"

"I don't know."

"You're sure they're not back under those vines?"

"No, I'm the only one here. They stopped hanging out here when the grapes were gone and it was too hard to get the others through the fence."

Bob was puzzled. "Then why are you hanging around?"

"I like your music. I hide under the vines and listen." There was a pause.

Bob's voice softened even more. "So you like my music. It's not too old fashioned?"

"No, I just like it a lot."

"You won't skip out on me tomorrow, will you? I'll be waiting for you so that I can introduce you to Manuel. We'll see tomorrow what his thoughts are and how you might repay him."

"Okay," answered Ryan. "What time do you want me here?"

"How about eight in the morning? That way if he likes the idea of your doing a little yard work, you can get started early and finish before it gets too hot. Do you think you can get here at that time?"

"Yes." Then Ryan looked down and between the old mans feet sat a miniature collie puppy. It sat there quietly, its tongue hanging out panting; it kinda looked as if there was a smile on its face. Ryan asked, "Is that your puppy?"

"Yes," said Bob.

"What's its name?" asked Ryan.

"I wanted to name her Little Bit, but Grace wants to call her Lady, like Lady and the Tramp. So I'll see you tomorrow then?"

Ryan said "Yes" one more time.

"Good, in the morning bright and early then," said Bob.

Ryan had made sure that his grandmother would get him up and out the door by 7:15 the next morning. Ryan walked around the block. He was more than a little apprehensive about doing this. He felt very visible, as if the whole neighborhood knew what he had done and where he was going and that all eyes were on him. Was it his imagination, or did he hear somebody say, "DEAD MAN WALKING?" In ten minutes he stood on Bob's porch. He raised his hand to knock, but before he could, the door opened. There, behind the screen door, stood Grace, Bob's wife. Ryan said "Hello" and introduced himself.

She smiled, nodded her head, then turned and walked back toward the living room and said, "You won the bet." She turned back to Ryan, smiled and then winked. She introduced herself as Mrs. Osborne and invited Ryan in. Then she said to him, "Bob said you liked his piano playing. What do you think about the singing?"

"Its good," said Ryan.

"It's good." A frown crossed her face, "Is that all it is? Well, I never!" She sounded disappointed. Then a big smile crossed her face. Ryan stood there in their front room not knowing what to say. Bob laid his hand on Ryan's shoulder and said, "Don't let her give you a bad time. She's a sore loser, and she owes me some chocolate chip cookies. Let's go next door and talk to Manuel." Ryan had been run out of the alley more than once by Manuel. Now he was going to have meet him face to face and that made Ryan kind of scared. Mr. Osborne still had his hand on Ryan's shoulder and kept it there all the way over to Manuel's house. He could feel Ryan's fear. "Don't be scared. Manuel is a good man, a little loud, but basically a good man." When they reached the door Ryan knocked on it. It opened and the owner of the big boots stood in the doorway. He looked down at Ryan. His face was wrinkled and his nose was big. When he opened his mouth to speak, his thick accent made it a little hard to understand him at first.

He said, "Good, you caught one of the alley rats that have been stealing my grapes." Ryan hung his head down and was staring at his feet.

Mr. Osborne said, "Wait a second. Ryan said he was only borrowing the grapes. And he is here to say something to you. Go ahead and tell him, Ryan."

Ryan started to stammer out an apology, but before he had gotten very far with it, Manuel cut him off. "I'm up here boy, I'm not on your shoes. Look me in the eyes. You're here as a man, so act like one," he said.

Ryan did just that, explaining what he and Mr. Osborne had discussed the day before. After he had finished, Ryan stuck his hand out and Manuel shook it. "It's a deal. Go around to the side gate, and I'll let you in and show you what I want you to do." Ryan turned to Mr. Osborne and placed his hand on top of the hand that was still on top of his shoulder. He started to lead Mr. Osborne back to his house.

"Wait a minute, where are you going?" Mr. Osborne asked.

"I'm taking you back home," said Ryan.

The old man unfolded a cane and said, "I'm fine. You go take care of what you need to and when you're done, come back to the house, okay?"

Ryan walked down the gravel driveway to the gate on the chain-link fence. There, waiting for him, was the real boss of today's fun. It wasn't Manuel but his wife. Manuel was there but his job was to translate her wishes. She must have been a direct descendant of Napoleon or some other sort of dictator. She marched along, pointing at weeds and other things in the garden. It seemed to Ryan that she only had one volume setting - loud. She would string out a whole bunch of words for five minutes or more, then Manuel would say, "She said, weed the flowerbed, water the vegetables, pick that up and put it over there." On and on and on she went. Ryan thought, Wow, all that noise just to say, pull that weed.

Ryan had been watching her finger point from one spot to another. Then he looked over at Manuel standing behind her. Manuel had his baseball cap turned sideways on his head, and his left hand was tucked in his flannel shirt, marching along. He was making funny faces. He was waving his other arm all over the place, pointing here and there. He even acted as though he were hitting her in the head with his free hand, then he acted as if he had broken his hand. Ryan was trying not to laugh. She spun around and bopped Manuel on top his head with the palm of her hand. Then she marched back into the house. Both Ryan and Manuel were laughing and Manuel was rubbing his head. He said in his heavy accent. "That hurt, she hit me right on the button." Removing his hat, he showed Ryan the button in the middle of the baseball cap.

They worked around the garden, pulling weeds and picking ripe tomatoes and other vegetables from the garden. They washed the vegetables and placed them in a wicker basket. Ryan really liked working with Manuel. He was funny. Before Ryan knew it, it was noon. Manuel's wife was standing at the screen door; she was yelling something in Italian. He looked over at Manuel, who was nodding his head over and over again. When she was finished, Manuel said, "It's dinner time. She wants us to go in," and adding, "I wish she would learn a little English some day."

Picking up the basket, they headed into the house. Manuel poured wine into two glasses and acted as if he were going to pour wine into the glass in front of Ryan. Then he pulled the wine bottle away and said, "No, I think milk for you," and gave Ryan a wink. The food was wonderful. Manuel's wife filled Ryan's plate full; as was Ryan by the time he had finished it. More food was put on his plate. He tried to finish it but couldn't. He sat there listening to Manuel and his wife talking back and forth in their own tongue. After they had finished eating, she started clearing the table. Manuel was finishing his glass of wine. He looked over at Ryan and said, "You did good today. You can have all the grapes you want, just ask. I really didn't care about the grapes in the alley, it's just I've seen your friends throwing them at each other. Never waste God's gifts, food, or your youth. Make life count, you understand?" Ryan nodded his head. "Maybe you're too young to understand, that's okay." As his wife went by, Manuel swatted her on the backside. She had a wooden spoon in her hand and popped him on top of the head and started talking to him real fast and shaking the spoon at him. Manuel held his head in his hands. Ryan heard him say, "Damn that button. Every time, she never misses."

Manuel and Ryan got up from the table and went out the front door. Manuel said, "My wife likes you."

Ryan asked, "Do you want me to come back tomorrow?"

"Hey, you trying to steal my girlfriend are you?" Manuel said while bringing his fists up and shuffling his feet around like boxer. Manuel's accent made this more than funny.

Ryan started laughing. "You're funny. I was scared of you before, now I like you. You're a nice guy."

Manuel whispered, "Could you please convince my wife of that? And to answer your question, you don't need to come back tomorrow. You paid your debt like a man. You're welcome anytime, please don't be a stranger. Oh, yeah, I think Bob said he wanted to see you when we got done." They were halfway up the driveway when Manuel turned around and headed back to the house. Ryan watched him go. Manuel had removed his hat and Ryan heard him say one last time, "Damn button," as he rubbed his head while walking away.

Ryan went next door to the Osborne's house and knocked on the door. The door opened and he was again invited in by Mrs. Osborne and offered a chair at the dining room table. A plate of fresh chocolate chip cookies and a large glass of milk was placed in front of Ryan. Mr. Osborne said, "It's only right that you shared in the winnings," referring to the bet with his wife. Ryan forced himself to eat a couple cookies and drink the glass of milk. The puppy pulled at Ryan's pant leg and tugged on his shoe strings.

Ryan asked if it would be okay if he played with the puppy. He was told that, yes, it would be okay. Ryan got down on the floor and rolled around and played with the puppy. The laughter and barking filled the house. The old couple sat there and listened. To them this was music that they longed for, the sound of a playing child. They were never able to conceive and now it was too late in life. But one doesn't need to own an instrument or to know how to play one to love the sound of the music it makes. After awhile, Mr. Osborne asked Ryan if he wanted to hear some music. Ryan answered, "Yes." They all went to the detached garage where Mr. Osborne worked on the pianos. Four pianos were sitting in the cramped quarters of the converted garage.

"Are all these yours?" asked Ryan.

"No, two of them were, but I sold that one yesterday to a young couple in Oakdale. I buy and sell pianos and other musical instruments. After I sell them, the new owners usually take me to their homes and have me re-tune their piano after its delivery. Sometimes it's necessary, other times it's not, but that's all part of the service. Now let's open that side door and these windows and get some air in here."

"Why do you have to go and re-tune them?" asked Ryan.

Mr. Osborne explained, "Moving them sometimes changes things and humidity swells and warps wood ever so slightly, changing tonal quality of the instrument. Even though there is a huge cast-iron frame in a piano, things still move around. Anything that has strings and is made of wood will do the same. Sometimes I have to tune a piano to the room where it will be played. Even the shape of the room changes the sound. I was doing that when I met my bride. I was asked if I would go to the rectory of St. Stanislaus and tune their piano. Well, I was there tuning their piano when I heard some loudmouth outside talking with a priest. It was a female's voice, it seems that she had come to give a confession and afterwards stayed to debate women's rights. She and the priest joked back and forth. Her wit was sharp and at times even coarse, but funny nonetheless. I could hear the priest saying more than once, 'But Grace, Grace, Grace, I can't change anything. This is the way the world is.' When the priest opened the door, I played a song for her. When I finished she asked me to marry her. Being blind I only had a couple dates in my entire life, and now this crazy woman was asking me to marry her. I knew that there would be a big debate if I said no, so I called her bluff and said yes. Grace started laughing. So far it's worked out good, she still is a pistol."

With her hand she was messing up what little hair that Bob had on the top of his head. Then she said, "Play something, you old coot. It's too hot to stay in here for very long." They played a couple of songs. She was right, it was too hot, so they closed everything up. They told Ryan to come back anytime.

Before Ryan left to go home, he thanked them both, calling them Mr. and Mrs. Osborne. Mr. Osborne said, "Call me Bob."

Ryan shook his head. "No, it's Mr. Osborne," was all he said as he left. Ryan had many questions but he hardly ever asked them. He would wait and watch to see if he could find the answers by himself. One of his questions would take eight years to answer. What song did Mr. Osborne play to win Mrs. Osborne's heart? Eight years is a long time for a kid to remember this type of question, but Ryan did. He occasionally would stop by and visit, but the closer he got to being a teenager, the time between visits grew further apart.

Ryan had just turned sixteen years old when he heard the news. He was at the neighborhood store and Lady, Mr. Osborne's collie, was standing at the store's door with her basket. Mrs. Osborne used to take Lady to the store everyday and in time Lady could be sent to the store by herself with her basket. She would walk to the store, carrying a basket with money and a note. It was a great trick. Everybody in the neighborhood knew this, and she was free to come and go unmolested. So it wasn't out of the ordinary to see her there with her basket. Ryan open the door, bent down, took the basket from her and removed the note and money from it. He handed the note to Edgar behind the counter. Edger read the note and asked Ryan to get the items from the shelves and bring them to the counter. While Edger was ringing up the goods, Ryan heard him say, "It's a shame."

"What's a shame?" asked Ryan.

"Don't you know? Mrs. Osborne's not doing too good. She's not expected to live much longer."

Everything was placed in the basket and handed back over the counter to Ryan. Ryan looked out the glass on the store's front door to where Lady sat wagging her tail and smiling. Ryan opened the door and handed the basket to Lady. She took the basket and headed home. Ryan followed. Lady was proudly walking with her head high and chest out. Ryan followed, his shoulders slumped and his head down. He had lost three aunts and two uncles, including one of his favorite uncles, Uncle Walter, plus he had also lost his grandmother, all in that same year. He just couldn't handle any more. He followed the dog home and stood at the end of the driveway. She scratched at the front door until Mr. Osborne opened it to let her in. She hesitated going in, looking back at Ryan. Mr. Osborne asked if anyone was there. Ryan, to his shame, didn't answer, he just couldn't. In a few days, Ryan did go by for a visit and helped with chores. Once a week he'd stop by. No matter how you cut it, it still hurt. Mrs. Osborne lasted until mid-summer.

It was on one summer evening, when Ryan's mother asked him to shoot the mockingbird that sat on the telephone pole behind their house. Its nightly singing was bothering her when she was trying to sleep. He told her he really didn't want to, but she kept on asking until he agreed. That night, he lay there on his sleeping bag, pellet gun on one side and his dog on the other. After dark, the mockingbird started singing. Ryan held a flashlight in one hand and his gun in the other. He had decided to shoot the pole just under the bird; maybe he could scare it away that way. He must have shot that pole ninety-times that night. Every time the bird began to sing, he'd shoot the post. Somewhere around 4:30 in the morning Ryan fell asleep. It was about 7:00 a.m. when a spray of water hit him in the face. Ryan awoke with a start. Confused, he wondered if this was a personal statement that his dog was making about his shooting performance the night before. Looking around, he saw his neighbor, Mrs. Prince, standing there with smile on her face and a water hose in her hand.

"Hey, what's that for?" shouted Ryan.

"You're lying out here shooting the sparrows on my feeder again, aren't you?"

"No, mom wanted me to shot that mockingbird. It makes so much noise that it keeps her awake, that's all."

"That's all! Please don't shoot that beautiful bird. Don't you understand he's only singing to his mate, his love? She's on the nest in the Cypress out front. He sings to her all night, reassuring her from the darkness that he is near, and in the morning, he'll take her place on the nest so she can go and eat."

Ryan was struck dumb. He made a connection, and an old question was answered. He thought about the day that Mrs. Osborne passed away. It seems that she died in the morning. Mr. Osborne cleaned her body, then put her best dress on her. He sat there with her all day and into the evening. He went out to the garage around 7:00 that evening. Ryan remembered it, and now he could hear it clearly, but emotionally, he felt it deeper now than he had that evening. Something was wrong.

When Mrs. Osborne first became ill, Mr. Osborne would play the piano outside and she would sing inside. A week before she passed away, she became too weak to sing, so there was only the sound of the piano each evening. That particular evening was cooler that most for that time of year, and Mr. Osborne played louder than usual. This time, he sang while he played, something definitely was wrong. He played until 10:30 that night. There was a pause, and then he started playing Amazing Grace. Now Ryan wondered, Could this be the song that Mr. Osborne won her heart with so long ago? It was if Mr. Osborne, who knew only darkness, except for the one light that seemed to illuminate his soul, now gone. The old man was cast into a darker place than he had ever been before. He sang from his darkness to where his bride had gone. Then there was an uneasy silence. All who had heard knew that something was wrong. Ryan sensed that this was the song that had won her heart and now Mr. Osborne was playing it to say good by to his love, his light.

The day after Mrs. Osborne's funeral, Ryan took a big platter of fried chicken that his mother made and gave it to Mr. Osborne. He invited Ryan in and offered him a chair at the table. Mr. Osborne seemed aged; he looked so much older and smaller than Ryan had remembered. They sat there several minutes before Mr. Osborne broke the awkward silence. He started talking about his wife.

"My Grace was a pistol. Her hair was red and being big boned and all; she was the brunt of all the other kids' jokes when she was growing up. This gave her that sense of humor I loved so much. She could handle anyone, disarming them with her stunning or stinging wit, depending on who or what was said. She was so plucky that day with the priest; she had me even before she proposed to me. On our wedding night, her skin was a love novel that I and only I had read by touch. I couldn't see; she was my eyes, she was my light, she was my one love."

They sat there for a long time before Ryan got up from the table, walked over to Mr. Osborne, gave his shoulder a squeeze, and said, "Whatever you need, like mowing your lawn, whatever, just ask." He gave the old man's shoulder another squeeze, and as he left, he said, "Thank you, Bob."

After this, the music was gone. The music was replaced by the plunk and plinks of Mr. Osborne tuning the pianos. When fall came and the last leaf had fallen from the vine, Mr. Osborne also passed on. His music was gone, replaced in time by the sound of boom boxes and the thump of soulless noise. From that day on, Ryan would think of these good people every time he heard the song of the mockingbird.

When Ryan was twenty-eight years old, he went on a trip with his friends, Wes and Corel, to Mount Shasta. Wes's mother, Dodie and his stepfather, Frank, lived twenty miles north of the mountain. Ryan, Wes, and Corel, spent three days fishing and hiking around the area. One day, at Cassel Crags Lake, they witnessed bald eagles mating in free fall. The last day, Wes and Ryan went to the lava tubes called the Pluto Caves. Borrowing a couple of flashlights from Frank. They entered the cave and walked about a mile or so. Here and there the ceiling had fallen in and shafts of sunlight fell through the holes and rested on the silent floor. Ryan and Wes squinted their eyes into slits against the contrasts between the harshness of the light and the blackness of the cave. They walked farther into the entrails of the mountain, a place of absolute darkness. The darkness of the cave and the muted color and porosity of the volcanic rock swallowed the light from the flash lights. There was little to reflect it back to the two of them. The floor was mostly rock. But occasionally there in a patches of dust others who come through the cave had scratched arrows and initials indicating who they were and which direction they had gone. But without leaving any dates it didn't make much sense to Ryan. He thought that if they came through here and hadn't return the same way to rub out their names, who knows, their bones could still be laying on the cave's floor someplace.

After an hour and a half, Ryan's flashlight was going dead, then Wes's started to fade. They had no idea how old their batteries were when they started and hadn't taken the time to change them. Spare batteries were right there with the flashlights. Why hadn't they stuck them in their pockets when they walked out the door? Now they were in big trouble.

Ryan thought maybe they should have scratched their names in the dust somewhere because now they were deep inside this dark cave. Before Wes's light failed, they heard something from the darkness. There ahead and out of sight came the sound of a mockingbird singing. When they rounded the corner, they saw there in the middle of the cave, an island of light and life. There was a mound of dirt where the ceiling had fallen in. Growing on that mound was a tuft of tall green grass and an aspen tree, in its limbs was a mockingbird. Ryan and Wes climbed the steep sides of the cave to the desert plateau above. As they cleared the rim Wes heard Ryan say, "Thanks Bob." Wes didn't ask Ryan why he had said this; he only held the question in his mind. Ryan surveyed the plateau; it was as sharp a contrast, a contrast of the dark lifeless cave and that of the island of life and light below, and sage brush and junipers above. Ryan felt like he had crawled out of mother earth's womb, and had taken his first breath, to be reborn that day, born again with his eyes open.

Sitting in the barn, Ryan's mind returned from the memory that to which the Steller's jay had sent him, to the day that was at hand. He would soon make another connection between birds and another turning point in his life. He again remembered what Reverend Richards said that Sunday so long ago, God even knows when the sparrow falls. Maybe it counts after all?

CHAPTER SIX

BENEATH ARCHERS TREE

Ryan stood up from the table, leaving his memories stirring in the dust where they lay. Evening would soon turn into night and Ryan needed to make a place to sleep in the bed of the pickup. He rolled out his sleeping bag on top of an old mattress he had brought along, so that he wouldn't need to lie on the cold metal pickup bed. A tarp was folded up neatly and placed in a corner next to the cab; it would be used in case a weather front moved in. Ryan placed the ice chest under an oak tree, where they would be in the shade and out of the suns direct heat. After Ryan had squared away and double checked everything, he took a moment to string his bow and check his arrow shafts and broad heads. He looked over the bow's string for any fraying; it still looked good for its age. The string was the original that had come with the bow. Tied to the string between the nock and the top limb-string notch, was a three-inch piece of frayed nylon string, Sam's handy work. He had seen Ryan, one day, practicing with the bow in the sand lot next to the station.

Sam quietly watched Ryan, who seemed to be a natural. His release was smooth and his arrow placement was good. Ryan's concentration was fully on what he was doing, so he was unaware of Sam's presence until he pulled his arrows from the target and turned to walk back to the place he had been shooting from.

"Getting ready for deer season?" asked Sam.

"Yeah, I was just trying to set the pin sights. Jack's Archery put them on for me when I bought the bow." Ryan's voice denoted his excitement about the new bow and seeing Sam again. He walked up to Sam and handed him the bow. A smile crossed Sam's face as he lifted the bow and drew the string back to full draw, sighting past the pins.

Sam slowly let the string back to its starting point. He then examined the bow more closely, commenting on the ornate arrow rest and the embossed name on the body of the bow. "Bear Alaskan - nice. Who made the camouflage covers for the limbs?"

"My Grandma but I made the string silencers. They'll help take the twang out of the string when it's released." Ryan pointed to the strands of rubber inner tube that were tied to the string."

"Well, you and your grandmother did a good job but you need one more thing." Sam walked to his truck and returned with a piece of nylon cord. Ryan watched, wondering what Sam was up to. Sam tied the cord to the bow string; next he reached into his pocket, fished out his pin knife, and opened its blade. He then began drawing the knife blade along the cord so that the cord frayed into finer and finer nylon fibers. These fibers soon looked more like down feathers from a goose than they did a piece of string. Sam looked over at Ryan and saw that Ryan had his head cocked to one side. He had a questioning look on his face. Sam brought the bow string close to his face and blew softly on the nylon fibers, making them move in the opposite direction, like a wind sock.

Ryan's face lit up. He realized what Sam had done, and exclaimed, "It's to tell what direction the wind is blowing, isn't it?"

"Yep! And it's light enough to tell you which direction a flea was facing when it farted. You'll always know what way the wind is blowing when you're stalking game. Keep the wind in your face and no animal will ever pick up your scent. Its kinda like the ones made of feathers our ancestors used." After saying this, Sam's smile was as big as Ryan's.

This would be Sam's last season. After Sam died, Ryan, in respect for Sam's memory, had removed the string and put it away for safekeeping. Until this day, it hadn't been strung to a bow. Ryan straightened the ball of nylon fibers and then blew softly on them, as Sam had on that day. He then hung the bow from a limb on the oak tree where the ice chests lay.

From the lid of one of the ice chests, he removed the rubber snubber. The snubber held the lid down and made it harder for raccoons to open. Ryan took a piece of fried chicken from the chest and replaced the snubber. He walked over to the tailgate of the truck, sat down on it and watched the sun set. All was right in his world-squared corners and tucked in tight.

Night came. There would be no fire, no light or smoke to betray his presence, just the stars and the clear night sky. The truck was in the middle of the bare dirt pad. This flat spot of dirt was where his mother wanted to build a house some day, but for lack of money, it never came to be. There wasn't anything to obstruct Ryan's view; eternity was at arm's reach. Ryan climbed into his sleeping bag and, lying on his back, he stared at the stars and wondered about what would come at the rising of the next day's sun. Had he forgotten anything? Sleep was shallow, with lots of dreams, then all at once he awoke with a start. "Sam!" Some one said "Sam." Ryan had heard the voice and recognized it immediately as that of Sam's, but he couldn't remember what the dream was about. Was Sam an answer to a question with in a dream? At one point, Ryan heard a crunching sound. Raising up he pointed his flashlight it in the direction of the noise and turned it on. The light split the darkness and in its beam was a possum eating the chicken bones where Ryan had thrown them. The possum flashed Ryan a toothy approval of his choice in cuisine.

The night passed slowly, with Ryan waking often to check the sky. He knew that when the constellation Orion was centered in the sky, it was now time to get ready and now. Getting up, he stripped his clothes that he had slept in and changed into camouflage clothes that had been washed in non-whitening, unscented soap. All to hide the offensive smell of man.

Ryan took the bow from the tree and walked into the darkness. He could easily see well enough to follow the game trail below the pasture and find his way to his deer stand. When he reached the stand, he checked the wind and placed himself downwind from this trail's intersection with another. Ryan sat there waiting behind cover for daylight. The air became colder, as it always seems to do just before daylight. The blush in the east announced the coming of the light. Hours passed, as did many does and yearlings. The only bucks were spikes, which were illegal to shoot; they'd have to be forked horn or better to be legal in California. Time for Plan B.

It was time to stretch his legs anyway, so Ryan stood up slowly and surveyed the area for anything that he might have missed from his sitting position. He decided to take a walk and cover some ground that he had hunted when he was a kid. He crossed over his property line and the Old Greek Mine Road onto the Lynch property to an old logging road. These roads are called skid roads; this one had been abandoned long before Ryan was born. Now it was partially overgrown, and erosion would caused it to disappear here and pick back up again over there. It girdled the mountain. Ryan moved slowly and with great stealth, he passed well below a house that had been built on the property since his last visit some twenty years earlier. He had permission then, but now it was anyone's guess who now owned this piece of property. Ryan crossed many such unmarked and unfenced property lines. Should I be doing this? The thought crossed his mind many times, "Who now owns this land?" As he went deeper into the canyon toward the creek, he'd jump a deer here and there from their bedding areas. There wasn't any opportunity for a shot through all the brush that had encroached onto the skid road. With a rifle, he might have been able to take a shot at one small buck when it stopped in an opening about two hundred yards down hill, with a bow, it was impossible. When using a bow, it's important to make a clean shot and a clean kill. This usually means that the game needs to be standing still and within fifty yards. Even this isn't a guarantee of a hit if the game jumps the string. This happens when the arrow is released and the string makes a twang sound. Even the muted thud made by a silenced string is enough to cause game to flinch or jump, ending in a miss.

In some places, the brush was so bad that Ryan spent a lot of time crawling on his hands and knees. It was 10:00 a.m. when he reached a clear piece of road. As he stood in the clearing, Ryan caught a movement in the corner of his eye, a kind of flash. Ryan slowly turned his head. At first, nothing appeared to be there. Then sunlight reflected off the tip of an antler, it was a Western-count four-point buck. That meant that the buck had four points on each main beams, not counting the brow tines over his eyes. This buck was in his prime. The buck stood stone still and looked in Ryan's direction. He was standing behind a dead snag that once was a pine tree. Old timers call these snags widow makers, because you never know when one of them will fall over and make your wife a widow. Had the buck seen Ryan? The only thing to do was to wait and see. After ten minutes, the buck went back to browsing his breakfast. Ryan gauged the distance to be a hundred yards or so, an easy shot for a rifle but much too far for Ryan's bow. If it had been forty yards he would have had a chance to make a good, clean, killing shot. Ryan checked the wind indicator on the string. Even though there was no perceptible wind, it showed that a faint breeze was present. As luck would have the breeze was coming from the direction of the buck. Now Ryan had to figure out which was the best course to take in order to make a successful stalk. This technique, called still stalking, is where Ryan moves slowly and, at times, stopping occasionally and remaining motionless for varying lengths of time. If he was in the middle of taking a step, he would have to stop mid-stride, sometimes balancing on one leg for fifteen minutes or more at a time.

Ryan looked over the terrain. Between him and the buck was a steep ravine with a lot of open ground to cross. Ryan remained fixed to the spot where he stood waiting for the buck to move. He didn't want to push a bad position and spook the animal. He watched the buck move slowly along nibbling at a bush here and there, spending a lot of time on a wedge-leaf Ceanothus, pruning only its most tender of tips and leaving the woody stems. Ryan knew all the plants that grew here and he knew that the buck would move on when he had browsed down to the more woody stems. Soon the buck moved behind a bush, and Ryan started his stalk. He would keep the bush between himself and the buck as long as he could. Every step was calculated. He walked on the balls of his feet, minding not to step on twigs. He lowered his weight slowly when stepping on dry leaves, silently compressing them underfoot or moving them aside to reach the dirt below. He closed in to seventy five yards. Ryan crossed the first ravine and a new obstacle came into view in the form of a shallow gully, it was an opening with little to hide behind. Then the unexpected happened.

A band of does, yearlings and fawns, came up the gully from out of the live oaks in the ravine below. There was an alpha doe; she was the leader and the eyes and ears of the herd. Yes, she was the boss. She came up the hill first, followed by the others. She gave the buck little acknowledgement other than a disapproving grunt for his being there. The wind was still in Ryan's favor. If the doe had gotten a whiff of him, this stalk would have been all over. The other deer filtered one by one into the clearing and followed the alpha doe uphill, all but one, a young buck. He was too young to have antlers, just the little nubs hunters call buttons where next seasons antlers would grow. He was a button buck. The young'n stopped in front of the older buck and froze. He stood there stiff legged, staring at the older buck.

Ryan watched with great interest and was more than a little surprised at what happened next. The older buck advanced toward the younger animal. They walked around each other kinda stiff legged, sort of sizing each other. The young buck acted much like a mature, antlered buck would during mating season, during rut. Was this a challenge? Ryan could only wonder. The old buck had the advantage but for some strange reason he took off running west and away from the younger buck and Ryan. What the heck, thought Ryan, had he been seen? The younger buck bounded off after the older one, caught up with him and lightly butted him in the flanks with his head. He then spun around and took off in the opposite direction with the older buck following. It's a game of tag, Ryan thought. He had seen other animals play this game but never deer. They had played for only a few moments when the lead doe bounded down the hill and put an end to their game. She positioned herself between the two and began swatting the yearling in the rear haunch with her foreleg. She made grunting sounds to show her displeasure at the young'ns lack of respect for her authority. She headed him up hill and soon he was bedded down in the mountain misery with the others.

While the group rested, the lead doe was on duty and ever vigilant. She presented Ryan with his greatest challenge, how would he get past her? Ryan would have to cross the open ground below the herd. There were times when Ryan started to make a move and she would turn and look in his direction. Ryan would freeze in whatever position he was in at the time. He would remain motionless standing stock still on one leg. His breathing was slow and deep, his heart pounded in his chest and in his ears. The lead doe finally lay down, only her ears could be seen. Ryan could see that she was still alert by the way she positioned her ears, one forwards and one towards the rear, so she could hear to the front and behind at the same time. The four-point continued to browse for awhile and then bedded down some fifty yards to the west and below the others. He picked a small clump of cedars, there to sleep safe under the watchful eye of the lead doe.

The next obstacle to pop up was another stellar jay. It landed in a sapling just yards in front of Ryan. For ten minutes, Ryan froze in place, then the jay flew off without raising the alarm. Ryan felt invisible for the second time in two days. He crossed the open ground in an hour. Because of the density of the saplings, Ryan was able to close to within fifteen yards and eased in a little closer. He was slightly downhill from the sleeping buck. Ryan was clear for a shot. He nocked an arrow and drew his bow, the string came to cheek. Looking down the shaft, Ryan saw movement beneath the buck's eyelids. His eyes flickered and his nostrils flared, as he made little noises. Ryan realized that the animal was in a deep sleep and dreaming. All that was needed now was for the fingers holding the bow string to release and the buck would die in his sleep, in the middle of a dream. Ryan watched and thought how much this reminded him of a sleeping puppy. Then Ryan thought, what does a deer or even a puppy dream about, anyway, where do they go? This struck a chord in Ryan and he let the bow string slowly come back to rest at its starting point. Silently, he watched in what could only be described as that of awe and reverence for this moment. Ryan thought maybe this was what Sam had felt, which might explain why Sam was the way he was. He felt a connection not only with the sleeping buck but with everything everywhere, being totally alive and electrically aware, aware to all but one thing.

He hadn't felt it, but there was a change in the wind. It was the change that happens on every mountain every afternoon when the sun heats the mountain slopes and creates updrafts. The lead doe caught a whiff of Ryan. She bolted upright to her feet and bounced downhill towards Ryan, snorting her discontent at his penetration into her protected space. The buck awoke, still in a semi-sleeping state and stared at Ryan as if questioning what was Ryan doing in his dream? A split second later, the buck was on his feet and bouncing downhill. Ryan started to draw on him again but fought the instinct to shoot at the running animal. The buck soon got behind cover and kept it that way as he crashed his way to freedom. He would live and add his genes to the waters of life.

Ryan stood there listening to the deer bounding off in the opposite direction. Now questions started crashing around inside his head. As he walked back to the ranch, Ryan tried to get a handle on the moment. Why hadn't he shot? He had spent four hours of stalking and had nothing to show for it.

The confusion continued, then the day seemed to get even stranger. On the clearest portion of the logging road, Ryan felt something flip the hair on the back of his neck, then a rush of wind followed. It was almost as if someone had shot an arrow and or had swung a baseball bat at him, just missing his head. Ryan spun around, but nothing was there. Then it happened again. Ryan spun and again nothing. What the hell was going on? It was like when someone taps you on the right shoulder and then pops up on your left side. It happened once more. This time Ryan didn't turn, but with eyes looking straight ahead, he caught an image in his peripheral vision, the image of a falcon's body and its sharp pointed wing as it dove past him and through the trees, then over the side of the road. Jim Bird had once told him that this sometimes happens near a nest during nesting season. Jim had said that birds of prey will swoop in and use their talons to pull or flip the hair on the back of one's neck, but this was the wrong time of year. That was the bird's last pass. The question about what had flipped his hair was now answered, yet added another for his collection of this day's whys?

Ryan walked back to the Old Greek Mine Road, just one more hill to climb to make it back to the truck. About halfway up the hill, Ryan sat down in a large patch of mountain misery, he was exhausted. This was a good place to rest. Lying back and immersing his tired body into the pungent fragrance of the fern-like plants, he shut his eyes. In a few minutes, Ryan's body started to cramp up, his feet and legs cramped the most. Stretching his legs out straight and pulling his toes up started to bring relief. Then, as suddenly as they came the cramps left. He felt a floating sensation, then there was a crackling and buzzing in his ears like the sound made by high-voltage electric lines. Next there was the rushing. It was like being pulled at high speed through a water hose, being pulled someplace, but where? It was kinda like that warm afternoon when Sam had startled him while he was looking through the telescope, when his spirit had soared in a cinnabar sky, except this time he was headed toward a place of light. A moment later he felt an old, yet familiar sensation, the sensation that a sleeping child feels when he is carried by a loving parent and gently laid down on his bed to sleep.

He now became aware that he was sitting up with his back against a smooth, cool surface. His eyes were still closed, but he was very aware of his surroundings. When Ryan opened his eyes, he was no longer on the hill at the ranch but he hadn't a clue as to where he was. Ryan always prided himself on being able to survive anyplace, under any situation. His first instinct was to check out what resources were available to him. Then he rationalized that this was just a dream, it had to be a dream, so he decided to go with the flow. Now he started to take in what was around him. Soon he was so immersed in his new surroundings that his rational adult mind seemed to be slipping away. Then a part of his mind that had lain dormant since childhood started to awaken, and a deep breath entered his lungs. He was lost in the total experience, like an empty vessel being filled. The feeling of bliss flowed in filling the void to over flowing, almost overwhelming Ryan's emotions.

The surface that his back rested against was the trunk of an ancient tree. The leaves looked like those of a dogwood tree. The trunk was smooth in places and rough in others. Over all, it wasn't as tall as most dogwood, sort of short and squatty. It had lots of blossoms and the flowers had a fragrance that could be described only as having an almost narcotic-like effect. Every breath drew in its intoxicating perfumes, sweet and almost heavy enough to see it suspended in the air. The blossoms moved in the light breeze. When the blossoms touched each other, they made a tinkling sound like that made by glass wind chimes. After a bit, Ryan got to his feet and walked out from under the low canopy of the tree and into the light under a vibrant blue sky. The grass was super green, as were all the colors he saw here. The colors seemed to make sounds unto themselves, each separate and distinct from the next. With his senses awash and the analytical part of his thinking shut down, it would take awhile for Ryan to regain his ability to think straight. He turned around to see that the tree was rooted at the rim of a shallow gully. The ground was covered with lush grass that swayed in the breeze. At the bottom of the gully, Ryan saw something sparkle. From where he stood, it appeared to be a spring complete with reeds or cattails.

Ryan then noticed that the light came from all directions. There was no one light source like the sun, it was as if everything here contributed to the illumination. Was this a vision? Sam talked about visions - a time when one becomes one with everything. Or maybe this was heaven. Maybe I died, Ryan thought. He walked down the slope of the gully to where the spring was bubbling out of the ground. Drinking the water, Ryan noticed that it was sweet and as cool as it looked. He felt an effect he hadn't anticipated. The water seemed to be coursing though his veins into every cell. Then, out of a clear sky, came a shower of large water droplets. As the rain struck Ryan, large sores erupted on his body. For a moment, Ryan started to panic. Then he saw that, as the drops ran off his body, so did the sores, leaving smooth skin behind. When a drop hit the ground, a flower sprouted, bright in color and perfect in symmetry. Ryan now stood on a small island of flowers surrounded by a vast sea of grass.

Then, to all the other sounds, another was added - the sound of a hoofed animal running, galloping somewhere above the rim. Over the rim came a horse, kicking up sod behind him as he came. The horse trotted up to Ryan. Ryan thought the horse looked safe enough, so he reached out and touched it. He patted the horse all over while walking around and looking him over. He was a fine horse; chestnut colored and had a white blaze that ran down his forehead, between his eyes. All in all he was in good health.

The horse started walking down the draw and Ryan followed. They had traveled a couple hundred yards when they came across a red-wing blackbird. The bird sang as it hung onto a cattail. As he looked at the bird, a thought ran through Ryan's mind. How many of your kin did I kill just for the fun of it when I was a kid? Somehow it didn't seem to matter any more. A closer examination revealed that this bird was different from any other red-wing that Ryan had ever seen. What made it different was that, under the red patch of feathers on the shoulder of its wing, there was also a band of yellow feathers. This marking made the bird unlike any of the red-wings where Ryan grew up. The bird joined Ryan and the horse as they traveled. It would fly ahead and sing its song while waiting for the others to catch up. Then Ryan heard something else, a klee-klee-klee sound from high in the air above them. Looking up, he could just make out a spot high in the sky. It looked like a hawk or a falcon; it was too high to tell for sure which it was.

The spring was getting wider and the gully started dropping away more sharply to become more ravine like for a half-a-mile or so. It then opened up onto a narrow beach. The water of the spring flowed into a large, flat expanse of water that seemed to reflect light as if it were an endless mirror or made of liquid mercury. Was this the great circle of waters that Sam had talked about? At the beach, there were signs that others had passed that way. The footprints were fresh and when the trio reached the water's edge, they could look down the beach to see some sort of gathering. They walked along, heading to where the group had formed. Upon reaching this place, Ryan looked around at those who had assembled there. All things living seemed to be represented in one form or another. Even in the water there was life, such as whales and seals, and other creatures of the waters. There were many animals but, as for humans, they were few and far between. Ryan started to think and to question why was he here. What was this about? Questions, questions and more questions.

Then came a voice, low, clear, and compelling, like a familiar whispering in Ryan's ears. The voice seemed to be coming from an undefined form sitting atop the only rock on the beach. It was kinda like being at a lecture where the speaker seemed to be reading your mind and answering your questions as you thought them. The voice was supplemented by stunning pictures in Ryan's head, illustrating what was being said. Fast and furious, as the information started flooding in. Ryan could hardly keep up. It was as if somebody was holding a deck of playing cards in front of his face and then squeezing each end of the deck and spraying the cards into his face. Each card had a picture and information on it and as it hit Ryan, he could understand the information on it.

Then, all of a sudden, the water started to shimmer, causing the form on the rock to appear as though its edges were being defused into the shimmering reflection and into the water's light. Soon the whole image was hiding in the reflection. The shimmering stopped and the form was gone. Bewilderment and abandonment replaced the wonder of it all. The gathering began to slowly disband and slowly walked away going in different directions. This time Ryan chose the way back to the tree, so he and the horse and the black bird headed over the sand dunes and onto the rolling grassy hills beyond. They traveled in a southeasterly direction. Off in the distance, Ryan heard a low, rumbling noise and a cloud of dust arose in the distance. The horse gave Ryan a playful nudge with its head. Ryan stroked the horse's nose and gave it a swat on the rump as it headed towards the cloud of dust. It turned out that, at the head of the cloud, was a herd of horses. Now there was only Ryan and the bird left. The bird flew ahead, as he had before and landed in the tall grass. He hung sideways from the heavier stalks of grass, only this time he didn't sing as he had before. They had traveled a half-mile when the sky darkened and the silence was broken by the sound of thousands of wings that churned the air above. The bird sang a single note then took to the air, following the flock. Ryan was now alone. He had never felt as alone as he did at that moment. When he reached the tree, he sat under it. He felt even more bewildered, lonely, and abandoned. Ryan looked out from beneath its limbs, from here he could see other patches of flowers here and there just like the ones he left. "Why hadn't I seen those before?" Ryan thought aloud. "Who else passed this way, leaving flowers behind?"

Then the same soft, clear voice from the beach said, "Wouldn't it not be better to ask who left the tree that you now sit beneath?" Ryan then, as suddenly as before, felt himself being pulled again through the void, only this time he was headed back to where he started. It felt as though his spirit was a liquid and was being poured in at his head to run down to his feet. It was like water sloshing back and forth from head to toe. Ryan awoke with a start. His eyes wouldn't focus at first but he could make out a dark form to his right. Squinting, Ryan could see that it was a human. As his vision cleared, he saw an Oriental man squatting over him. The stranger was dressed in brand new camouflage from his head to his feet. Ryan looked the stranger's clothes over for a forgotten price tag. Ryan thought that the stranger looked like an Oriental Minnie Pearl, kinda out of place, as though he were off the cover of G.Q. This guy was fresh out of the package. Then the stranger said "Howdy. Are you okay?"

"Yeah." Ryan couldn't help but laugh and reply with a howdy of his own. The stranger offered Ryan a hand to help him up. Standing, Ryan shook the stranger's hand and introduced himself.

" Kami"(Commie), replied the stranger and then added, "I saw you from the road," pointing toward the Old Greek Mine Road. "I thought you might be hurt." Then a crooked smile crossed his face. "Who knows, you might have been dead and I could always use another bow and some extra shafts." They both laughed.

"Would you like to come up to my camp and have lunch with me?" asked Ryan.

"Yes, that's if it isn't too much trouble," replied Kami.

"No problem, no problem at all. I've got plenty and could use the company. Just follow me up the hill." As they walked silently up the hill to where the pickup was parked, Ryan was wondering to himself, trying to remember. There was something about a dream. For some reason, he couldn't remember the dream. What was it?

A small band of does and fawns crossed the trail up the hill from them. Both men stopped, like terra cotta soldiers, they stood watching the animals. The deer hadn't seen or smelled them, so they continued up the hill unhurried, on the same trail that the men were on. The men followed slowly behind, watching the animals ahead. When the lead doe saw the pickup on the flat, she froze, as did the others. The wind was coming from the direction of the truck, so she could smell the residual scent of man. She slowly left the cover of the brush and walked over to the vehicle and sniffed around. She looked back at the others, snorted, and the rest left the brush single file, trotting past the truck, down the road, towards the barn. They made almost no noise as they passed, like ghosts they disappeared back into the brush past the barn. The lead doe was the last to leave. The men watched it all from their vantage point. Ryan motioned for Kami to follow him. When they reached the truck, Ryan asked his guest to give him a hand with the ice chest and they carried the chest to the truck. Ryan removed the snubber and took out a box of chicken that he had bought at the Chicken Barn on McHenry Avenue while leaving town. Soon paper plates and cups plus a two-liter bottle of Sam's Choice cola were on the tailgate, the table was set. Ryan handed a plate to Kami, as he did this, he cautioned Kami not to lose the plastic fork because they were getting rare, he had only one left.

Kami stood up straight and held the plate in front of him, both hands forward, palms up, and with his arms slightly bent. Kami bowed at the waist and said, "I'm honored." The expression on his face was that of seriousness.

Ryan laughed. "Heck, it's not the last plastic fork on the planet; it's just the last one I have with me. We can go into Mountain Ranch if we need more." Then he placed his own plate down on the tailgate and Kami did the same. Ryan opened the box of chicken and said, "Help yourself." Kami hesitated, as though he was uncertain of what to do, so Ryan reached in and fished out a couple pieces and one of the small containers of Valley Dressing. Then he put a little coleslaw on his plate. Ryan poured some of the dressing over the chicken and then handed the dressing to Kami, who did the same. Ryan poured them both a cup of coke, then, he picked up his plate and sat down on the tailgate, took a piece of chicken, and bit into it. "Ummm, that's good. You can't get chicken better than this, except when it was fresh out of the frier, that is. The only thing better would be the chicken that my mom and grandmother used to make." His guest copied Ryan's every move. They sat on the tailgate eating and making primal noises of satisfaction. They started to exaggerate these sounds, improving and refining their tonal qualities, basically acting like kids, laughing and having a good old time. After they had finished with their meal, Ryan gathered the plates together and placed the bones in a pile about twenty feet from the truck. Kami looked as if he had a question but didn't quite know how to ask it.

Ryan broke the silence asking, "Would you like to hunt the ranch with me this afternoon?" It had been a common practice in the past to offer this courtesy to other landowners or fellow hunters. This practice had all but disappeared because of lawsuits against landowners by hunters who had accidents while hunting. This is the reason why access to land is denied to so many hunters across the nation today. Ryan felt that he could trust this stranger. There was something different about him, something Ryan couldn't put his finger on, yet he was sure he could trust him.

Kami nodded his head yes and said, "Thank you, thank you very much." The look on his face hadn't changed though. He still looked a bit bewildered, kinda like he still had something on his mind. Then he raised his hand and pointed toward one of the larger oak trees. Beneath the tree was the hulking olive-drab hull of the good ship, Billy G. "Is that a boat?" They both walked over to it. Kami put his hand against the hull. He closed his eyes and walked the length of the boat, his fingers lightly touching and tracing their way in the dust as he went. He paused at the other end and said, "This boat was in a war."

"Yes, it was. It belongs to a friend of the family, Bill Gilstrap. He needed a place to store it, so we let him bring it up here. Heck, when he dropped it off, the oak it's leaning against was a sapling about two inches around." Ryan chuckled. "It's been here so long that half the time I don't even see it anymore. It's now just part of the landscape."

Kami was smiling and shaking his head. "I was going to ask you, just exactly how high does the water get around here? That's one big boat." They both laughed.

Ryan noticed that his guest's English had taken on a more Southern accent, almost with the same inflection as Bill Gilstrap's or any number of neighbor's from the west side of town. It sounded kind of strange coming from an oriental. "Yeah, Bill bought it from the Army Surplus. He was trying to rebuild it into a sea-going vessel. Bill had a dream of running away from home, off to the seven seas, or maybe just hanging out in the Delta where his wife couldn't find him. Like most people where I grew up, he had a dream. Its kinda like my mom's dream to build a house on this flat spot we're standing on. So the boat sits here, some day to turn to rust and dust, and, you see, in the not-too-distant future, the brush will take back this little patch of flat dirt. Hey, I just noticed something; your English has suddenly gone south, or in other words Southern. You got a little south in ya."

"No, I just seem to pick up on other people's accents. It's kind of a curse where I come from."

Ryan couldn't hear the accent in his own speech, but Kami, when he spoke the southern taint, seemed strange. And his new friend didn't seemed to have an accent until he had touched the boat hull. It was almost as if he had picked up the essences of Bill's speech, and even his delivery was like that of Bill's, all from just a touch. For a moment, Kami sounded just like Bill. This surprised Ryan and caused him to almost believe that, in touching the boat, Kami had made a direct connection with its owner.

They walked over to what was left of the pump house. Kami asked, "What happened here and what was this structure?"

Ryan stuck both of his hands in his pockets and looked down at the concrete where the pump house once stood. It was as clean as if it had been swept. He paused, rocking back and forth on his heels, shrugged his shoulders and started to speak. In his voice could be heard the echo of a memory. In an apologetic tone, Ryan said, "This is what's left of the pump house. Dad built it. It's not one of his best works. My grandfather wouldn't have let Dad build it the way he did. Grandpa was a master carpenter and taught my father the right way to put up buildings-buildings of any size. He was the only one that could change Mom's mind once she made a decision, such as a remodeling job or, in this case, the pump house. He had already passed when this was built. About halfway through the project, Mom redesigned it. That was when Dad's pump house turned into the Leaning Tower of Mom. What was to be a single story, fifteen-by-fifteen foot pump house, turned into a fifteen square foot bottom to a twenty-by-twenty second floor building? The five feet of overhang on the north and on the east side of it was going to be a screened in porch. The key words here are, 'was going to be.' It didn't take Mom long to change that. She had Dad turn it into a twenty-by-fifteen foot bedroom and a five-by-twenty foot tack room on top. Heavy wooded beams were placed underneath to support the overhangs. This helped for awhile, but slowly the building started to lean and, for the last five years, it was unsafe to enter. Then this last winter it blew over and set down just as you see it. The top room is fairly intact. I have a couple of friends that have tractors with front loaders on them, and we're going to lift it up and put blocks under it. I couldn't keep it from falling, but maybe I can level it up again."

They walked around to the south side of the pump house. On the ground was the wall that once held up the top portion. Ryan noticed that some of the old linoleum floor tile was still stuck to the outside of the wall. He hopped up on what was left of the wall, squatted down and pointed to the piece of tile. "Would you look at that? That piece of linoleum has been glued to that piece of flooring probably more than fifty years."

"So, what was a wall, now is a floor again?" question Kami.

"It has been both. Everything on this property has had at least one other life. This wall was once the floor of a school." Ryan pointed up to the pump house roof. "Those trusses up there were from the same school, it was the old Robert's Ferry School. Dad, Grandpa, and I tore it down over twenty-five years ago to make room for what is now the new Robert's Ferry School. We were doing salvage demolition and saving all this great old wood. This kind of wood you can't even find in most lumberyards anymore. It was dry, straight, full-cut, clear-grained with very few knots.

We sold most of it at about half of what new lumber was going for and still made money. What didn't sell, we brought up here, and we used it. Come on, walk with me."

They headed up the dirt road, paying attention not to disturb the tracks of the deer that had traveled the road since Ryan had driven down it the day before. There in the dust was today's news. Ryan could read the signs easier than a newspaper; he started to read them as they went along. "Look here! The does walked over a buck's tracks. He came up out of that ravine, probably this morning when I was clear down at the other end of the very same ravine. I must have made a mistake somewhere in my program and he picked me up and came back up this way."

Kami pointed to a track and asked, "What's this one?"

"That's an opossum's track and would you look at this? A coyote was following it. I wonder if it was the same possum that dropped in for dinner last night. The coyote hung back here." Ryan pointed to a bushy clump of live oak suckers sprouting out of a stump. He was watching from this cover, waiting for the possum to finish his meal. He let the possum pass, then, he moved out onto the road. He moved slowly at first, he's almost stepping in his own footsteps. See, here the coyote squatted down. See where the hair on his tail made these marks in the dust? The marks are a little harder to see because of where the deer had walked over this set of tracks. See, here he has started to move faster. He's kicking up dirt, and it's falling back behind the heel of its pad. Over here the possum turns around, confronting the coyote, and here is where the coyote threw on the brakes. The possum started backing up, and the coyote followed. Then he tried to pounce once here, then once again there. The possum kept its tail tucked and slowly backed his way over to this tree and, more than likely, climbed the tree and hung out there until the coyote got bored and left. The coyote was probably a juvenile. Look there on that piece of rock. He's deposited his opinion about the service in this restaurant. It looks like he didn't get the possum-wrapped-around-chicken-bones dinner he had ordered. He made his feelings quite clear but look, he still left a tip. We probably won't get a good review in the Coyote Culinary Gazette." On top of the rock, the coyote had relieved itself. "That is what they call scat." Ryan picked up a stick and poked the remains of what was once one of the coyote's meals. "You see here, he had been eating manzanita berries and what looks like the remains of a wood rat. Why didn't I hear all of this? I must have been sound a sleep, dead to the world."

Kami rubbed his chin with his right hand. "That's one heck of a story. Now who taught you how to read signs like this?" he asked.

"I've learned from my father and every hunter I've ever hunted with. Heck, even the Boy Scouts taught me a little about tracking. Then there was Sam Bird and Jim, his son. They probably showed me the most," Ryan answered.

When they reached the barn, Kami said, "Look at all this great stuff. If it's all right, may I take a look at it?" Ryan saw Kami's excitement and nodded his head. Kami walked into the shadow of the barn. There he started picking up things that were stacked on top of what was left of the trailer. He picked up this and that, it was as if he had never seen junk like this before. An old two-quart bulk-oil can seemed to hold his attention for a moment. He looked into its open mouth, and put his eye to the spout as though he were trying to peer into it like a periscope.

Ryan started laughing. "See any dinosaurs, captain? It's an oil can. You'd crank oil into it from a bulk oil dispenser. Filling it to the line would give you two quarts. Then you'd haul it out to your customer's car and tip the spout and let it dump into the engine. The customers that used bulk oil, their vehicles usually leaked out about half as much oil as you'd dump in it. At times, I thought they must have been watching me and waiting because it never failed that when I'd get my broom and soap out and have half the islands washed, they'd drive in and park over the clean spot. They'd want two dollars worth of gas and two quarts of bulk. So there I'd be cleaning the same piece of concrete all over again, sometimes two or three times a day."

Kami had a questioning look on his face. He elevated the can in a pouring fashion, like a coffee pot, then, he put the spout to his lips as if he were going to take a drink from it.

"No, not like that! Level the can, grab the spout, and now push down." The mischievous smile crossed Kami's face again. "I think you're messing with me, man," Ryan said.

Kami put the oil can down and picked up a couple other items, examined them and put them back where he had gotten them. He paused for a moment and looked at the ground. He stared at the things that had stirred Ryan's emotions the day before. Kami knelt down and picked each item up and dusted it off, in what could only be described as a respectful manner. He then placed each one back on the trailer. Neither man said a word. To Ryan, it was almost like this new friend was experiencing Ryan's thoughts and feelings from the day before. Could he? After all, he seemed to pick up impressions off of Bill's boat.

When Kami had finished, he looked up in the northeast corner of the barn, something in the rafters caught his eye. Ryan looked in the same direction. There, staring back at him, was something that he had tried to put out of his mind long ago. This object shook him, Ryan then said, "Let's get out of here. Come on, let's take a walk up the road."

For a while there was only silence. Their footsteps were the only sounds to be heard. Ryan couldn't even hear this sound, just the reverberation of a distant emotional storm, a storm where he had become the center of the tempest, a moment long ago when Ryan had almost lost control and crossed into a place where there is no return and little chance of redemption. Kami placed his hand on Ryan's shoulder bringing him back to the present. "It's okay, friend. It's okay."

They continued up the road, passing all the rusting equipment and the ranch house past the neighbors driveways, to reach Baker Riley Road. At this point, there were only two directions they could go, right or left. Ryan chose the direction and Kami followed. A hundred yards down the road and another choice had to be made, whether to head to the main road or down the Old Greek Mine Road. Again, they went to the right. One of the neighbors was standing at the mail boxes. He gave them a friendly wave and a "Howdy." Ryan and Kami returned the greeting but didn't stop, they just continued down the road. Ryan's mood had changed, and he was now walking along, telling stories about hunting along this piece of dirt road. Kami said little. He seemed content just to follow and listen. They had traveled about a quarter of a mile when the road took an abrupt turn and headed downhill. This is where Ryan stopped at the fence of an old friend. There wasn't anyone home; no one had been there for many years. This was the boarded-up home of one of Ryan's friends and mentors. Ryan and Kami leaned over the white wooden fence in front of the house, resting their fore arms on its top rail.

Kami asked, "Whose home is this?"

"This was the weekend home of Hayward Richardson and his wife, Bernice. Two of the best people that I've had the pleasure to have ever met."

"Why is it boarded up"?

"I can only speculate, but after Mr. Richardson died, maybe there were too many memories and the family had a hard time dealing with the loss. I can understand it because when I found out about his passing, it really shook me up. I couldn't really believe that he was gone." "Tell me more. What were your friends like?" asked Kami.

"Hayward was one of the smartest men that I've ever come across. He taught me many things. He worked for Stanford University. I don't know what he did there, all that mattered was that he was a friend, and his wife, Bernice, was a gracious lady. Hayward had never built so much as a birdhouse house before he built this place. He bought the plans for this home and a book on carpentry. He and his sons, plus his grandkids, worked weekends and vacations until it was finished. At first there was quite a buzz about these new neighbors. Most of the noise came from one local contractor, Al was his name. Al didn't like the idea of "those kind of people living here."

"What did he mean by these kind of people? You make it sound bad?"

"Well, you know, black folks." There was distaste in Ryan's voice.

"Again, I hear something in the way you answered. Did something about my question bother you? You seemed to be a little upset at the barn and again here. Are you okay?"

"Yeah, I'm okay. I've just had a couple things on my mind the last couple of days. Just now your question made me remember something in the way Al described the Richardson's. I was with my Dad when Al broke the terrible news about who had bought the property that we now stand in front of. Al used words, racist words, words that I choose not to use, words of a bigot, to describe their ethnic background. You see, because of them being black, it didn't make any difference to me. I really don't feel comfortable to even use the word black or red or any color to identify a friend. Al said that he had gone over to offer them his highly skilled talents. Of course, they were offered these talents for a nominal fee, and would you believe, they turned his offer down? He laughed and said that they looked like a bunch of ants crawling around on that house. I know you probably don't have racism were you come from."

In a low, almost monotone voice, Kami spoke. "I know. In Nipon where I grew up, there was much the same kind of attitude. Social class of a family was determined by what the father did, such as a fisherman or carpenter. This defined their class, his status and that of his family would remain so forever, from birth until death, forever. Even though we were all of the same race, there were always those that were born of privilege and rank and then there were those without power and in poverty. The lowest classes were those that dealt with and in the death of animals and the byproducts of those animals, leather and meats. When they ventured beyond their social boundaries, they would politely be reminded of their proper place. They could marry only within their station; to do otherwise was considered a great breach of etiquette. It was social suicide for both bride and groom. Both families would be shamed." In Kami's voice Ryan could hear both embarrassment and pain.

"For a minute there, you made it sound like you were talking about something that had happened a long time ago. I thought Japan was more liberal than that. It seems that the enlightened East and the barbaric West aren't so far apart after all. Maybe the polite approach is easier to swallow, but isn't easy to digest or any less destructive to the individual?" asked Ryan.

"No, in my home country, society instills in us that the individual is not important, only that the class in which we were born be maintained to serve the class above us. Never complain, just politely agree and go your way. It seems to have changed little in both our countries if what I heard was correct. I do not believe that this way is right, and I could hear in your voice that you and I are of like minds. Maybe you're right. East and West are closer together than we realize. How did you become friends with this family anyway?"

"Well, when they were building this house, I was in the seventh grade, and I always used that hill where you met me to go and come from the ranch. So, for the first couple years, I only knew of them what I heard from Al. It was my freshman year before I met Mr. Richardson, at this very spot."

Ryan leaned back, away from the fence. Only the palms of his hands touched the rail. He lightly tapped up and down on the rail, causing it to vibrate. Ryan stared at the house and started to speak in a soft voice. It was kinda like he was watching a film playing in his head and interpreting what he was seeing to Kami. "It was kinda like he was waiting for me right here that day, his arms resting on this very rail." I was headed back to the ranch. I had broken my leg in a football game. I had a cast clear up to my hip and it was too hard to use my usual trail to the ranch. It was late and evening was coming on. I was putting past here on my crutches, focusing on the ground in front of me. I hadn't seen him, I just heard his voice from behind the rail.

"See anything?' he asked. I was a little startled at first, then I looked over and there he stood. He was a big man with even a bigger smile. I didn't respond at first, just shook my head. Since it was deer season, I had my rifle slung across my back and I was a little self-conscious about traveling the road with a loaded rifle. Then he asked, "What kind of gun do you have there, son?'

"Remington 742 Wood Master 308," I said, then gimped over to where he was.

"Can I have a look at it?"

I said, "Yes." Then, I propped my crutches against his fence and peeled off the rifle. I unloaded and cleared the chamber and then handed it to him. He also checked the chamber before he shouldered it and sighted down its barrel.

"It shoulders nicely and the sight picture is perfect; nice rifle." He then turned it over and looked at my makeshift sling fashioned from a belt, "Functional and innovative. I like it. By the way, I'm Hayward Richardson." Then Ryan stuck out his hand over the rail like Mr. Richardson had those many years before.

I reached out and took hold of his hand. His grip was firm and I introduced myself. "Pleased to finally meet you," he said. I must have had a confused look on my face, like a why-would-he-be-wanting-to-meet me kind of look?" He went on to explain. "I've seen you almost every weekend going up or down this road, and my curiosity had the best of me, and now I've got to meet the young man that passed here armed to the teeth and on crutches." Maybe he thought I was going to pull a limp-by or something like a drive-by, only slower. He then said, "I've seen you go by very early, but before I could get outside you're gone. I've walked down the road in the direction that you had gone and you were nowhere in sight. I figured that you left the road at some point, but where? Twice I've seen you at or just before daylight and today I finely caught you and its almost dark. Have you been out there all day?'

I said. "Yes."

He then asked me if I had eaten? He put his hand on my shoulder, and said "You must be hungry." I shook my head. He then asked me if I would like to come in and have some dinner with him and his wife. I thanked him, then told him that my Dad and Mom were waiting for me and I had better get going. Before I could leave, he again asked me where I went and exactly how far I had traveled and what I was hunting for. I told him about some old skid roads that I hunt and pointed at the brush near his corner post. Back then the brush next to his corner fence post looked like a solid wall. Ryan turned to his right and pointed his finger to where a fairly new road had now been pushed in with a bulldozer.

"Mr. Richardson didn't know that all you had to do was to step around to the right side of the brush, duck under, and crawl to a small game trail. The trail opened up about ten yards in and leads to an old logging road that went to an abandoned ranch house. I told him about the trail and where it went. He laughed and said, "Man, for a while there, I thought you were a ghost or a figment of my imagination. How far is this ranch house?" I told him it was a little over a mile. He stood there shaking his head. "A mile! That means that a round trip is over two miles and on crutches and in the mountains! That's got to be hard. You're a tougher man than me, McDuff. What's the farthest in one day that you estimate that you've traveled on those sticks?" I told him somewhere around eight miles, adding that this was a round-trip number. He continued shaking his head in disbelief. "Eight miles! Eight miles! That's amazing! What are you hunting for, anyway? This seems like a lot of work. What's the reward?"

"It's deer season," I said. I was surprised that he didn't know what season it was. This must have registered in my voice, because he then said, "I wasn't aware that it was deer season. We leave from the Bay Area and it's always after dark on Friday when we get here. When we go home Sunday, it's also after dark so I haven't noticed the traffic that one usually associates with deer season. Matter of fact you're the only person I've seen hunting here. But now that I think about it, this is all private property, and you wouldn't have the traffic that you see around the National Forest during deer season." "I apologized and asked if I had offended him in the way my answer came across." "No, no, I was just surprised, as it seems you were, that I didn't know that it was deer season. You see, I've been a little preoccupied for the last thirty or so years. It's that thing called work. That's why we built this place. It's where we're going to retire and learn to live again."

"In time, the Richardson's and my family became close. I have many good memories of great meals and kind of potluck affairs where other neighbors gathered here, with hours of storytelling after dinner. There were times where Mr. Richardson and I would sit and talk about things that were either on his mind or on mine. I learned a lot about life issues and the view through his eyes. He never talked down to me but more as an equal. He would ask thought-provoking questions that caused me to think. The way he posed his questions forced me to evaluate the way I believed things worked. He was like another friend, Sam Bird. They had a lot in common. They both taught me that for the most part, when I was questioning something, the answers were usually to be found inside myself, especially when the questions were of the workings of the darker side of mankind."

Kami reiterated Ryan's earlier statement by saying, "This man sounds like he was not only intelligent but wise."

In a respectful tune Ryan said "Yes, and do you know, he had such a way with people that he became good friends with Al and his extended family. When Hayward passed away, the person that seemed to feel it most was Al. He moped around for most of a year. A once-bigot heart was broken; he lost his best friend, more like a brother. He was a bigot no more. Hayward was a positive influence on all who were lucky enough to know him. He was proof that Sam was right - it's better to make friends of a perceived enemy than to keep him an enemy forever."

The two men rested there for a few more minutes. After a bit, it was Ryan who broke the silence, saying, "Let's head back." They walked down the road in the direction that they had come. They had traveled only a little more than fifty yards when Ryan stopped. He just remembered something that happened on the spot at the bend in the road before them. "Right here, right on this spot, I was out hunting. Night had fallen and I could hear them coming. They were laughing and talking loud like people do when they're afraid." Ryan was pointing north up Old Greek Mine Road toward Baker Riley Road.

"I had taken a flashlight with me that morning because I knew that I'd probably be coming back after dark. Anyway, I recognized one of the voices; it was my brother, Shawn. It was also Halloween and they were going trick-or-treating with the foster kids that Al was taking care of. Shawn was the oldest of the group, so he was their leader. They were headed for the Richardson's. Shawn and his partner Larry, Larry who was one of the older foster kids that lived at Al's, had been telling the younger kids ghost stories. Shawn had told one of his favorite stories about a haunted bush. The story always changed, if there were more trees, it was about trees, if there was more bushes then it was a bush. Ryan looked around and smiled, it was the bush version that night. The story went like this; the bush was haunted by an evil spirit of a mad man. He was a serial killer who lusted after the blood of children. When the bush was ready to attack, the glowing face of the killer could be seen coming out of its branches. Branches would come jumping out to grab the victim and drag him into its center. There he would be drained of his blood. The bush then was able to use the voice of its victim to lure the victim's friends into their own horrible deaths. The younger kids were so spooked by the time they made it to this corner that they were ready to run at the sound of the acorns dropping. Shawn and his partner in crime were in front of the group. They were tossing rocks into the brush and making low, scary sounds. They were taking rocks from their pants pockets and kinda giving them a little wrist toss into the brush so the little ones wouldn't see them throw the rocks. Then Shawn and Larry would react like they were scared of the sounds and the thing following in the brush. Nobody had seen me, so I got back in the brush and waited for them to come in close. I waited until they came to with in around five yards or so of me. Then I jumped out of my hiding spot. I put the flashlight under my chin, turned it on, and started howling like a banshee. The kids scattered in all directions. Shawn and his partner ran into each other knocking each other to the ground. They had so many rocks in their pockets that they couldn't get to their feet easily. They looked kinda like chimpanzees scrambling in the dust, screaming and yelling. They ended up on all fours, using their arms and legs, trying to run, trying to get away. This made them look even more chimp-like. Shawn was doing pretty good, Larry, well he had a real problem. He kept stumbling and falling back to his knees. He didn't have a belt, and he was wearing a pair of oversize hand-me-down pants from Al. The added weight of so many rocks in his pockets kept his pants falling to his ankles. He was just too easy to catch, and after I caught him, I almost wished that I hadn't. I grabbed him and he screamed so loud that I thought I'd to have permanent hearing loss. When he finally quieted down, I came to the realization that I now had a bunch of kids scattered out in the woods on a moonless night. I could hear them out there kinda crying and whimpering. I was only trying to scare my brother and ended up creating a problem for myself. The problem now was how to gather them all up again. I found Shawn and had him go up to the road where his buddy was waiting. He tried to call the kids back. We waited for a while - nothing. The youngsters thought that the possessed bush was using Shawn's voice to trick them. I tried to follow the sound of their crying. I felt terrible and every time that I would get close to one of them, they would hear me and become quiet. It was over an hour later before they were all back up on the road." All the time Ryan was telling his story, he was acting out all the parts in this play. Both he and Kami were laughing; Kami was even holding his side.

Kami, still laughing, asked Ryan "I can see it - how funny. Did your brother ever get over it? And what's Halloween anyway?"

Ryan was surprised that Kami didn't know about Halloween. Kami's English was now so good that Ryan had stopped thinking of Kami as being Japanese. Heck, with his Southern accent, he sounded more American than anything else. "I don't think Shawn suffered any permanent damage from that night but as for the rest of his life; he inflicted his own style of injury and misery on himself - just like the rest of us. As for your other question, I hadn't really thought about it. But why would you know about Halloween? You probably don't celebrate it in your country. Halloween is on the night of All Hallow's Eve or Witches Eve. Some say it was a pagan thing or a druid thing or just a wacky thing, who knows? We hollow out pumpkins and carve them into jack-o-lantern faces and we place candles inside so they glow in the dark. The kids get dressed up to look like scary spirits or monsters. They go house to house, knocking on doors, and calling out, trick or treat. The kids are usually rewarded with candy."

Kami paused, took a deep breath. "My country is a land of ghost. Spirits are everywhere - in rocks and in trees. The air is thick with ancestors watching and controlling our destinies. We use masks and costumes in dance to tell stories of the spirits, both of the good and the bad, and their effects on the living. We are very superstitious. The tough thing is not allowing one's life to be completely controlled by these superstitions. This had a great effect on me as a child. I was a lot like those children that you just talked about. My first years were controlled by fear. I was always afraid that my ancestors were watching all my mistakes, and to disgrace them was to humiliate not only myself but all who were before me and all those that would follow. This was supposed to be an honor; instead it was a burden when I was young. When I matured a little, it became a comfortable, peaceful place; a place where the air at times seemed to gather around me, to embrace my soul and refresh my spirit."

These words made Ryan think. Was God watching the day he killed his first sparrow? Was it God or ancestors watching the day when an ancient whistle caused tears to streak an old man's cheeks? Then there was the night the coyotes sang for an old soul that was returning to a place where he believed the great waters gathered. Each of these events had made significant changes in the way Ryan thought about life and the responsibilities of his actions.

"Yeah, I think I know what you mean," was all that Ryan said.

They spent the rest of the afternoon hunting together. Ryan noticed how his new friend moved; each step was very direct in its execution; as quiet as any animal in the woods. Ryan was impressed. At the end of the day they returned to Ryan's camp and finished off the chicken. After their meal they talked briefly about getting together the next day to hunt.

Kami thanked Ryan and then excused himself, saying, "It's time for me to leave."

Ryan then asked his guest, "Where's your camp?" Kami pointed toward the west in the direction of a very steep hill that the Olson's called the Razorback, after the wild hog of the same name. The Razorback was a little more than a mile and a half by road and in the dark, it would seem even farther. "It's pretty dark out there. Would you like to use my spare flashlight?" Ryan handed Kami the light. Kami thanked Ryan again. He then turned and headed back up the driveway toward Baker Riley Road. Ryan watched him go up the hill, then, for some reason, he felt compelled to follow Kami. Calling after him, Ryan said, "Wait up! I'll walk you to the road." They walked quietly up the hill, the beam from their flashlights splitting the darkness. When they reached the road, Ryan was the only one to speak. "Watch out for the demonic monster bush, and since tomorrow's Sunday, I'll see you in church. Oh yeah, don't worry. The clothes you have on are fine for the church I go to." Kami smiled, nodded his head, and then turned and headed up the road. Ryan watched him until he went around the bend and out of sight. He thought that there was something quite different about his new friend; maybe it was something in his voice.

Ryan made his way back to his camp, stopping only to shine his light into the far corner of the barn, into the place where he didn't want to look earlier in the day. Staring back at him was the bony object that had unhinged him so. He brought the beam back to the ground in front of his feet and stared at the ground for a few minutes before proceeding to his truck. Before crawling into his sleeping bag, Ryan leaned against the truck bed and watched the ridge top along the Razorback. There was a light. If it was Kami's flashlight he had made good time. The light moved along the ridge, it appeared to be floating, almost as though it were tied to a balloon that was traveling on the breeze. Ryan thought it had to be Kami, and if it was him, would he turn the light in Ryan's direction to signal that he had made it to his camp? At that moment, the light swung toward Ryan. It was almost as if Kami had heard Ryan's thoughts. The light went off and on three times; Ryan did the same with his flashlight. Ryan climbed into the back of the truck and into his sleeping bag, soon to sleep and to dream, dreams of frozen moments and fluid insights.

CHAPTER SEVEN

BONES AND BRIGHT PLACES: THE DAY HE KILLED GRANNY

Sleep, sleep, fast and deep, quick to dream, a past deed repeat. Hollow, bony brow, empty orbits, scornful scowl, lipless smile, silent scream, whispers softly a life's story unfold, once held prisoner in shame's embrace, now be told, story of a time and a life lived in grace.

Ryan dreamed a fitful dream, a dream of family, friends and a moment of shame. That day started with a phone call. Ryan grabbed a rifle and headed to the ranch. He was prepared to take life; from that first sparrow to a human-did it really matter? He parked out on Baker Riley Road and walked into the ranch. He slipped the magazine into the mini-fourteen, slid the bolt back, racking (chambering) a round up the spout. He placed the gun on safety and walked up the dirt driveway. He quietly approached the barn, hoping to find them still together and wishing he were somewhere else. He was afraid of what he would find. Ryan made it to the barn unnoticed and found her alone. This was worse than he thought. His anger roused, he brought the rifle to his cheek; the stock rested into the hollow of his cheekbone. Peering through the scope at such close range the field of view was nothing but the white hair on the back of her neck. Ryan slipped his finger into the trigger guard, and pushed his finger forward taking the safety off. She didn't acknowledge the click. Taking a deep breath, Ryan slowly released the air from his lungs while increasing the pressure on the trigger. Inside the confines of the barn, there was a deafening blast. The muzzle flash lit up the dark corners of the barn. Behind her, through the open door, a cloud of blood and red dust erupted. White hair swirled in the air where she had fallen. Dust knocked from the rafters and gunpowder mixed, stinging Ryan's nose. The rifle's report echoed back across the canyon announcing the death of a grand lady.

Ryan bent over and picked up the spent cartridge and placed it in his pocket. He walked the few yards that separated them. As he stood over her, suddenly her leg jerked; her body was in its final death throws. The leg kicked and flailed the air. It was as if the puppet master had lost all control of the strings except one and was now trying to pull Granny back to her feet. Ryan squatted and placed his left hand under her head, cradling it. With his right hand, he slowly stroked her head. Ryan asked for forgiveness and wished her peace. He remembered the life that he had just taken and the first day he met her. Ryan's family had a habit of adopting friends, turning them into family members and Granny became part of the family in this way.

That first day, Ryan walked from his house to his parents which was only three doors down. He picked a rose from one of his mother's many rose bushes that lined the driveway and yard and went through the side gate to the back yard where the family was gathered. That's when he first saw her. She walked over to meet Ryan, and he noticed how white her hair was. He thought that the years had been good to her considering what she had been through. She stood in front of him, bringing the rose from behind his back where he was hiding it, he offered her the flower. She gently took the rose, placed her head to his hip and with great enjoyment, quietly chewed her gift while Ryan scratched her head. Granny was a registered Nubian milk goat. Ryan's father had bought Granny from a goat farm. The goat farm was just outside the city of Ripon, north of Modesto. She was old and her milk production was down, so she was going to be destroyed if nobody was willing to buy her. The Olson's often would bought goats like Granny. They weren't much use to the goat farms, but to the Olson's, they were invaluable-they were brush control engineers. Goats would eat the poison oak as if it were candy. They even ate the manzanita, which other animals such as deer wouldn't touch. Goats also were great at pruning the oaks from the ground to as high as they could stand on their hind legs. This was great for fire control.

Granny was held in a pen in the corner of the Olson's back yard for two weeks. This would be her new home while the Olson's checked out her health. She was injected with vaccines and cleared of parasites so she wouldn't infect the other goats at the ranch. The family soon learned that Granny must have been reincarnated and that Granny in a previous life was Hudini. She seemed to be able to escape the pen any time she wanted. Granny was an escape artist. Once, when Ryan's nieces were in the backyard playing, one of their friends came through the side gate, leaving it open. Granny had gotten out of her pen and crashed the tea party, she loving all the attention she was receiving from the kids. The next party crasher was another child's dog. Granny placed herself between the children and the canine. When the dog got too close for Granny's liking, she stood up on her hind legs. She did a couple hops, lowered her head and slammed it into the dog's ribs. This sent the dog scrambling for the gate with Granny close behind, but she stopped just shy of the gate. Was she protecting the children from what she perceived to be a threat? Had she adopted them as her own? This was a trait that would be useful up on the mountain.

Ryan was in the den sitting in the recliner and talking with his father when they heard a strange noise. It was coming from the kitchen where Ryan's mother was doing dishes. She was at the sink looking out of the kitchen window, which faced the back yard. The noise wasn't loud at first but was getting louder by the second. Mingled in the sound were Ryan and his father's names. Mom, being a Christian woman, would never condone cussing, but the sounds coming out of her as she ran through the den wasn't exactly the Lord's Prayer. Besides their names, Ryan and his father heard the words "Granny" and "roses." They followed Mom to the back yard, where Granny was busy pruning the roses. Apparently, Ryan's mom didn't think they needed pruning. Granny on the other hand must have thought she needed to repay the Olson's hospitality; that it was her duty to prune and she wouldn't take no for an answer.

Mom started off with Plan A, Ryan recognized it right off. She used this technique on Ryan and his brother, Shawn, and it worked well on them up to age twelve or so, anyway. She would walk slowly in the general direction of her intended target. She made it appear as though the last thing on her mind was getting her hands around, in this case anyway, the critter's neck. Granny saw through this ploy, and Ryan's mom came up empty handed each time. Mom instituted Plan B, which consisted of running around while she waved her hands madly in the air, screaming for Ryan and his dad to come help. Ryan and his dad were having too much fun watching and laughing. She chased that goat from one end of the yard to the other. She was flailing her arms about and making so much noise that she looked like a juvenile albatross on its fledgling flight. Lots of noise not much altitude, while Granny, on the other hand, proved to be quite deft at bouncing along on her hind legs, snatching roses as she went. She could shuck and jive or jink with the best of them; she could put an NFL running back to shame. Mom had lost all composure, and not too long after that, she ran out of wind. It seems that she had come into the season a little out of shape. She ran out of gas and plopped herself down in the grass. Granny stopped running, walked over to Ryan's mother's side, and sat down next to her, chewing her last stolen rose. Ryan wished that Terry and Philip could have been there to see his mother's performance. They would have been impressed. Ryan had no idea that his mom even knew the bumblebee dance. Mom was one of the best; man she could really put on a show!

Sweat was dripping from the end of her nose. Her hand rested on Granny's back, and she was staring a hole through Ryan and his father. Their laughing, of course, wasn't helping in this matter. It looked like Ryan's dad might be doing the cooking from now on, which made the prospects of going to McDonald's for Thanksgiving an appealing, if not an appetizing, idea.

"Why didn't one of you help me?"

Mr. Olson stopped laughing long enough to say, "I asked your son if he wanted to get in on the action and he handed me a five-dollar bill. I told him that it wasn't right betting against his own mom, especially betting on a goat." Somehow this didn't seem to amuse Ryan's mother. She sat there for a few moments catching her breath; then she started laughing. Thanksgiving was saved. Granny laid her head across Ryan's mother's lap and closed her eyes. The next day Granny was taken to the ranch.

Granny was released into the pasture with the other goats and was greeted by a goaty chorus of welcome. Granny soon had a suitor, her first. It was one heck of a hand shake. She had always been artificially inseminated at the goat farm. The billy did his job well, and Granny eventually gave birth to a bouncing baby girl. All these things were new to Granny. It was her first taste of a relative kind of freedom within the fenced-in portion of the ranch. This was also the first time that she would be allowed to raise one of her babies. She took to motherhood, and she soon became the lead nanny.

Ryan sat there on the dirt floor of the barn holding her head. He looked at the entry wound; it was small but the exit wound was horrific. The 55 grain, soft nose bullet had almost decapitated her. There wasn't any pain, just an instant death. Only ebbing energy twitched its muscles one last time. He took a closer look at the damage that was done by the one who had been there before him. Granny was partially disemboweled; her intestines were hanging from her belly, and her left leg had been hamstrung and the tendon was dry. She was slowly dying when Ryan arrived. Ryan stood up and grabbed one of Granny's front legs and dragged her body from the barn. He had just started downhill when something caught his eye. It looked like a crimson piece of a rag. The closer Ryan came, the clearer it became that what he was looking at was the remains of Granny's baby. Her remains were scattered along the hillside. He dropped Granny's leg, gathered up what was left of the baby, and placed the fragments next to her mother. This wasn't a lion attack; no it was the neighbor's dogs. This wasn't for food but for fun. The dogs had played tug of war with the baby. Granny was the last of nearly a hundred and forty goats that had lived at the ranch, today's count was eleven; now all were dead.

Ryan walked back to the barn, picked up his rifle, and went to the dirt driveway to check out the tracks. There he found several different dog tracks and a set of human footprints. He followed the foot prints to Al's house. Ryan placed his weapon under some brush to hide it before heading up Al's driveway. Ryan went up to the house and knocked on the front door. Al's wife, Gladys, answered it. Her first words were, "Al's not home," and started to shut the door. This wasn't like her; she usually was very friendly and normally would have asked Ryan in.

Ryan stopped her and said, "I got an anonymous phone call today telling, me that dogs were killing our goats. I followed the only other set of human footprints to your door." She hung her head in shame, and started to tell her story.

"Al's been gone for a week, working on a remodel. It started on early Tuesday morning around two in the morning. Those terrible sounds, the sounds of your goats, they sounded scared. I walked over to your place when it got light enough, but I didn't see anything wrong. Then the next night the same thing happened. This time I walked our property line in the morning and on the back side where the fences meet; there was a pile of dead goats. Then this morning around nine, it started again. I grabbed Al's four-ten shotgun and went to your barn. Stan's Saint Bernard had one of the goats down in the barn. I shot into one of the posts trying to scare him off. He only went about half-way down the hill and stopped. The shotgun is only a single shot and I didn't have any more shells with me."

Seeing the tears building up in her eyes, Ryan put his hand on her shoulder and then asked her. "Why didn't you shoot the dog instead of the post? And why didn't you let me know who you were when you called?"

She stared at her feet and softly said, "I didn't want to get involved. Stan's dog has done this before and cost him over two thousand dollars in restitution. I just didn't want to have problems with him, he's my neighbor."

"Well, he's also my neighbor and I guess I'm going to have to pay him a visit. If I have to go to court, can I count on you to be a witness?"

"Please don't get me involved. Besides, after I called you I called Stan." This was the last thing Gladys said before Ryan left.

Ryan could only shake his head as he went down the driveway. He picked up his weapon and headed to Stan's house. It would only take a few minutes. He looked around Stan's driveway and there was fresh dog tracks everywhere. Ryan looked up to the house from the road and before he could even step onto Stan's property, Stan himself stepped out from behind a cedar tree.

"Can I help you?"

"I think you can, that's if your last name is Stan and these tracks belong to a Saint Bernard."

"I am Stan and who the hell are you? I don't even have a dog."

Ryan looked back at the house. There next to the porch was a doghouse.

"And what's that, your guest house? Now where the hell is your dog? I'm here to kill it." Ryan strained these words through clenched teeth.

"I told you, I don't have a dog. I had a dog, but for the past three weeks, it's been with my son in Stockton, and it's now his dog. So you're just wasting your time here and my time too, so just get on down the road."

Ryan paused. He was fighting his rage and the urge to bring the muzzle of the rifle up and point it at Stan and call him a liar. Then Ryan had a flash of insight. This was a no-win situation and if he were to follow through with his urge, he could end up in prison. He would never be able to carry a knife or a gun or even be able to hunt again for the rest of his life. Stan was right; there wasn't a thing he could do about it. Before he walked away, he called Stan a liar and left it at that. Ryan had gone a few yards when he turned around to see Stan walking up his drive. There was a pistol sticking out from his waistband in the small of his back. Al's wife had called Stan after Ryan left her house, warning him that Ryan was on his way.

Ryan awoke with a start; his heart was racing, pumping hard against his chest wall. Then he remembered the dream and what had set it off and, most of all, the hollow eye sockets of the skull that stared at him from the corner of the barn. What bothered him the most was that Granny's final place of rest was disturbed by a niece who had little or no respect for others. She was the one who had gone through the boxes and scattered everything on the floor of the barn. She was looking for something to sell for drugs. She had defiled this place and she would have sold the bones of her own grandparents if there had been a market for them. Granny's skull was worthless to her, so she left it where Ryan would eventually see it.

If Ryan had raised up from where he lay, he would have seen a form sitting at the edge of the clearing. It was the same form that sat on a rock on the beach in the other dream. Ryan looked up into the night sky and into the Milky Way and slowly drifted back to the deepest sleep of his life. He started off dreaming about what happened earlier in the day, before he awoke in that patch of mountain misery. His unconscious mind revisited the pleasant dream and meticulously evaluated all that he had experienced. This was a dream within a dream. It was like peeling an endless onion, each layer revealing something different yet still connected and still related to the unpeeled portion.

Ryan slowly awoke to a light shining into his face, only to fall back into a semi-sleeping state again. He was desperately trying to cling to the dream and pull it into his waking mind. Then there was the light again and now it was accompanied by Kami's voice and quiet chuckling, "Wake up! Come on it's getting light!" Yes, it was Kami.

Ryan sat up and, still holding pieces of the dream in his mind, he started to ramble on about the dream. "There was a horse and a red-wing black bird and a falcon and animals and people, and there was something else, what was it?" Ryan babbled.

Kami was now laughing. Then he said, "Hey slow up and wake up my friend. You need to get up if we're going to go hunting."

Ryan quickly got ready. While doing so, he continued trying to verbalize what he had seen. Kami listened; there was a slight smile on his face, and he nodded his head in an approving, knowing manner. Ryan had his head down, tying his shoes, and hadn't seen Kami's face, but, if he had, he might have gained some insight into the real reason Kami was there. They started out into the pre-dawn morning. They both moved as quietly as they had the day before. When they came to the stand where Ryan had sat the first day, Ryan motioned to Kami to look over to where the two deer trails intersected.

Ryan whispered, "This is a good spot, you stay here and I'll cross the road and go down this ravine about three hundred yards or so and hunt a couple exit trails that branch off these two trails. Around ten o'clock or so, I'll meet you back here, okay?" Kami nodded his head.

Ryan had given his guest the best stand, choosing the less likely and the least traveled for himself. Ryan headed down the ravine. He moved as stealthily as he could. Because the ravine dropped off sharply on that side of the road, it was hard to stay upright. A thick mat of dry oak leaves and acorns covered the ground. It was like walking on ball bearings and potato chips. This wasn't going to be easy. He did the best he could at being quiet and finding the escape trails before daylight. Escape trails are much narrower than main trails and, as the name implies, they're used to get away from danger. Sometimes deer will travel these trails just to check them out. There was also the possibility that if a buck picked up the scent of Kami, he might come this direction. Ryan found a good spot behind a dead fall for a ground blind and hunkered down to wait. Sitting there in the cool morning air, Ryan let his mind wander back to the puzzle of the dream. It was like having something stuck in a tooth, and you keep running your tongue over it until you either get it out or your tongue gets so raw you have to stop.

Ryan saw brilliant flashes of colors and heard sounds so pure that they vibrated his soul. Pictures flashed before him that held the spirit suspended in the ethereal plain where time seems to cease. Fragrant smells permeated a place where the soul and spirit live. Ryan had for a moment slipped into sleep and these thoughts and feelings left the taste of reality upon his waking thoughts. He smelled his sleeve; he could still smell the sweet perfume of the dog wood. His emotions started to come to the surface, and he reigned them back in. Why couldn't he remember all the details? It seemed that the harder he tried to hold onto the details, the quicker they slipped though his consciousness. To Ryan, it was like grabbing a fist full of water or, in this case, the harder you squeeze it, the less of it you have. He sat there pondering this event in the quiet coolness that surrounded him. The only thing to break the silence was the occasional bird or the sound of dropping acorns rolling down the hill.

The hours passed and only one doe had crossed on the other side of the ravine. It was now time to head back up the hill to where Kami was hunting. Ryan chose a route that would allow him to go to the other stand and not scare any deer that might be in any of its shooting lanes. The route would take him past an old mine shaft that his family had named The Leprechaun. Ryan passed this landmark and, as he crested the shoulder of the rise across and above Kami, he saw a very nice buck and only few yards from where Kami was hidden. Ryan lay on his belly and waited for Kami to shoot. After many minutes of waiting the buck wandered away. Ryan was perplexed. It was quite a respectable buck. This old buck would have been a prize for most hunters. Why had Kami let it pass? Ryan rose to his feet and walked to the stand. Kami appeared to be asleep or meditating or something. He wasn't slumped over; he was sitting straight-backed, and his hands were placed palms down on his knees. Ryan spoke. "Hey! Hey, wake up!" Kami's eyes slowly opened. "Man, there was a huge buck that was so close to you. Maybe you had better check your shoes he might have tied your shoe laces together." Kami raised his left eyebrow and smiled. He smiled in a way that made Ryan wonder if his guest might have seen the buck and just didn't take his shot. Was he really there to hunt? Maybe this stranger wasn't what he appeared to be. After all he was a little slow at first, almost as if he was learning English for the first time, but now he seemed very comfortable with the language as though he had spoken it all his life. Then again, the day before, in the same situation, Ryan had done the very same thing; he had passed up an opportunity for a sure kill.

Ryan gave Kami a hand up. Standing there, Kami looked over Ryan's shoulder, up the hill in the direction from which Ryan had come. "What's over the hill?" asked Kami.

"Nothing much, just another ravine and a lot of poison oak and an old mine shaft. Why? If you want, we can walk over there and take a look," answered Ryan. Kami nodded his head. Both men walked over the hill. When they reached the mine, Kami squatted down, his butt touching his heels. As he stared into the hole, he seemed very deep in thought. The men hadn't spoken since they had left the stand and now Ryan though something must be playing out in Kami's head. Maybe the mine reminded him of something. Ryan finally spoke up. "It's called The Leprechaun. My dad named it after a rhyme he made up about my brother. It went, 'Shawn, Shawn the leprechaun, stole a pig and away he run.'"

"How far in does it go? Who dug it, and what were they looking for?" asked Kami.

"Nobody knows any more. It was here when we bought the property. We kinda think that it was high graders trying to snipe a little color. We think this because they took their tailings with them. Even though it only goes back in the hill a couple hundred feet or so, there isn't enough dirt and tailings out here to account for that much of a hole. High graders were thieves that would steal gold ore and nuggets from sluice boxes; in this case, they would dig among or near proven mining claims. So it appears that here they were trying to be first to reach the main stringer or vein of gold ore ahead of the Greek mine. At one time, mining law allowed any valid claim owner to follow a vein of gold that he discovered underground even under another person's claim or property. But to me, it looks like this hole reminds you of something or someplace else."

"It does; another time, another place, another story." Kami took in a deep breath and sighed.

To Ryan it seemed that his friend didn't want to talk about whatever it was that was on his mind. Ryan let the brief explanation stand without prying for more detail. "Let's head back to the camp. I'm going to go into Mountain Ranch and pick up some food and ice from Sender's Market. If you want to, you can come along, you're more than welcome."

"That sounds good. I would like to see as much of this land as I can in the time that I have left. I would also like to thank you. You have been a gracious host. You my friend seem to be very well brought up and represent your family well." Kami's statement embarrassed Ryan.

"Thank you. I wish you could have known my family. I think you would have liked them. Now let's get up the hill and go to town. I'll give you the quarter tour."

The trip to the truck was uneventful. They hung their bows and emptied the water from the ice chests, combined the contents of both ice chests and placed the empty one in the back of the truck. Ryan pulled out anything that might blow out of the back of the truck and placed it next to his bow. Ryan unlocked the door on the passenger side and opened it so that Kami could get in. Ryan went around to the other side of the truck and got in, fastened his seat belt, and was ready to go, except for one thing - Kami wasn't in yet. Kami just stood there looking at the truck door as if he was scrutinizing everything about the door. Ryan told him to climb in. Kami did as he was asked and then Ryan then told him to buckle up. Kami seemed confused by this term, so Ryan unbuckled his own seatbelt and then buckled back up. Kami followed Ryan's lead. Kami looked over at Ryan; a look of confusion was on his face. Ryan thought that there was something strange about what had just happened. It was as though his guest had never ridden in a pickup before - or any vehicle for that matter. It's just plain strange, thought, Ryan, because there is no way that a person could go through life without knowing how things worked in this world. It was as if he had fallen from the sky and had landed in the middle of the ranch. Ryan put the key in the ignition and started the engine. When the truck started, the radio came alive blasting. Somehow, the volume knob had gotten bumped and was turned up to the max. As fast as he could, Ryan turned the volume down. Looking over at his passenger, Kami had the look of a deer caught in the headlights look on his face. "That will stretch you're ear drums." Then Ryan started laughing as did Kami, although Kami's laughter was a bit strained, to say the least. When the truck started to move, Kami's eyes got even wider, and he sat bolt upright, his legs pushing at the floorboards. He was as rigid as a statue.

"Relax, I'll take it slow. You know, you almost make me think that you haven't ridden in a Dodge before. Heck, it could be worse; we could be in a Ford." Kami relaxed and started to enjoy the ride as he listened to Ryan's rolling commentary. They were about half - way up the grade above Jesus Maria Creek when Ryan pointed to the right over the side of the hill to a house and a barn and said, "That's where Sherrie Windsor lived. He moved here from Hawaii. He sold a ranch in Hawaii and was able to buy six ranches here for what one was worth there. I asked him once why he would leave paradise to move to these dry hills." I was surprised at his answer. Sherrie said, "You know, mainlanders visit the islands and want to stay. It seems that wherever you go on vacation, it's nicer than where you live, so you want to stay forever. The people that live where you're vacationing are probably going to go on vacation, and they'll probably end up where you live and have the same thoughts you have; how great it would be to live here. You make your own paradise. I love it here.'

"He was one of the best swimmers that I've ever seen. He could swim circles around a friend of mine, James Bradis. James's parents John and Audrey Bradis, owned the Silver Spur Bar and Grill. They also were the only ones on this side of the hill with a swimming pool. Sherrie loved to swim, and, at that time, James and I were freshmen in high school. James had trained all that summer to make the swim team. Sherrie coached James. Sherrie was a sixty-plus-year old man who could out swim teenagers in their prime. Sherrie impressed me; he was friendly, easy going. He was also friends to Johnny Weissmuller, the best known of the Tarzans. Sherrie also grew up surfing with Duke Kahananamku, the original Big Kahona. Sherrie, Weissmuller, and Duke hung out together in Hawaii. Sherrie had pictures of them together. The young men in the pictures were strong, at their peak, with full lives ahead of them."

Kami asked, "Have you stayed in contact with any of these friends?"

"No, Sherrie passed away and not long after his passing, James's father died, he was the last living member of the original Navy Top Hats. James's mother sold the Spur and most of the property. After awhile we drifted into our own lives and lost touch, but every time I pass here, I think of them. I wonder what happened to Audrey, James, and his brother Michael, and their sister Darlene. The last time I heard from Darlene was over twenty years ago. She was working at a hospital in Stockton, and everyone else had moved away. Look over here to the left - there's the Spur. It's now a convenience store."

They were about half-way to Mountain Ranch when Ryan pointed to his right again. "See that hill over there, at its base is lake M-24. That's where James and I spent many hours fishing for black bass. Man, we had some great times fishing. One summer James spent half the summer down in Modesto, and I spent half the summer up here."

Kami asked, "Can we go over to the lake that you talked about?"

"No, the original M-24 ranch was broken up into lots and sold. Now you have to be a property owner or have a key to get in. I wish we could get in there and see the lake. Lake heck, its only a fifty-acre pond, caught a lot of fish there, I really would like to see how it's changed."

Pulling into Sender's Market, they stepped out of the truck and walked up to the door. Before entering the store, Ryan stopped, and looked over the bulletin board. "Well, well. Would you look at this? Between the lost German Shepherd and the potbellied pig that's for sale, there's one for a lost Oriental fellow who responds to the name Kami," joked Ryan. Then he continued into the store. As he opened the door, Ryan looked back towards the bulletin board. Kami was stranding there scratching his head; he didn't get it. Ryan laughed to himself, shook his head and continued into the store. Kami followed him in. As they walked through the store, Ryan placed items into the basket occasionally asking Kami what brand he liked. Kami would just shrug his shoulders indicating that he didn't know. He didn't seemed to have any idea what Ryan was asking. He was wide-eyed and speechless, as if he was seeing this all for the first time. Ryan noticed his friend's peculiar behavior; it seemed that this was new territory to him. It was as though Kami not only was culturally and geographically removed from here but also time removed. Like he was from a different time and place and dropped here with contemporary clothes and equipment. Ryan stopped asking questions and went about his shopping. Kami stood smiling in front of the produce section. He had found something he liked.

"This is wonderful, all so fresh," Kami said and went though the produce section touching and smelling all that this section offered, all the fresh fruits and vegetables.

Ryan asked, "Is there anything in particular that you would like?" Kami pointed to the oranges.

"Can we have some of these?"

"I don't see any problem with that. Let's also get a watermelon and a couple pounds of grapes. You know, I don't think either of us is into hunting, so let's get some steaks and have a barbeque."

Kami smiled and nodded his head, showing an enthusiastic approval of Ryan's suggestion. Ryan seemed to relax after making that statement. He wasn't pressured anymore into finding a deer for himself or for filling Kami's tag. As they cruised the aisles, Ryan watched Kami more closely than he had before. Kami really was seeing this for the first time. How could this be thought Ryan, because like the truck, there wasn't a person on the planet who hadn't seen modern processed foods in one form or another?

Ryan paid for the food and ice; then on an impulse, he purchased an assortment of candy bars. They went back to the truck where Ryan placed everything into the empty ice chest. Shutting the lid, Ryan paused, looked at the store, then over at Kami, and said, "You know, this store didn't used to look like this. When I was a kid, this building was a two-story with a tin roof. Its walls were stucco over-rock two foot thick. It was built around eighteen sixty-five. There was a little bar in the back and the store was up in front. God, I remember the night that the piano ended up out in the street. The town used to hold a combination street fair and mountain-man rendezvous. Hell, it was probably just an excuse to celebrate another year of community survival. The celebration started on Friday and lasted until Sunday afternoon. Three days of good food and dance and games - games from baseball to lumber jacking and even woodsmen skills, black powder shooting and hatchet throwing. There were lights strung along the streets and the party went until two in the morning. People were dressed in Western-style clothing or they dressed as trappers or miners. James and I were walking along giving the girls a good looking over, when a guy stopped me right about there." Ryan was pointing across the street toward a small white building. "That used to be the Post Office. Anyway, this guy stopped me and asked me for a match. I told him that I didn't smoke and didn't have a match. He was dressed in cowboy duds and he had a gun holstered on his side. He asked me one more time, and I repeated the same answer. He then pulled the pistol and pointed it at me. There was still a little daylight left, so I figured he was bluffing. I just stood there. He pushed the barrel into my ribs. Then I told him that I still didn't have a match and the gun didn't make one magically appear in my pocket. I just told him to put it away; better yet, put it back in his car before somebody told one of the sheriffs that were walking through the crowds. An hour later we saw the guy and his gun was gone. On Saturday night he came back and sometime around midnight, he was arrested in the middle of the street, shooting the damn thing up in the air. Crap like this makes it hard for people like me and other people who are responsible gun owners."

"Did he scare you? What did your friend James do?" asked Kami.

"Well, James stuck by me and didn't flinch. As for being scared, I really don't know - there wasn't time to be scared. Maybe we were lucky. Today it could be a different story if the same thing happened to me."

"Do we have time to walk around and look the town over a little? Please tell me more about this place." There was sincerity in Kami's voice. He really wanted to know more about Ryan and the town of Mountain Ranch.

"This is Garibaldi Street and it's the main street." Ryan pointed up and down the road that they stood on. They walked over to one of the two closed buildings on this street and stopped in front of one of the old buildings. "This building is one of the oldest in town and it also was a store at one time. Its plaster-over-rock-wall construction like Sender's used to be, only its a single story. When I was a kid, this store was still open. Anyway, up this street there were booths set up. It was kind of a swap meet, arts-and-craft-fair atmosphere. Across the street, that wooden building used to be kind of an unofficial museum; on special occasions it would be open to the public. I can't tell you the last time it was open." Ryan seemed quite pleased at his new role as tour guide.

"Show me some more. Did everything happen only on this street?"

"No, the whole town was used and, for that matter, outlying towns were used by out of towners for lodging. Come on, let's walk on over here. This is Washington Street. Tables were also set up here and things were sold." They walked down the street and at the corner of Washington and Blacksmith Street was the community hall. Pausing there Ryan, looked at the hall and a Cheshire-cat smile crossed his face.

"Heck, you asked me if I was scared when that dumb ass pulled the gun on me. I said that I didn't have time to be scared. That same Saturday night, James and I walked down here to use the restroom and something happened on this porch right here that scared me. They had a couple benches out here on the porch and there was a line for both restrooms. We stood in line, waiting our turn to go in. We finally made it up on the porch and sat down on the bench. The way it worked was when a person would leave the restroom, the end person would leave the bench and everybody else would slide down one. Things were sliding along smoothly, you might say, when this absolutely gorgeous young woman walked up and onto the porch. She was breathtaking. She was what every so-called red American male-wanted, wanted at least until you got to know her better, anyway. She stood there looking her prospects over. She knew that she could pick and choose any man on that porch. She started to move. There was a deliberateness in her presence - she was on a mission. She could be described only as a sexual, sensual animal and she had made a choice. She walked over to where I sat and placed her hand on top of my head. Mussing up my hair, she allowed her arm to slide around my neck. Pulling my face forward into her midriff and parts north of there, she slowly lowered her body and sat on my right leg. I was afraid to open my eyes. When I did, her face was only inches away from mine. She said, 'My name is Sandy. It's my birthday and I want a birthday kiss.' She started kissing my cheeks and then she planted the very first, and the biggest, wettest, kiss that I had ever had. It was my first grown up kiss. One hand was running through my hair while the other was running wild. Sandy pulled away only long enough to invite me to the back seat of her car. Then there was a great shadow over us. Something was standing between us and the single light bulb that lit the porch. It was huge. Its name was 'husband' or was it 'Oh, shit, my husband?' Anyway, he reached down and separated us. At thirteen, there wasn't much life to flash before my eyes. Shoot, it went by so fast that it could have run by one more time and there still would have been plenty of time left to see my beating heart as it was ripped out. This guy was big. He looked like a combination power lifter and lumber jack. He could have blocked the sun at high noon. He gently held that beautiful thing he called 'wife' in his arms. She looked so vulnerable there and as fragile as a baby bird that had fallen from its nest. He looked down at me and there were tears running down his cheeks. I felt sorry for this tree that walked like a man. Then, in a soft tone, he was apologizing - apologizing all over himself, apologizing to me for his wife's actions saying. 'She only acts like this when she drinks.'"

"I swallowed hard and two of the three Adam's apples that had migrated up into my throat went back down, heading south for the winter. I felt sorry for him and I felt embarrassed for us both. When James and I got back to his house, somehow everybody there had already heard what had happened. And you know something strange? James's sister, Darlene, was mad as heck at me. I had no clue as to why she should be mad. She was kinda like my own sister - that's if I had a sister, anyway."

Kami was laughing, stopping only long enough to ask, "I wish I could have seen it. Do they still celebrate like they used to? Did you ever see that couple again?"

"I don't know if they celebrate anymore like they use to, but, they do have some sort of shindig some where around August 26. That night, I do know that after that idiot started shooting his gun in the middle of the street, he was arrested and that's when the sheriffs tried to shut the party down. The crowd protested and kept the officers at bay. Somehow, the power was shut off and the music and lights died. That still didn't stop the party. Soon the piano was removed from the bar and placed in the middle of the street. Somebody sat down and began to play; it was some of the best honky-tonk piano that I've ever heard. Then, around two in the morning, the sheriffs called in back-up and tear gassed the place. The party was over and, as for the husband and wife, I never saw them again. I did hear that they later divorced."

Ryan and Kami continued on down the street. After they passed the new Post Office on the left hand side of the street, Ryan pointed over to an open field. "There's where they would set up the pioneer camp. Teepees and a (u-ma-cha) bark house were put up or built there, also. They would show how to build shelters and how to tan hides. There was traditional cooking; both native and pioneer food being prepared. A place was set aside for archery and black-powder shooting. Kids were allowed to give either a try and were given strict instructions on the safety and proper use of these weapons. History was alive and well. I remember one man; he was a Native American Indian. He gave lessons on traditional medicines. He had plants that grew locally; most of them I already knew some of their uses. A friend of mine, Sam Bird, had shown me when I was a kid. Oh yeah, there was one guy, a craftsman, showing how to use antique tools. With a tree-limb lathe he was demonstrating how to turn wood and make furniture. Again, he, like the others, was telling the history of each tool he was using. The lathe was neat, no electricity was needed. The lathe's frame had a tree limb attached to its base. The limb was bent over the top of the lathe in an arc, and a rope was attached to the end of it. The rope was pulled down and wrapped around the turning shaft, or what is called the live head. Three turns were put around the shaft and the end of the rope was then attached to a treadle on the frame. The limb was now bowed and it would work like a leaf spring. The man would step down on the treadle, pulling the rope and limb down. This caused the shaft to rotate. Then, when he let his foot come back up, the limb did the same. This caused the shaft to rotate in the opposite direction. The tools were designed to cut both directions. It was ingenious." Ryan then pointed across the highway and added, "They barbecued and played baseball on the other side of the road. Hell, it might have been gone forever because of one idiot a gun and a bunch of drunks."

"You sound as if you miss it."

"I was there, I saw it, but there has been more than a couple generations that will not have had the privilege of having this experience." Ryan's voice reflected the feeling of loss he felt.

As they walked back to the truck, they passed a house where it sounded like there was a fight going on. Kami stopped and he and Ryan peered into the front-room window. There was an elderly couple watching television, and on the screen was big-time professional wrestling. The couple was screaming at the TV, warning their champion that his opponent's partner was sneaking up behind him with a chair. Ryan and Kami watched through the window as the champion was beaten about the head and shoulders with the chair. Ryan was laughing, but Kami had a shocked look on his face.

"Is this real? Is he killing that man? Why are you laughing?" There was real concern in the way Kami asked his questions.

"I don't think he's going to be killed. Heck he's the good guy. He'll probably end up winning, he and the other guys will be having dinner and drinks after the match. The reason I was laughing, is that the old couple there sounded a lot like my grandparents. They loved big-time wrestling. Oh, man, would they ever get into watching this stuff. They were fanatics, yelling and screaming at the TV. Let's get out of here and head back to the ranch."

Ryan chose another route back to the ranch. This time they would be using Whiskey Slide Road. Kami seemed fascinated with the radio. He poked the buttons, trying to make it work. Ryan watched him for a while, letting him figure it out for himself. Kami wasn't getting anywhere, so Ryan reached over and turned on the power and increased the volume. They listened until the radio signal was lost in the canyon. Ryan pulled over and stopped.

Ryan reached across to the glove compartment and grabbed a handful of tapes. "Okay, I can't believe that you've never seen a radio or a tape deck, but here's how it works. All you have to do is place the tape into the tape deck with the open side of the tape on this side of the deck. Now when you want to change tapes, push this button and it will eject the tape, then pop in another tape. If you think you got it, knock yourself out."

"Yes. Is it, okay if I put a tape in now?" asked Kami

Ryan thought for a moment. "I want to apologize. I must have sounded like an ass. It just seemed like everything is new to you. Here you are my guest and I'm treating you like you've never seen any of this before, this is terrible and condescending. I'm a terrible host-please forgive me."

"Please, my friend, I am, in some ways, as you put it, new to all this. You have welcomed me onto your property to hunt with you and you shared your food with me. You have told me entertaining stories of your youth. This, in definition, is what makes you a good host. It isn't necessary to apologize. You honor your family." There was a firmness in Kami's voice. Ryan nodded his head, acknowledging that he understood what Kami meant.

The music played all the way back to the ranch. Ryan kept quiet most of the way. Kami seemed to enjoy the energy of the rock and roll; he even seemed to enjoy some of the jazz. Among the tapes was a couple classical tapes, one of which was one called "Ode To Joy." Ryan looked over at his guest, who had become quiet. Kami's eyes were closed. Then Ryan heard Kami say in a low voice, "The colors-so beautiful." Ryan smiled.

CHAPTER EIGHT

SPIRIT DANCE

The trip back to the ranch was a pleasant one, but as for conversation it was a quiet one, with only the music and an occasional word or two by Kami. Ryan observed the way that the music affected Kami. It seemed that he was savoring the music, holding it on his pallet and swirling it, tasting its emotional essence. Kami used single words such as "earth," "water," "wind," "fire," and "void" to describe the hiss sound during transitions in the music. He was attaching colors to sounds. At times it was as though he were describing a meal or a painting. Kami found patterns, structure and symmetry in the chaos of the wilder rock-n-roll music or jazz on one of the tapes. If this stile of music was a meal, the last piece of music and the only one he played to its entirety, "Ode to Joy," was the dessert. He was almost like a cat with a ball of catnip; Kami seemed to immerse himself emotionally and roll in it. Unusual, thought Ryan, to talk of music like this and react to it in this manner. When the truck came to a stop, they removed the ice chest from the pickup and placed it next to the other one, replacing the rubber snubber.

Ryan walked toward the barn with Kami in tow. When they reached the barn, Ryan finally spoke. "I know you said that I need not apologize for the way I acted here at the barn. This isn't an apology, but I feel I owe you an explanation of my behavior yesterday. You see, I've been away from the place for awhile, and when I first pulled in, things weren't where I had left them. I had heard from one of the neighbors that my niece and some of her druggie friends had been coming onto the property. They had been stealing whatever they could from the ranch and neighbors houses. Here they have stolen chain saws, welding tanks, torches, tools, etc., including the antique iron bed that was my father's when he was a boy. Gone, just gone, family history sold. Boxes rifled through and contents scattered in the dirt. They took everything they thought had any value. When you pointed out the skull in the corner, I just felt an intense rage because something special had been violated. The skull was Granny's; it had been taken from her place of rest--probably left because it had little value."

"Who was Granny? Why was she special? Was there something else besides her remains being moved?" There was genuine concern on Kami's face as he asked these questions.

Ryan took in a deep breath and told how and why he had to put down the injured animal. As he told his story, shame was reflected in his voice. Ryan told how he tracked down the dog that was responsible for her injuries and how he was tempted to do something stupid. He paused, thought for a moment and told a little of what it was like growing up along the river and with his friends, Phillip and Terry. He told the story of how the bumble bee dance came about. Ryan now was laughing as he talked of Granny's life and her dance with Ryan's mother. He paused, almost like a child staring at the bottom of an empty cream bowl. He looked at the ground, shrugged his shoulders, and said, "All gone."

When Ryan finished, Kami was nodding his head in manner showing he understood. Then he asked, "Who was the neighbor that the dog belonged to? Does he still live nearby?"

"We waved at him yesterday at the mailboxes."

"That was him? You didn't seem to be holding a grudge. You even seemed to have made peace with this person. So is your niece the one you're upset with?"

"Yes and no. For a moment, I was upset with my nieces and myself. The day I killed Granny, like I said, I was so close to doing something stupid. I almost pointed a weapon at another human being. Some of those feelings came to the surface again when I saw what my niece and her friends had done. Just for a moment, I wanted to hurt these people, and that's something my parents wouldn't have wanted. I was ashamed of myself and of those who did this. Damn it! I hate what drugs are doing to this country!" There was disgust in Ryan's voice and on his face the look of distress, distressed at being unable to do something to prevent these events and to protect this place.

"I understand my friend. You needn't explain any more." Kami truly cared; it could be heard in his voice.

"Well, I really didn't bring you over here to confess my sins. I need your help moving the barbecue grill and gathering wood to cook with. My father cut a bunch of oak; it's dry and will work well for what we'll be doing." They made many trips back and forth, up and down the hill, hauling wood and stacking it on the bare ground next to the to were the grill was placed. The grill was rectangular in shape, low to the ground, opened at the bottom and at one end. Its sheet metal panels enclosed three of it's sides and its expanded metal top was rusty. Ryan placed a small amount of very dry kindling on the ground under the barbecue. He retrieved one of the grocery bags and a lighter from the truck, placed the bag and a little more kindling inside the pit and lit it. Kami watched with interest. Ryan rose from the pit and said, "Let's get some chairs from Mom's garden." Kami hadn't realized that they had walked past Ryan's mother's garden several times while picking up the wood. What was left of the garden lay under the oaks that straddled the dirt drive way. There, enclosed behind the iron fence post and chicken wire, were roaming roses. They were, for the most part, now wild and dependent on rain for water. They were unpruned which made them appear more vine-like than bush. Here and there could be seen a flower or two. In front of the roses, on a pallet of brick, were two concrete planter boxes. One box was turned on top of the other, creating a crypt where the ashes of family members could be placed. Ryan's parent's ashes were entombed there. Ryan stopped and, for a moment, stared at the place were his mother and father now rested. Kami stood next to him. Ryan spoke first, "Kami, this is my mom and dad, Don and Pat Olson. I didn't have enough money to place their ashes anywhere else, this is all I could afford, the best I could do. I even had to do a do-it-yourself cremation for Mom."Kami nodded his head. Kami's eyes followed the water hose to a nearby ranch house and asked, "Who lives there?"

"That's where my parents lived out their last years. It's mine now - on paper anyway. I've held onto it for the rest of the family, even my nieces and nephew and their kids. Then there's my kids and grandkids. I'm trying to keep it in the family, for all the family. That's the promise I made my mother before she passed away. Dad once told me, 'If you ever get your hands on a piece of dirt, hold on to it because they aren't making any more of it. Because if you sell it the money will soon be gone and there won't be anything to show for it.' So, you see, this is family dirt. As long as it's respected, it's here for the family," Ryan said with conviction.

Looking a little confused, Kami asked, "Why are you sleeping in your truck and not in your house?"

"Well, after my mother passed away, my youngest nieces wanted to stay here. You see, my parents moved up here after my mother retired and father became semi disabled. They had raised my brother's two daughters until they were adults - at least in age anyway. The youngest was only six months old when they took them in. They all lived in Modesto until the oldest niece was in high school. Mom and Dad found out that she was trying to get jumped into a gang, so they moved from Modesto to here and continued to raise them."

Ryan paused, looking lovingly at the crypt. Soft were the words when they left his lips. "God, Mom was strong. When she was told that she would die from lung cancer within six months, she asked the doctor for the truth and if there was anything that would extend her time here? To his credit, he told her the truth. Anything that they could try would only degrade the quality of what little life that was left to her. He agreed to help her with the pain, but that was really all he could do. Mom lasted six weeks. My youngest niece, to her credit, did help her grandmother at this time and, as for Hospice, there isn't enough good words for them. But I'm rambling; all I probably should have said was that the house is in an unlivable condition after my nieces wrecked it. It's in great need of repair. When I say nieces, they both lived here and after the oldest one got out of jail and rehab, I gave them a chance to prove themselves, and to grow up. The oldest stole everything she could get her hands on, even her grandmother's car. When I asked her why she had taken it, she said,'Grandma's dead and she don't need it anymore.'"

"I wanted to press charges but didn't have enough evidence so I ended up getting screwed. When I say screwed, it wasn't just the car but thousands of dollars worth of bills, bills for the phone and electricity. Hell, I couldn't even run the pump to water Mom's roses."

"I see, there's no need to explain any further," was all Kami said.

They picked up the plastic lawn chairs and walked back to the barbecue, setting the chairs up by the truck. Ryan stoked the fire with bigger pieces of wood; he then walked over to the truck and retrieved a steel-bristle brush. Both then took a chair and sat down. Ryan pointed to the fire and said, "The wood has seasoned, Dad cut it more than six years ago. We won't have to worry about popping and flying embers. It's kinda funny. You see, Dad knew he was on borrowed time when they moved up here, or at least he had a hint. After all, he had six heart attacks and a tumor on his pituitary. Dad made it through all those heart attacks. He was released from the hospital and at home, then two days later he sneezed and went blind. That's when they found the tumor pressing on his optic nerve. He went through radiation and chemo with little trouble. When he could see again, it was in triple vision. He taught himself how to drive again even better than before. Well, maybe not better - faster is more like it. One day when I was riding with him, I asked him if he was seeing triple, how could he drive?

He said, "Heck, I just drive right through the middle."

"He could drive all day, but when it came to walking, his stamina was compromised. He was so limited, that in just walking a few yards, he would have to stop and rest. This was a man who could repair just about anything and always had energy to spare and he was reduced to this. He couldn't see well enough to do repairs on his own cars. This was something he believed he should have been able to do even with his eyes closed. This touched a place in his soul, while breaking his spirit. He felt worthless and of little use." Ryan pointed over to all the old equipment rusting away.

"Dad bought some more goats, which raised his spirits. The goats gave him company, and when he had problems walking, would you believe that two of the largest goats would push on both sides of him to help steady him? Before long they were going for short walks. Dad would kinda hold on to their collars and they would pull him up the hill. Later he traded something for two jackasses; their names were Jack and Mack. Dad bought them to help keep the dogs away from the goats and it did help, for a little while anyway. They even ran off a mountain lion one night. I'll be damned, but one day I was in the barn working when I saw Mack lower his curly tufted forehead into the middle of Dad's back and help the goats push Dad up the hill. After a while Dad, started to feel a little better. One day he grabbed a chain saw and went up the hill above the house and cut down a tree for fire wood. You know, it was great to see him and the goats, heading into the woods. He'd cut down a clump of oaks. Like those live oaks over there." Ryan pointed over to a bunch of trees. Dad was just thinning them a little. As soon as a tree hit the ground, the goats would rush in to eat the leaves. I can still see him and those goats. From that day on, the goats would come running as soon as they saw Dad and his saw. You see, Dad hadn't given up, he wasn't really beaten. The way he put it, "I've just slowed down a little."

"When Dad finally passed away, one of his best friends, Billy Buck, said to me, 'I can't believe that Don's gone. I figured that they would have to hold Don down and drive a stake through his heart to kill him. Now he's gone - I can't believe it.' He was crying as he walked away."

"This Billy Buck, he's not the owner of the boat. You said his name was Billy Gillstrap, right?" asked Kami.

"Yes, but Billy Buck and Bill Gillstrap lived next door to each other. Both lived on the same block as my parents. Both of these guys were good people. Bill Gillstrap used to take Phil and me deer hunting. Billy Buck was a notorious neighborhood drunk with a huge heart. Heck, both men did. Two things that sticks out in my mind about Billy Buck was his way of dealing with his rowdy sons. When a fight broke out, he'd order them to put on boxing gloves, go into the back yard and beat the hell out of each other. When they finally stopped, he would make them kiss each other. That's the last thing they wanted to do. This cut way down on the fighting, at least until they were teenagers. That's when Bill put two knives on the table and said, "We'll bury the loser." That put an end to it.

"The other thing that sticks in my mind was when a neighbor, Ms. Wane," a smile crossed Ryan's face. "Well, anyway, she asked Billy Buck if he'd watch her dog Tuffy, while she went to visit her daughter in Southern California, for a month or so. What made all this worthwhile was the fact that, for as long as I could remember, there had been a war going on between those two. So, when she came to Billy and asked him this favor, it surprised everyone, especially Billy. Lord knows why she asked Billy, but she did, and Billy said yes. She brought Billy into her house to give him instructions for taking care of her Tuffy. She sat him down at the table and poured him a cup of coffee. She then went to the refrigerator, took out a big steak, placed it into a hot frying pan and cooked it to perfection. She set the steak in all its glory on the table in front of Billy; his eyes were already tasting it. She then cut it into bite size pieces. Billy could hardly wait, his stomach was rumbling, and his mouth was watering. But this was going to be a lesson in canine care that he could really sink his teeth into. Mrs. Wane then picked the plate up and went out the back door. She poured the warm meat into Tuffy's dish. Billy was heart broken. Mrs. Wane explained that this is the way Tuffy liked his steak, medium rare. She led Billy to the back porch, she opened the freezers door. There, stacked from top to bottom, was clean white butcher paper covered steaks - a cubic yard of steak. She had been feeding her dog nothing but steak. When she left for her visit, Billy went to the store and bought a hundred pounds of dry dog food. He fried up those steaks twice a day as instructed and he ate those same, fore mentioned steaks himself. Before he dug in to that first steak, he looked out the screen door to where Tuffy sat, and said, 'This is the way Billy Buck likes his steak.' Tuffy ended up eating dry dog food and drippings from the steak. Tuffy seemed to like it, anyway Tuffy didn't complain - or tell, for that matter."

Both men had a good laugh. After a moment, Ryan picked up a piece of oak and said, "Dad had cut enough firewood to heat the house for four winters. There's still plenty of wood scattered along the hillsides. Its kinda like he's still here giving us his warmth. Today he is helping us cook dinner and his stories and friends fill my memory." There was more than a little pride in Ryan's voice. "Your parents were good people, I see now where you get your hospitality and perhaps your sense of humor. I'd like to hear more about your family. It must have been fun to grow up in a family like yours. My upbringing was much different. There wasn't very much laughing. I found more laughter in the two days as your guest than in all of my childhood. Thank you." Kami smiled as he said this.

Ryan smiled back. "Yeah, you're probably right. They say the fruit doesn't fall far from the tree. But, then, neither does the nut, which is probably more accurate in my case. I do have to agree with you about my family. Heck, the entertainment value alone made it worth being part of my family. We didn't do anything normal. We had adventures. If you're interested, after dinner ask me any questions you like. Now I need to brush the grill and get the steaks and corn ready."

"Yes, that would be great. Is there anything that I can help you with?" asked Kami.

"Thanks. I think I've got it under control. Sit down and take it easy. Then again, if you see a lot of flames and me running past you, try to catch up and stay up with me." Ryan chuckled as he said this.

Ryan prepared the grill by brushing vigorously with the wire brush he had brought from home. He had also brought onions and seasoning salts in case he had fresh back strap or liver to cook. Because he had let his best chance to harvest an animal run down a hill, there wouldn't be any venison. Steak would have to do. Soon the steaks were on the grill and seasoned with seasoning salt. The aroma coming from the grill was wonderful. Ryan turned the meat and occasionally made sure that it was cooking evenly. When the steaks were done, he placed them on paper plates and handed one to Kami, he placed the other on one of the chairs. Taking his hunting knife, Ryan cut into Kami's steak and asked, "Is this done enough for you? I can put it back on the fire if you like."

"This is good, just the way I like it. I think Billy and Tuffy would also approve." Kami's stomach rumbled in agreement.

Ryan handed Kami his hunting knife, saying, "Go ahead and cut your meat while I put the corn on the grill." Ryan rolled the corn still in its husk on top the grill. When he looked back over at Kami, Kami hadn't cut up his meat yet. Kami was more interested in the blade in his hand. Ryan reached into his pocket and fished out a small pocket knife. Walking back over to his chair, he picked up his plate and started carving up his steak. "Don't worry, it's sharp and clean. Just don't cut yourself, or did you lose your fork?" Ryan goaded.

Kami woke up to Ryan's voice. "Right, yes, yes. I was just looking at your knife. It's nice, very nice. I haven't held a blade for a long time." There was something in the way Kami said this that caused Ryan to wonder once again about his guest. Unusual he thought.

They both began eating their dinners; they sat there quietly enjoying the evening air. Occasionally, Ryan would rise and roll the corn on top the grill. After finishing their first course, Ryan picked up one of the ears of corn and pulled its husk back. After examining it, Ryan placed it back on the grill. He then walked over to the ice chest and removed something. Returning and unwrapping what he had retrieved he placed it on his used paper plate. Kami eyed the new item on the menu-a yellow rectangular cube. Ryan rolled two ears to the cooler end of the grill, then removed the other two. He quickly husked them, removing the silk, and then picked up the plate with the cube. He placed the warm ear of corn on top of the cube and twisted and rolled it back and forth. Kami watched intently. When Ryan had finished coating both ears, he picked up the same seasoning salt that he used on the meat, sprinkling it over both. Ryan handed one to Kami, then raised his piece to his mouth as he took a deep breath, inhaling the fragrance. He then began to eat, starting with the first couple rows of kernels at one end and eating his way to the other. Kami did the same and, as he did so, Ryan watched the expression on Kami's face. It was the look of satisfaction.

"I didn't know how well the corn was going to turn out. Normally I would only put salt and pepper on my corn, so this combination was new to me. It's little garlicky but not bad. You see, I put a little garlic and pepper in my seasoning salt. That way it works well with meat. I've never tried it on vegetables - not bad!" Ryan seemed pleased.

"That was the best meal I've had in a very long time. This was special, thank you. I don't know how to repay you for your hospitality." Kami extended his hand.

Ryan shook his new friend's hand and said, "That's enough of a payment, consider me paid in full. Oh, heck, the other ears!" Ryan ran over and pulled them off the grill. After husking them, Ryan looked them over. Some of the kernels were almost black and others looked overcooked. "Well, what the hell, let's give them a try." Ryan buttered and seasoned them, then handed one to his guest. They both tried a little taste. To Ryan's surprise the flavor had change for the better. Both men smiled, enjoying the corn and the quiet before nightfall.

Ryan gathered up the paper plates and husks and placed them in the fire along with a couple of logs. "That's it, the dishes are done. Now let's have some dessert. You want to give me a hand?"

Kami nodded his head and followed Ryan over to the truck. Ryan removed a sack of fruit and walked over to the ice chest that held the soft drinks. He picked up one end and Kami the other; together they carried the chest over to the chairs and set it down between them. Ryan opened the chest and brought out the Coke and two cups. He poured the glasses full, offering one to his guest. They both sat down and watched the sun set, as they drank their soft drinks and ate oranges and the other snacks that they had bought.

The sky was dynamic, stunning in color, rich in texture. To the west, clouds over the coast range were held back by the heat of the central valley. To the east, the evaporated waters of the valley had condensed into clouds over the Sierras, billowed up along its summit. Condensation trails from commercial aircraft streaked the sky from east to west, from horizon to horizon, all painted in the colors of the setting sun. Ryan broke the silence. "I haven't any colors on my pallet to paint this, nor words to describe it, except only one sound and that sound being a sigh." This was a first for Ryan. He might have thought these thoughts before to himself, but to say it out loud and in front of someone else, no-never.

Kami listen to Ryan while watching the evening sky. Saying nothing, he merely gazed and smiled. They sat there caught in a web, a web spun against a tapestry woven by God. Into the evening, both minds were suspended in the bliss of the evening's void. They sat there, until the light of the fire and the dark of night grappled for dominance. Neither light nor dark winning the fight, but became balanced and settled into a dance. A waltz that could be seen in the dancing shadows among the leaves of the live oaks.

Ryan stoked the fire again, then moved his chair so that the fire would be between him and Kami. "I was wondering, would you tell me more of your childhood and what it was like growing up?" There was genuine interest and curiosity in the way Kami's asked this question.

"Heck, I've been talking all day. You're either a glutton for punishment or you have a high tolerance for pain. I figured by now you would be begging me to shut up. My life is boring. What would you like to hear first?"

"I would like to hear about your earliest memories. After all you did say that the entertainment value alone was worth being part of your family. Then you said something about adventure, so please start somewhere toward the front and work toward this end", Kami kiddingly chided.

"Well you asked for it. If you want to hear about my family, I guess my grandparents would be a good place to start." Ryan talked in general about his grandmother's home and his father's early drinking problem. Ryan went on to tell Kami about the river and how broke they were and the irony of the arch - the arch with those four words, water, wealth, contentment and health. Then on how it was growing up in west Modesto. Ryan talked about the family get-togethers and those who were there and how stories rich in family history were told late into the night. Ryan paused for a moment, looked to the stars, took a deep breath, and started to speak in less general terms.

"My grandmother, at least by the pictures that I have seen of her, was a beauty in her youth. She was pure wisdom in her waning years and self-empowered, she lived life on her own terms. She taught me many things, things that most grandmothers wouldn't have known or even experienced. She was a wild thing in her early years. She hunted, fished and she was as wild as the horses she broke. Of course, Grandma wasn't one to brag, so I learned most of this by listening to aunts and uncles as they talked among themselves at family gatherings. These get-togethers usually centered around a visit by Uncle Walter and his family. Uncle Walter was a government hunter and trapper, so to hear him praise Grandma's hunting and fishing abilities really surprised me. Then one of my aunts admitted that, still to that day, she couldn't eat rabbit, because when times were hard, Grandma fed the family almost exclusively on rabbits and prairie chickens that she shot. At one of these get-togethers, a friend of my dad's showed up. Bill Stickle was his name. He was a professional bull rider. Hearing that Bill was a real rodeo star, Uncle Walt couldn't resist telling Bill that his little sister was the best horse breaker that he had ever seen. I sat there and listened to the stories of Grandmother's exploits and how she could break a horse in half the time it would take any other bronco buster."

"Uncle Walt said that what amazed him the most was the way she could green break a horse. It seemed that she could gentle a horse down just with her voice. She would stand in the corral and wait, letting the horse come to her. Then she would talk to it softly, charming it, almost like she put a spell on it. Then, ever so slowly, she would start touching it, patting it along its sides and down its flanks. Before the horse knew what was happening, she would have a blanket on its back. Within a day or two, she would be riding it. She knew the other ways of breaking horses, the snubbing post and sacking plus hobbling, but she would never do that. Uncle Walt paused as he told this story, then said, "I was gone the day she was nearly stomped to death. The bronc was one that others had tried to break. They had tried every trick in the book to break this horse, but his spirit was too strong. Most of those tricks were tried by an old boy that was known not only for breaking horses but also their spirits as well. Whana was warned to leave that horse alone; he was made mean by those who had tried to break him. She went into the corral and apparently had her back to the horse when he ran her down and stomped her. She lay there, for how long was anybody's guess, since nobody saw her enter the corral. When she was found she was crumpled into a ball, and anyone who tried to reach her was run out of there. Finally, somebody shot the damned thing. Whana was taken into the house and the Doc was called, but he couldn't make it out to the homestead until the next day. Doc set her bones and wrapped her broken ribs; he shook his head and said there wasn't anything else he could do. Then he added that we should make arrangements because he didn't think she would make it. She sure the heck made a liar out of him, he didn't know Whana. When she came to, she was worried about the horse. We waited until she was well enough to tell her that the horse had been destroyed. Boy was she mad! She still wanted to break the damned thing. She felt responsible for the horse's death and never broke another horse again."

"About that time, Grandma came out of the house with a platter of food. Uncle Walt put his finger to his lips and shook his head, indicating that Bill shouldn't say anything to Grandma about what had just been said."

Picking up a twig and snapping it into pieces Kami asked, "Your Grandmother's name was Whana and she broke horses?" The expression on Kami's face showed that he was somewhat confused as to the term of broke or the breaking of horses.

"No, not like that. She would do what was called green breaking wild horses to where they would be ridable. She told me what it was like to use a snubbing post and how to calm a horse by just using your voice. She told me many stories about the prairies and the hills of Colorado. They were great stories, that's all they were until one day when she was sick and she asked me to rub some lineament on her back. She was sitting up, and when she pulled up her night shirt, I saw something that I will remember the rest of my life. There on her side was a large scar, a scar where they had to remove one of her kidneys. This was years after she had been stomped. She also had knots on her ribs where they had healed and fused together. I couldn't help it, I had to ask her. All she said was, 'I had a little run-in with a horse.'"

"I guess she was the person who started opening me up to racial and physical differences in all of us and to appreciate those differences. She was married three times; this fact must have embarrassed her. I found this out long after she died, from my Aunt Doris. Grandmother's first husband was a house painter and ended up having his fingers shot off by his hunting dog. He was posing for a picture with his dog and the day's limit of prairie chickens at his feet. His hands were over the open end of the barrel and the stock was on the ground in front of him, his dog was at his side. The dog pawed at his pant leg, then somehow his paw hit the trigger firing the loaded shotgun. Grandmother's husband lost most of his fingers on one hand, and the other hand was also badly injured. He went into a severe depression, driving my Grandmother away. She would have stayed otherwise. Grandma never mentioned that this was her husband, only that he was a friend, when she used this lesson to help teach me firearm safety. She showed great empathy for those who were physically impaired or had a different skin color. I saw her cry only three times. The first time was when Uncle Walter died, then when Kennedy was killed, and next when Dr. Martin Luther King was killed. The last was the worst. It broke her heart, it was as if a wound had been reopened, perhaps an old wound? That day I came home from school and found her sitting at the kitchen table sobbing. When I asked her what was wrong, she told me about Dr. King. To my shame I couldn't understand what the big deal was, and I said so. Grandmother was shocked. She stopped crying and gave me a stern look. Then her face softened and she gave me a hug.

"Her voice was soft and compelling as she started telling me about her second husband, my grandfather. Your grandfather was a U.S. Marshall for the Craig Colorado area. There was a family that lived out of town and the father was known as a wife beater. He was jealous and on the rare occasions that he would bring his wife to town, she would stay in the wagon until she was ordered to get down and follow her husband into the store. She always held her head down and heaven forbid if she looked up and there was a man in the direction she was looking. If that happened, there would be hell to pay. To her husband this was a punishable offense for which she was beaten on many occasions. Usually this was done out of sight, back at their homestead. One time they were in town and a stranger stopped them to ask for directions, which the husband provided. When the stranger walked away he said 'good day,' the husband said the same and with her head down, she spoke, also saying 'good day.' Her husband grabbed her by the arm and pulled her into the alley, where he beat her. She never made a noise, she just accepted his rage. When they left the alley, she could hardly walk. Her bonnet was pulled down to hide her face. Somebody saw what had happened in the alley and went to get your grandfather. He caught them as they were leaving town. He stepped between the team of horses and stopped the wagon. He asked the wife to raise her bonnet. She wouldn't at first, but when she finally did, your grandfather was shocked. He knew this woman before she married this monster. She was once one of the prettiest ladies in the county. Now her nose was off to one side, it had been broken many times. Her lip was split open and both eyes were black, there was a pleading look in them. This image stayed with your grandfather for many years. At that time, it was okay for a husband to beat his wife, there wasn't any law against it. Your grandfather could only warn him, but, hell, he threatened to kill the bastard. This was the first time that I heard my grandmother use strong language. From that time on, the husband came into town by himself."

"Then one day, the wife walked into town. She could barley stand. She told your grandfather that her husband had been beating her children and molesting them, so he and a deputy headed out to get the children and arrest the husband. After they had arrested the husband, the deputy got in the wagon with the children. He headed back to town with the kids as he had been ordered. Your grandfather and the husband were on horse back. Your grandfather decided to take a shortcut back to town."

She paused here, her voice held shame, "He arrived in town without the husband. He said that his prisoner escaped and he took a couple shots at him. Somebody found the husband's body in an abandoned line shack. There was no investigation." Grandma then asked me how I felt about that. I just shrugged my shoulders. She waited to see if I would say anything, but I didn't know what to say. She stared into her coffee cup, now cold. When she started to talk again, the tone of her voice changed, like she was even more ashamed about her next revelation.

"Do you know what a porter is?" I shook my head no. "Well they work on trains, carrying luggage and helping passengers and providing other services. Back in those days, porters were all black and they never left the trains. One day the train left and one of the porters stayed behind. Maybe it was his day off, or maybe he just wanted a meal and to sleep on a bed that wasn't moving - nobody will ever know. All I know is that the good God-fearing citizens of Craig should be ashamed. Not a single one them would even give the poor man so much as a drink of water, much less rent him a room for the night. A train would be coming through the next day, so he must have figured that he would wait in town until it arrived. He wandered around town all day, smiling and trying to strike up a conversation, but there weren't any takers. He just sat alone on the bench at the train station until dark. We lived outside of town and it was unusual for your grandfather to show up early for dinner. Even though we were several miles from town, he'd almost always head back to town after dinner. This night he didn't. I should have known that something was up. The next day, me and the kids went into town. Those "good" Christians had hung that poor man. When I asked passerby's to help me cut him down, there was either silence or they'd say something like, "The nigger should have known better than to be in town after dark!" Your grandfather helped me cut him down. Now I knew why he'd stayed home that night. I was so mad I asked him if he was going to do something about it. He looked at me with a blank expression on his face and asked, "What do you want me to do? Arrest the whole town?"

"Nothing was done. I later found out that he must have been cold. He came back into town and somehow found an old discarded horse blanket and was caught with it on his way back to the station. All he was asking for was the minimum assistance that should be afforded any human being or animal, for that matter. He was killed for the color of his skin and for stealing from the garbage an old horse blanket. Now what do you think?"

I shrugged my shoulders again. After thinking a moment, I said, "that I wasn't sure about the first story, but the second wasn't right. Dad has a lot of black friends and friends of all races, and so do I." She then told me what Dr. King was all about and it was still all about minimum respect and equality. These were the needs of all things, not just blacks, but all humans and because the majority of people believe that something's right or justified, that doesn't mean it is right.

It wasn't until I was in my early teens that I found out a secret about my grandmother, she was part American Indian. I found this out only when Sam Bird asked me one day, "What tribe is your Grandmother from?" My reaction was that of denial, and I said, "She's not Indian, she's a Gypsy." Sam laughed and patted me on the shoulder and said, "Okay."

Sam's question caused me to wonder why my grandmother always gave a pat answer about being a Gypsy when she was asked her ethnic background. It was Sam who later gave me the answer to this nagging question. He had stopped in to get gas and I asked him why he thought my grandmother was Indian/Native American.

He smiled and said, "I just know, and I also understand why she answers those questions the way she does. You see, when she was growing up, being an Indian wasn't what most people wanted to be, much less half an Indian. Do you understand that Indians, as a class, were considered to be the lowest form of human being, even lower than Blacks of that time? During the early history of this country, Blacks were property, they had value. Later the Chinese were even more welcome than us, they helped build the railroad. With the railroad, came the market hunters and the end of the Free Indian Nations. The only value our people had was a small piece of fur, like the coyotes, there was a bounty on our scalps. Now things are different and you'll probably see in your time that history will be rewritten and the truth will be shown."

Ryan looked down at his shoes, shaking his head. "It was at this point that I had a reason to feel ashamed. I remembered playing cowboys and Indians in my grandmother's front yard, and none of us wanted to be one of those stinking, dirty fighting, dog eating Indians. We said things like this in front of that wonderful dear lady. My shame pierced deep into my soul. I never had the nerve to ask the truth. She and Uncle Walt had skin bordering on reddish, going into the olive tones. Their eyes were hazel green with brown dots. I still had some reservations. Then Mr. Hayward came along, a black man with blueish eyes and a wife who had freckles and hazel green eyes. The clincher was a friend of mine, Joel Hagen's mother, Mrs. Eloise Hagen. She and I would sit and talk for hours under the plum tree. She's wonderful to listen to, she has stories of her family and its history. One day after listening to me talk about my grandmother and my doubts about being part Indian, she told me a story about her father.

"She said, 'My father was a lawyer in Scranton, North Dakota. Of course, you knew that already but I didn't, or maybe I did, tell you about one of his clients. Well, anyway, one of his clients was a tribe of Indians. They were the Nandate Tribe, which is an offshoot branch of the Lakota Sioux. I was a little girl the first time I saw one of the members of that tribe. I thought how strange he looked, he was almost olive skinned, and he had freckles and hazel eyes. It seems that Welch trappers had come into the tribe and had been absorbed through marriage and their offspring carried these genetic traits. So I don't think it's so far fetched that your grandmother was of native background.' This made sense to me. Oh, by the way her farther was William A. Fleming, and he was one of the first to introduce ring neck pheasants into his state. To me he is a hero; he did something for the future generations that would fallow." Ryan stopped talking, then quickly looked first to his left and then to his right.

"What's wrong?" asked Kami.

"Nothing, nothing. As I was talking, I kept seeing things out of the corners of my eyes. It was kinda like somebody was sitting over there at the edge of the light, or maybe the form of someone or something. Heck, I must be tired."

"Are there any other stories you remember about your grandmother? There must be more," Kami said, trying to divert Ryan's attention back to the fire.

"Yes, there is. My father told me lots of stories about mom. He always called Grandma 'Mom'. They were still in Colorado when she and a neighbor's wife hatched a plan to become bandits. Sometime near the holidays, I don't know whether it was Thanksgiving or Christmas

- anyway, they planned to raid another neighbor's turkey ranch and steal a couple birds. My grandfather, the Marshall, caught wind of their plan and contacted the rancher and told him what was going to happen. He asked the rancher to let them get their birds and to let them get out of range before he started yelling and shooting into the air. The women ran back home laughing and flush with the excitement of the stolen fruit. They were like the Dalton's or the James Gang after a bank robbery. Like the old saying, it's the stolen watermelon that tastes the sweetest or in this case the turkeys anyway. Grandfather's part of the deal to the rancher was to pay for the turkeys. Grandfather never told grandmother that he had made a deal with the rancher, he told only the kids and made them swear to keep it a secret."

"The other story Dad liked to tell was about an Indian whose name was James Whitehorse. He was a regular Sunday dinner guest at the homestead. Every Sunday James chided my grandmother, saying, 'You white folks throw away the best part of the chicken.' Then one Sunday, after he had placed a bunch of chicken on his plate, Grandma reached over and removed his plate saying, 'I've got something special for you,' and went to the kitchen. When she returned, she had a cloth covered plate in her hand. Passing the plate under his nose, she placed it on the table in front of him. James removed the cloth to display the entrails of a chicken, all rolled up and fried. The claws were also fried and sticking up from the center of it all. James pushed himself away from the table and walked out the door not saying a word. Granddad was mad. 'How could even think of offending a dinner guest like this?'

"Grandma's answer surprised him. 'I don't know what his problem is. He's the one who asked for it and I cleaned everything real good before I fried them.' Within three weeks, James feet were back under grandma's table. It seems that Grandma's fried chicken and mountain butter gravy was a meal that was hard to resist which made it easer to forget her previous little prank. "

"You say that your grandfather was your grandmother's second husband. Why did she leave him?" asked Kami.

"My father told me that my real grandfather was an alcoholic and that he and James Whitehorse were the biggest moonshiners in the state. Now combine that with a mean disposition and you have a formula for failure.

The last straw was when Grandfather was cooking breakfast one morning. My father said something that made Grandfather mad, so he hit my dad across the face with a hot pancake griddle. Grandma packed up the kids and headed to California and ended up in Modesto. They lived on Seventh Street, not far from the arch. Grandma found work plucking chickens for fifteen cents an hour. That and shooting rabbits kept a roof over their heads and put something on the table. The man I consider my grandfather was my grandmother's third husband. His name was Howard Stout.

"He had divorced his wife and followed Grandma to California and later married her. The poor man was shunned by his own family and his children turned against him. One of his teenage children went as far as to write Howard with a threat to kill him if he should ever show his face in his home state. Grandmother made sure that Howard's child support was paid first before any other bills. This still would not appease his ex-wife and the hate she had for my family. When Howard went home to bury his mother, his ex-wife had him arrested for non-support. She made him sign over any inheritance he would receive to get out of jail and bury his mother. Grandma had warned Howard about paying his support in cash but his ex insisted on cash only; there wouldn't be any record this way. My dad also hated Howard at first, but later he learned to love him. Howard was a very loving man with a great sense of humor. He taught me that the same tool that builds a house is the same tool that can tear it down. This also applied to out-houses and countries. Unfortunately, his real kids missed out on someone I loved and sometimes took for granted. I somehow thought he would always be there. Precious few of my family are still here, and those who have passed, I miss terribly."

"Every time I see a yellow rose, I think of Grandma, she loved yellow roses. I have vivid memories of Grandma. Sometimes the smell of food, like a warm piece of toast, triggers a memory. Thoughts, like sitting in Woolworth and sharing half a ham-on-toast sandwich and afterwards going to Sears to make a payment on her bill. While she was doing this, I would always go down the stairs to the basement. Over in the corner by the paint was the gun rack. She could always find me, there among the walnut stalks, so smooth to the touch, immersed in the smells of paint and gun solvent. On the way home, we'd always stop at Merry Gardens. Merry Gardens was a combination second-hand thrift store and roller rink. She let me watch the kids skate in the roller rink next door while she shopped. She'd shop for used clothes and a now and again she'd pick up a toy or two. We didn't have money for skating, but it was fun to watch anyway. Another memory was setting in her kitchen, listening to Ramona's party line. It was like a yard sale over the radio. Grandma was always looking for bargains. There wasn't any extra money until Dad opened the station. One of my best memories is when I was little. I would lie across her lap, and she would scratch my back. I can still feel Grandma's fingers scratching my bare back, and the back of my neck. She would also run her fingers through my hair. Grandma, like I guess most grandmas are, was pure love." As Ryan spoke, he noticed in his peripheral vision what appeared to be a couple more apparitions. This time he passed them off as a trick of the campfire light.

"Would you say that your grandparents and other family members were your heroes as well as this fellow Sam?" asked Kami.

After taking time to think for a moment, Ryan said, "Yes, I guess you could say that. Family fed me, clothed me, and taught me right from wrong. They gave me the tools to succeed. No one else, no sports stars or other public figures, just family. I don't know when it became unpopular to have parents or other family members as heroes. Because of family, I'm a success. That doesn't mean that I'm rich or famous. It means that I'm able to support myself. That's all the responsibility that a parent has in this world."

"Sam said it like this, 'Look at a mother bird. She raises her young'ns until they're old enough to leave the nest. Her responsibility ends pretty much there. She might show them where to find a little food here and there, but that's about it. Now it's up to the fledgling to find out everything else it will need to survive and to live successfully. But, let's say that the young bird is caught and eaten by a kitten learning how to hunt. Does this diminish the role that the mother bird played? Was she a failure? Does it reflect on her as a parent? After all, the kitten was learning to hunt and survive. Humans aren't very smart; we take years to learn what a bird learns in a matter of months. We are victims of our inability to learn from others mistakes and to take responsibility for our own mistakes.' Yes, Sam was one of my heroes. He had a way of explaining life simply, in a way that I could understand. "

"Who else would you call a hero? Or maybe there are many others that you consider to be heroes? Somehow, I have a feeling that perhaps there are many."Kami smiled.

Ryan was taken aback by this question. Nobody had ever asked him this question before. Ryan thought for a moment then said, "Teachers, yes. Teachers, every one of my heroes taught me something. Friends like Dennis Barbour, he's more like family, anyway he helped me keep this place. He also has helped raise money for good causes, by barbecuing. He helped to raise many thousands of dollars doing this for a disabled truck driver. Dennis will cook up to thirty turkeys at a time on holidays, all for friends and employees and even for the homeless. He's an average guy with a huge heart. This shows what a guy with a big heart and a big barbecue or even a bunch of guys with little barbecues can do. Hero, yeah, he's one." Ryan paused, then started by telling other stories about Sam and James and stories about Charlie and Skeeter. They taught me by being both good examples and good examples of bad examples. Kami laughed with Ryan as he told how a poodle with pink bows and red painted toenails was able to get a badger named Bump out of a barrel. He talked about the majesty of the birds of prey. Ryan spoke in depth and in detail. His mood became gradually somber.

Looking over at an oak tree, he watched the light play among the leaves and limbs. "You know, Skeeter turned out to be smarter than most people had thought. It was as if his IQ was lowered by the people he hung out with. Skeeter became a poet and began living the life he was born for. He was smart enough to say no and not to stay with Charlie and get caught up in trafficking drugs the way Charlie had. Charlie was taken from the freedom of the woods to a lonely existence behind the walls of a prison. So who was smarter, Skeeter, who is still alive, or Charlie, who died in prison of a drug overdose? Each taught me something different. Charlie taught me that, if you're doing things wrong or illegal, you will always get caught. Skeeter, he taught me, that nobody can find his true self while playing the fool, or, by not challenging one's self, or having a more dominate personality. This is what cages the spirit, and damages the soul."

Kami had an understanding look on his face, as he said to Ryan, "Keep going, I want to hear more."

"Ok, if you want more, here it goes. Stop me when you've had enough.

When Sam first took interest in me, I was a super religious Christian hiding behind my Christian Son glasses. My eyes were shut to the spirituality of all things. At first, what Sam was saying was quite alien to me. The idea that all living things are connected and that all things are circular and are a part of something called the great wheel or circle of life. Don't get me wrong, there's nothing wrong with those who call themselves Christians if they value other's rights as they value their own. I've looked over many religions and it's as good as any. There's a story that Reverend Bizzard once told me. It went like this.

"There was this minister; he had one heck of a fellowship. People came from all over to hear this man's sermons. The church was always filled to capacity and after every fellowship; he was the first out of the church and to the bottom of the steps. There he shook everybody's hand. One Sunday while doing this, he was listening to the small groups of worshipers who had gathered nearby. As he was listening he heard words, glowing words of praise about his sermons and how lucky they were to have him as a minister. They felt sorry for the other churches that had other ministers who weren't as good as theirs. They told how they left other ministries to come to this one and why. The minister's head was swimming. He was filled with great pride in his ability to teach and preach. Then it struck him that he was allowing his pride to give him a big head. He went over to the group and in the most humble way that he could, he said, 'I was listening to you talk about my ministry as compared to others in the county. I thank you all for your belief in my teachings, but I'm reminded of one teacher I had and a lesson that I will always remember. I'll illustrate what he said to me.' The minister pointed his finger to different individuals and said, 'You grow tobacco and you grow cotton' and so on and on to the different farmers. There were growers from all over the county there. 'You live in the east end of the county, and you live in the west, and the buyer lives in the south end. Now the cotton gin is in the middle and the growers are surrounding the gin from all corners of the county, right?' The farmers nodded their heads. 'When you all bring your crops in, does the buyer pay you more because you traveled farther than anyone else?' The farmers shook their heads, no. 'Right,' the minister said. 'He only wants to know what and how much you brought and in the end he'll decide the quality, right? You see, there are many roads, and in the end it's still only the quality and quantity that counts. The other ministers are saying something right and it touches their congregations. I'm proud to be placed in their company.'"

"Sam taught me about nature and the true nature of man. He said, 'There are really only four types of people, those that look at a plate glass window and see only the flaws in the glass and dirt on the window. When the purpose of the window is to let light in so you can see the glory of the world outside. The next type isn't even able to see the glass at all; they are too absorbed in the outside. They might even walk into the window. Then there are those who fall in the middle, which is most of us, those who are able to see the beauty and the utility at the same time.' I've added one more type or level to this. They're the ones who believe that the window is after all only an illusion the rest is potential. The illusion that we believe to be solid, tangible and without any further thought real, or are they, who's to say?"

"He also taught me that we as a species aren't that far removed from the animal part of our past. Like birds nests, our homes are mostly made of sticks and mud in the form of wood and stucco. Just consider our houses as merely another type of cave. He also said that we are predators and when we remove our natural prey, we prey on ourselves. He was right, and now with denser populations, there is higher social stress and it's only getting worse. Gangs are preying on the weak and holding entire neighborhoods hostage. We have poisoned one in ten of our children by using drugs or alcohol before their births. This poisoning has caused mental illness, fetal alcoholism, drug-addicted babies and children who have behavioral problems, some with violent personalities, due to this poisoning. They become the violence. In most cases, guns or knifes are used against others. The sins of the parents are visited upon the child. What the parents can't put down, the children will pick up, be it smoking, drinking or drugs, violent lifestyles such as gangs or the KKK, dumb isn't it? They are pitiful, desperate to connect to be part of something, even if it hurts others."

"There is a trend toward removing all weapons. Sam saw this coming and said, 'I've got to believe that when we give up our ability to defend ourselves, we'll become a society of sheep. When the population of sheep rises, the population of wolves will also rise, that's the nature of the beast. A person allowed to legally bare arms is a citizen; one who isn't is a subject.'"

"He was right, that's the way nature works. The more we try to remove ourselves from the nature within us, the more nature shows us what kind of animals we really are. Maybe the only answer is to have a cop for every man, woman, and child." There was a bitterness in Ryan's voice. He paused, and then said "Sam and my grandmother also taught me not to kill anything that I didn't plan to eat. Maybe that's the answer, make them eat whatever or whoever they've have killed."

"Sam also taught me that humans are arrogant. It's been said, that maybe we created God in our own image so he no longer would exist in nature. God's being held prisoner in our churches and for a small fee, you can go and hear about him. Man has lost touch with his balance and where he belongs in the natural world. This all may sound like it puts a poor light on mankind, but it's to illuminate man's place in nature and the nature in man. Man's impact is neither negative nor positive when he's in balance. If humans were gone tomorrow, the sun would still shine and the world would still go on. We are just fleas on the world's back, with inflated delusions of grandeur. Unlike parasites, we're aware of our effect on our host. If we cause negative effects on the host and the host can no longer support us and dies, we also die. It boils down to cause and effect. But the world will still go on, it's just that simple. Maybe humans are the opening act, comedians holding the stage, while waiting for the main players to hit their spots, creating a laugh track for a cosmic comedy not yet written. Maybe we're just background noise or animated arrogance, daring to dream that we are God's chosen."

"Karma. Karma plays a big part in my country and in my beliefs. Some of what you said about cause and effect sounds as though you believe in karma or maybe Sam did," Kami said softly.

Ryan looked surprise, knowing that Kami had made the same connection that he had. He smiled and said, "Yeah," then continued on where he had left off.

"Sam also pointed out another arrogance. That man has long assumed that he had a monopoly on this ability to communicate both in language and emotions. Whoever or whatever doesn't speak our language is inferior and that at one point in history, they didn't even possess a soul. This made it easy to enslave others or kill them, using language or religious or cultural differences to justify their actions. To Sam, the earth was a living thing, as were its waters, rocks, heck; even the air had its own spirit. This is the way he was taught and the way he would teach anyone who would listen."

"My grandmother said it this way, 'If you can't find God in an open field or the woods, among his best works, then why would you expect to find him in a building built by man?' She had this necklace and attached to it was a glass orb. Inside the orb was a single mustard seed. She said that, 'If you have faith, even if it was as small as a mustard seed, God could find you.' Sam would have agreed with her. He also said that, 'No man has all the answers.' Sam then scratched his chin and asked me a question, 'What do you think God or the Creator needs humans for. He made everything but some believe that he sits around and obsesses over us and why would he have to? So what does he really need us for?'"

"I didn't have an answer then but I think I understand now. As for Sam, Grandma and my parents having all the answers, I'll be damned that as time goes on they were more right than wrong. Here's an example of the language thing. Not long ago, a lowland gorilla named Michael was taught sign language. Using sign language, Michael told a story about his mother being killed and butchered and eaten in front of him. We now recognize that most life on this planet communicates in some form. I would like to extend that to all life forms. Sam once said that vegetarians were wrapped in that same arrogance of language. It's just arrogance in a new suit. Even vegetables feel and, who knows, maybe they scream when they're put in boiling water. He believed that, after death, our bodies should feed the grass and trees to complete the circle."

"It sounds as though you might have a problem with religion," injected Kami. "Nah! It's ignorance and arrogance that I have a problem with, people who follow something blindly without thinking. I've studied many religions and beliefs. For the most part, people are followers and go blindly where they're led. Sometimes their leaders wish to force their own morals on society, saying that they are speaking for God. This kinda gives me a rash. They try to pass laws to secure rights for themselves while limiting the rights of others."

"Grandma once said in reference to this kind of belief and that sort of sentiment, 'Anything limiting those who are different or those who love differently, limits our ability to grow and understand what God wants of us. There has always been more than enough hate in this world and not nearly enough love. Hate blinds the possessor and limits God. So, leave those alone, who have found a love that they can call their own. Heaven knows we need as much love as we can find in this world. There's so precious little of it.' Grandma used an elderly lady at the end of the street and her gentleman caller to illustrate this." A huge smile crossed Ryan's face as something he hadn't thought about for a while crossed his mind.

"Well, what's on your mind? It must be something good." Kami's smile was as big as Ryan's.

"I hadn't thought of this for years. I remember the first time I became aware that there was something different about the relationship the widow lady on the corner had with her gentleman friend. Ms. Sunny was one of six widows who lived at my end of the street and she had the dirt on everybody. In this world of mass communication, we had telephone, television, and tele-Sunny. One day my mother was catching up on the neighborhood news and gossip with Ms. Sunny. We were standing out in front of Sunny's house next to the street when we saw him. He had gotten off the bus on Sutter Avenue at the end of Avalon. At a distance you could easily see that he carried a carpet bag in each hand. Sunny pointed him out saying, 'There's that carpet bagging, traveling salesman.' She had forgotten that I was there and proceeded to tell Mom the sordid tale of the goings on at the end of the street. I listened to her while watching him walk toward us. As he got closer, I could see a cigar in the corner of his mouth. He happily puffed away as he walked, looking like an old steam engine coming down the tracks. On top of his head was a wispy tuft of white hair. It blew around in the afternoon breeze and the smoke curled around his head. When he got to us I could see that he had a smile from ear to ear, he was on his way to see Gladys, his sweety. Sunny suspended her dissertation that took place at the sins on the corner, as the old man approached us tipped his head, and, said 'Good afternoon, ladies.' Both Mom and Sunny returned the greeting. As soon as he was out of hearing range, Sunny started back up. She hit her stride, telling the torrid tale of geriatric gymnastics at the end of the street. When I was older, I realized that there was a cycle to his arrivals and departures. He showed up in the spring, helping Gladys with her garden and he stayed until the last tomato came off the vine. I later learned that he had two other girlfriends and showed up at different seasons of the year for each and stayed four months.

Over the years, more information came to light, such as; all the ladies knew each other. Heck, they even kept in touch by phone with the old man and each other. They weren't jealous of each other and after four months, they were ready for him to move on to one of his other girlfriends. They all seemed to be happy with this setup including this man for all seasons. My grandma was friends with Gladys, the widow lady at the end of the street. She was the one that put the pieces of this puzzle together. After hearing what Ms. Sunny and the other widow ladies had to say about Gladys's boyfriend, I asked my grandma what she thought. She asked me what I knew or thought I knew. I told her and she honestly filled in the blanks. This was her way of teaching me tolerance and how not to judge others. This was one of her many lessons about how God wants us to respect each other and each other's way of loving. 'You might not understand it, but respect it no less. There's too much hate in this world and not enough love in this world. Those that have found love, let them be.' Grandma went back to her toast, coffee and Ramona's Party Line."

"So, how did your father and mother feel about God or religion?" The way Kami asked this question caused Ryan to pause a moment and think.

"Mom was a church-goer, while my father, on the other hand, was burnt so many times by those passing themselves off as being good Christians. Here's an example. Dad extended credit to these people who professed to be God fearing Christians and almost always they left him holding an unpaid bill for gas or car repairs. The ministers were the worst; they always expected Dad to donate goods and service. I once overheard one of them ask Dad, after having just finishing a motor overhaul, 'Would you please consider donating your service to the church. It's tax deductible, please help me do God's work?'

"Dad replied by telling them this story. The last time I was in a church, other than for some friend's funeral, was when I was a teenager. The minister passed the donation plate around four times during the service. Each time the plate was passed, the total was written on a chalkboard. Finally when this ear-banging, mine numbing service was stopped, the minister pushed up over the podium and warned the congregation, 'This service wouldn't continue until we have enough money for a down payment on a new car.' Would you believe that pompous ass said, 'I can't go to the meeting of ministers without a new car, this wouldn't reflect well on our church and this congregation.' He needed it so he wouldn't be embarrassed? My sister Doris and I walked to church. Our family didn't have a car and couldn't even afford to own one, for that matter. This minister had a Cadillac and wanted a new one. That was the last time I attended a regular church service. I've never really trusted ministers after that, but I've always gave them a chance, one chance only. You can pay in cash or on credit card, that's all I can do for you."

"There was exception to this rule and that was a black Reverend, Mr. Bisszared. He always paid his own way. Dad respected Mr Bisszared, he was a good man, but as for the others, they were given a chance and they almost always let Dad down, leaving him with a bill and a little less faith. Heck, Dad had more respect for one of the local prostitutes than all the rest of those ministers put together. The first time she came into the station, she wanted a fill-up but asked that Dad check her spare tire first. Dad opened the trunk and on the spare tire was a sign stating what she would do for a tank of gas. Dad shut her trunk, walked back up and politely declined her offer. He said to her 'I respect your business as much as I do my own, but the only business relationship we're going to have will be cash.' She smiled and handed him twenty dollars. When she had cash, she would come in and when she didn't, she went elsewhere, until Dad gave her credit. She respected my father and became a regular customer and a friend." Ryan opened his hands and stared at them as though he were trying to read his own future in his palms or maybe just looking for words.

"You know, the one event that really defines my dad happened at the service station. Dad was severely flawed as a businessman for his time or even this time for that matter. He gave credit pretty freely to those who proved to be trustworthy, no matter what they did or what color they were. He sponsored youth baseball teams and when a player couldn't afford a mitt, somehow one would show up. There was a rivalry between the so called, good side of town and the other side of the tracks, where we lived. When the Little League issued us equipment, we were given a bag full of stuff that the other teams didn't want. Dad bought new equipment, and would you believe that we went all the way to city championships? On the day of the championship game, the local paper's photographer had the other team come out onto the field. He took their picture and then he tried to leave the ball park. Dad caught him out in the parking lot and asked him why he hadn't taken our picture. The photographer said, 'I'm here only to take the winning team's picture. You're the underdogs, you aren't going to win. Just lose gracefully. I'm not wasting my film or my time.' Dad was talking loud enough that everyone in the ball park could hear, 'The game hasn't been played yet and you will take our team's picture.' The next time I saw the photographer, he was coming back across the infield. He was a lanky fellow and well over six feet tall. He apparently had changed his mind and was in a hurry. There was a jerky cadence in the way he was walking, he had a springiness to his step and some how he had grew two extra legs. That's when it became apparent that Dad was helping him along. My five-foot-nothing dad had him by the back of his shirt collar and waist band of his pants. The photographer took our picture and for our part we won the game and repeated it the next year, also."

"This isn't the story that I was going to tell you. Like I started to say, Dad had a different way of doing business. One day I had just finished scrubbing the islands and this oil leak on wheels rolled in and parked over my freshly cleaned concrete. I waited for what seemed like a long time while the husband and wife dug around in the glove compartment looking for change. I looked into the back seat and there sat a bunch of kids along with what looked to be all their worldly possessions. I was growing impatient when I heard my father speak. There they were standing in front of this heap, my dad was talking to the father, who had gotten out of the car and was checking his own oil. Then I heard something strange. In a low voice so the man's wife couldn't hear him, Dad was talking it up, heaping praise on this pile of rolling rust. Dad was telling the old boy a story about the good times he had in a car just like this one and how he missed it. Soon Dad was offering to buy the car. The stranger said that he couldn't, because, it was the only way they had to the fields and orchards. They were migrant farm workers who were traveling with the harvest. I thought that Dad's first offer was crazy, and then it happened. The next thing I heard was Dad offering one of the used cars that he had on the lot as trade. The husband said that he didn't have any money to make up the difference in a trade. That's when Dad said, 'Money? Money? Did I say anything about money? Ok, you drive a hard bargain. I'll tell you what I'm going to do. You see, I really want this car. I'll trade you that car over there, it's freshly rebuilt, and I'll even throw in a tank of gas.'"

"It was now confirmed, Dad was nuts. He had lost it. This car was nothing but a bunch of loose parts assembled around an oil leak. What was he thinking? Before it was over, the family drove out in their newly rebuilt used car. Dad bought shoes for the kids and two huge bags of groceries from the Paradise Market across the street. The tank was full and he had thrown in forty dollars to boot. By the time that family left, Dad had the father believing that Dad would be forever in his debt for letting him make this trade. That wasn't the first or the last time that I saw Dad do this kind of thing, but it was one of the most memorable because the family would always drop by the station when they were working in the near by orchards in the area. We watched their kids grow up. The father never asked about the car he had traded." Still staring into his hands, Ryan quietly said, "Dad had magic mechanical hands. His hands weren't really mechanical but they worked magic on machinery. They could resurrect a pile of rust and dust to running in no time at all. It was a thing of beauty. Oh, yeah, the car that he traded, left the station the next day dead on a hook. That is to say, it was hanging from a back of the wrecker, headed to the scrap yard. Dad didn't want to even give that one a try. You see, to Dad business wasn't just about profit, it was about people and one day that old car might have killed that family. This was also his way of paying off debts he felt he owed to those who had helped him out in the past when he was down on his luck. It was his way to honor God; it had nothing to do with religion, just God. He taught me by focusing on the good things, the positives, the heroes, there isn't any time left to be judgmental or to hate. When it's all over, it boils down to family, friends, love, and respect."

"He found the commonality in everyone, rich or poor. He taught me that anyone can be a hero and it doesn't necessarily mean fighting in a war or saving people from a burning building. Dad said, 'Even if you're broke and all you have left is a smile, you're rich enough to give it to somebody who is having a bad day. You might just save that persons life. You never know, your smile just might keep someone who's depressed from committing suicide.' I find new stories and heroes every day, each one teaching me about that special something in all of us. When Dad decided that he wanted a family more than he wanted a drink, he was a hero to me. I later came to understand that, in order to save someone else from drowning, you must first learn to swim. You need to be able to save yourself before you can save anyone else. With this also comes the understanding that a doctor doesn't need to have had the same illness to help in your healing. That's to say, if you have a broken bone the doctor needn't have his arm in a cast in order to set your broken limb, because after your bone is set the doctor has done his part. It's up to you to heal yourself."

"Yes, yes, I was right. You are a fine representative for your ancestors. They should be proud of your hospitality and generosity. There is a richness to your family. Keep going!" exclaimed Kami.

In the light of the fire, one would have to look hard and close, Ryan was blushing. He was embarrassed by Kami's praise. Kami continued, "Tell me your favorite stories about those adventures you mention."

"Most of our adventures happened when we were going someplace in the car. Maybe it was a flat tire or some strange noise. Dad would pull over to fix the problem; we would have a picnic and afterwards explore the area. You wouldn't believe the things that you drive past at sixty miles an hour without even noticing but when you stop and get out, there could be history under you feet. You just have to look. We once found an old Indian arrowhead and an old bottle stuck between the rocks of an old Chinese built fence on our way up to the area around Sonora or Columbia. Dad would tell about how things were built and would spin a story around what we had discovered. Mom loved to tell the history of things. They turned adversity into adventure and a learning experience. Whatever we discovered was left where we found it so it would be there for someone else's enjoyment. Besides these things weren't ours."

"Once, we were taking a dozer, into the hills when we had truck problems. The motor over heated and we had pulled over to let it cool down. Mom was following us in her car, with her were my two cousins, Lee and Lynn, also known as 'the twins.' While Mom set up the picnic, the twins and I went exploring. We soon discovered a stream and a bridge close by. The twins and I were on the bridge, hanging over the rail looking for fish and wildlife when a shadow covered us. I turned to see nothing but a face full of hair. At first, I thought it was a bear but bears usually aren't gray. This piece of gray fur was attached to the face of an old man with strikingly blue eyes. The beard attached to his chin was thick enough to hold a covey of quail. The beard and mustache parted, and a big smile appeared. His bright blue eyes sparkled as he asked, 'What ya lookin fer?' We were speechless. Dad joined us and after he and Dad shook hands, the old man introduced himself as the Mayor of Jupiter."

Kami stopped Ryan saying, "The Mayor of what?" and pointing to the brightest point of light to the right of Orion.

"No, it seems that at one time there was a town of Jupiter somewhere close to where we were, the way he talked it sounded like the town no longer existed. The old man went on to explain that he had jumped ship in San Francisco the day before the 1906 earthquake. After the quake, he headed into the hills ending up in the town of Jupiter. For awhile, he was the town drunk. He worked at the dry goods store, then he was the bar keeper, after that he was voted Mayor and postmaster. He was the last resident of the township of Jupiter. One day he walked away to live on his mining claim. He led us on a tour of his holdings. From the road, there was no way of knowing that anyone was living nearby. There wasn't any road or drive, just what looked like a game trail, that led to his shack. We followed him to the front door; he opened it to reveal a neat one-room cabin with a dirt floor. At the opposite end of the room was a tarp that covered the opening of a mine shaft that went back into the mountain. The old man lit a kerosene lantern and pulled the tarp aside. The air was cool. Not far into the shaft were two small rooms, one he called his locker, where the carcass of a deer hung, the other was his root cellar for vegetables and canned goods. Farther back into the shaft was a side shaft going to the back side of the hill. This allowed him to dump his dirt and tailings away from prying eyes. On the bank of the stream was his sluice box and rocker. When we left the mine and cabin, Dad took a close look at the roof. The old man said that the tin shingles were old institutional-size cans he picked up at the dump. The cans had both ends cut out and were split up the sides and flattened out to make a shingle. The old mans cabin was all that was left of the town of Jupiter. Time and the Forestry had removed all that was left of the town."

"We all went back to where Mom had the picnic waiting; we ate and listened as the old man spun more tails. I realized later how privileged we were to have had this chance meeting, because the Mayor wouldn't have had to reveal his presence. He seldom had visitors and when he did, it was on his terms. He could have stay back in the woods, and we wouldn't have known he was there." "What other stories do you have of these adventures?" Kami posed this question with what seemed to be a genuine interest.

"Here's a story that didn't involve car problems, which Dad loved to tell. This was before we had the service station and to make ends meet, Dad and Mom had a bait business. I was about four years old. We went up to Del Puerto Canyon to pick up the minnow traps. Dad had finished running the traps, and rebating and replacing the bait cans. We were preparing to have a picnic on a quilt that my mother had placed under the shade of an old oak tree that was growing out from the side of the hill below the truck. The tree had several dead limbs. It wasn't really the best place to have lunch but it was close to the truck and because my brother was only a year old, Mom decided to set the picnic up under its shade, besides, it was the only tree in the area. For some reason, cattle leave the grass under oaks alone. This always puzzled me because it stays greener longer in the drip zone under the oaks. Maybe the oaks make the grass bitter or something. Anyway, Dad and I were sitting on one of larger limbs that had grown out from the base of the trunk. The limb kinda swooped down toward the ground and then arched back up and over the quilt. We were watching Mom getting things ready, when Dad saw something out of the corner of his eye. It turned out to be a huge rattle snake. Dad, like others, had a fear of snakes, a fear fostered by television and folk lore. Dad jumped down from the limb, picked up a large stick and went after the reptile. He swung the stick as hard as he could. The stick was rotten and snapped off in his hand. He picked up another stick just as rotten as the first and tried again, with the same results. The snake had caught on to Dad's intent and started to crawl into a hollow at the base of the tree. Dad picked up another branch and this time he pushed it up into the hole where the snake had gone. This stick also broke off. It was about that time that Mom started screaming. Dad didn't realize that all he had succeeded in doing was to push the rattler up the limb that we were sitting on. The limb turned out to be hollow, and Dad had forced baby rattlers up the hollow limb. The babies started raining down from a hole where a branch had rotted out and fell on the quilt in front of Mom. Things were getting crazy fast. Mom grabbed my little brother, Shawn, and she was holding him and was running in place. In a time before workout videos, Mom was impressive. Her workout was interrupted when Dad picked up what he thought was a rock. Anybody who has grown up around livestock knows that not necessarily everything that looks like a rock is one. Dad, of all people, knew this, but in the excitement of the moment, he made a slight error in judgment. A misjudgment in specific density and mass, anyway. He threw this pretender to the throne as hard as he could."

"Now I know that out there somewhere is an engineer who has probably already figured or is in the process of figuring out the drag coefficient of a flying meadow muffin. He's doing this on a government grant to boot. Dad and I could have saved him the effort. Meadow muffins don't fly for darn. But when it does fly, its terminal velocity is relatively low. Somewhere about half way between Mom and Dad things were coming apart. Dad was aiming at the snakes and a small piece did hit in the general area of the quilt. We have all heard the expression about when this kind of stuff hits the fan. Or the other old expression 'let the chips fall where they may.' That's okay if you're not at the back end of the herd. Here's a word of warning, what ever you do, don't let them hit your mom. Well, a majority of the muffin did hit Mom right in the head. That's when Mom's snake dance came to an abrupt end. Dad was caught like a deer in the headlights, to be slowly micro-waved in Mom's glare. Mom stamped off to the truck, leaving me sitting out on the limb and Dad to pick up the picnic. Dad walked over to the quilt. The snakes had by then crawled away. They might have mistaken Mom's dance for a cattle stampede or maybe it was the earthy bouquet of semi-fresh meadow muffin. At any rate, they escaped down hill and into the creek bottom. By the time we made it back to the truck, Mom had settled down and we all had a good laugh."

"There it is again, a story worth passing down from father to child, from generation to generation. This is something to give your kids, a rich oral tradition of storytelling. Please continue, I want to hear more." Kami's voice reflected sincerity and a genuine caring. Ryan felt like maybe he was being guided along, but it didn't matter somehow. It felt therapeutic.

Ryan talked into the night, telling stories of other heroes. "It seems that over the years, I've opened up to expand my heroes to include people other than family and friends. I've added sports and movie stars, not for what they do on the field or move screen but how they help man and animals off the screen and the playing fields, people who take back their neighborhoods from gangs and druggies. "

"I've found that I'm looking up to more and more kids. For example one kid was only seven years old. Every year before school started, his parents bought him new clothes and a new winter coat. When it finally was cold enough he went off to school proudly wearing his new coat, but he came home without it. The next day he wore his old coat. When he returned home his mother noticed that he was wearing his old coat and asked him were his new coat was. He said 'At school.' His mother told him that he needed to bring it home. After a couple of weeks of almost daily questioning by his mother, she finally had enough and told his father. The boy had been warned that if he lost the coat, he would get a spanking. He came home the next day without the coat and was sent to his room to wait for his father and his punishment."

"When the boy's father got home, he went straight to his son's room. He asked his son if he knew where his coat was. The son nodded his head as tears ran down his cheeks. The father removed his belt and then asked, 'If you know where your coat is, why didn't you bring it home?' The son said, 'Tommy has it.'"

"The father was puzzled? 'Why does Tommy have your coat?' The kid was still sobbing as he said, 'He, he, his mother died when he was little and his dad doesn't have enough money for new clothes. They can afford only used clothes. He has never had a new coat and my old coat is still good so I, I, I gave him my new one. I can't ask him to give it back, Dad.' The boy turned and lay across his bed, preparing for his punishment, but the punishment didn't come. His father sat down on the bed next to his son. He picked the child up and hugged him and told him how proud he was of him. The father was in awe of his son, who was willing to stand his ground and take a paddling for his belief that what he had done was right. He had done something wonderfully unselfish for someone who was less fortunate than himself."

"There's a young lady who raises money for bullet-proof vests for police dogs. She started placing cans in stores and shops to collecting pennies to buy these vests after a police dog had been shot and killed. She found power in pennies to make a positive impact, to make a difference. Another young man who builds birdhouses to sell, raising money for the homeless. People are offering to read to people who can't and to be mentors to those in need of support and encouragement. These are just regular people like my Aunt Doris, who volunteers to work with cancer patients. They help us realize that all the bad stuff we read and hear about isn't all that's happening. I believe that there is a whole lot more good going on in this world than bad. Someone once said that we're all teachers, and that we're also students. We do this exchange along with taking on parent and child roles, exchanging these roles as we go. Teachers can learn from their students."

"Ryan told of a teacher in Petaluma who has students involved in cleaning up Petaluma Creek in order to release steelhead trout they had raised as a class project. Steelhead had not been seen in the creek for some twenty years. The kids cleaned the creek, policed it and made sure that no one polluted the place where their steelhead would return to spawn. Then the state shut down the school hatchery that they had set up in an old greenhouse, citing earthquake hazard as the reason. The students raised money for a state-of-the-art hatchery. Now, every year there is a special class reunion where past students, some even taking their own children, and current students gather along the creek bank to witness the returning steelhead. The creek stays clean, because the kids are watching. They've become stewards of this little creek. Every graduation class across this country, the top students address their classmates and declare that their generation will make a difference. They'll most likely end up doing what every other graduating classes has done before. Get a job and earn a living. That's not a bad thing but falls way short of the promise. But those kids in Petaluma did make a difference."

Ryan told of others who have taught kids about the outdoors and fishing and hunting. He talked about hunters and sportsmen who respect other living things, both human and animal and the planet in general. To the general public, however, these guys are vilified.

"I have a friend named Red, who's helping the stripped bass in California. Red manages a little restaurant out east of town on 132, it's called Joanne's Country Kitchen. He puts in long hours and still finds time to lobby for fishermen's rights and the rights of the fish themselves. You see, laws were passed defining the rights of water districts, farmers, and cities, as for fish and wildlife they were left out of the equation. Red and others are lobbying into law the rights of fish and wildlife to their basic needs, water and habitat. Heroes are very personal and these are some of mine. They try to correct the image of sportsmen, in the minds of the general public. Those that think we only take and don't put anything back. There are thousands like Red, they are the ones helping to put things right, by improving and giving habitat back to nature. They're helping to heal an image tarnished by market hunters and those who hurt the honest sportsmen such as Charlie and his kind. They try to educate. There it is again, teachers. I've had some bad teachers, but they are far outweighed by the good ones. I had two great ones."

Ryan talked about Ms. Foret and Mr. Dailey and how they were the teachers, in the right place at the right time, who helped him to succeed in school, how they opened up another world to him, a world of the written word. They, along with others like, Sam, helped him to understand the diversity of life. They unchained his imagination, opening him up to learning. Making a difference in his or her life and perhaps its direction.

The light of the campfire was dwindling and Ryan once again stoked the fire. Kami had listened in silence while Ryan talked. As Ryan was stoking the fire, Kami asked, "Were there any others in the neighborhood besides family who had an influence on you?"

"Why don't you tell me about yourself and your family and your heroes? It's only fair I've told you about mine, how about telling me about yours. Besides, you have to be tired listening to me rattle on."

"Maybe in a little bit, but I'm happy to listen to your stories. We've had a wonderful meal, fresh fruit and for dessert my host has served up stories that are rich, heady, and full of color. Please continue," said Kami.

Ryan spoke of a Mr. Osborne and Manuel, who both taught him about honesty and the responsibility for properly using God's gifts, how that same blind man and a mockingbird, helped him understand about a special love. He told about that warm night, when the smell of concord grapes and the way the music moved his emotions. The night when the passing of a friend lowered another into darkness. He explained about a bond that had been stretched but had stayed unbroken. When Ryan finished this story, Kami asked, "When you hear this music or a mockingbird at night, what do you think of?"

"The mockingbird reminds me of Mr. and Mrs. Osborne. The music, the song, Amazing Grace, well that also reminds me of Mr. Osborne, and a cousin of mine, Bill Hager. Bill was a fireman, and I guess all firemen are heroes even though they'll tell you that they're just doing their job. In my book, they're heroes. Anyway, I went to the hospital to visit Bill. He had cancer and knew that he had only a couple weeks to live. When I walked into his room, his first words expressed concern for my health. He had heard that I had an accident in my truck and had almost left this world ahead of him. That's just the way he was, he thought of others before himself. At his funeral service, I found out how special he really was. He was a battalion chief, the boss, but his men called him 'Dad.' They told about how they could always go to him for advice. Sometimes on holidays, Bill and his family would go to the fire station to have dinner with his men. They recalled the times when Bill could have been home with his own family but chose to let one of his guys off to mend things with his wife or to take care of some personal business. Bill would take the place of that person himself rather than shuffling others around to cover. He led his men by example; they would have followed him anywhere."

"Bill's casket was placed on a fire truck and the hundreds who had gathered followed him on his last ride on a fire truck. The caravan stretched out for more than two miles. At every major intersection there were two hook-and-ladder-trucks, their ladders extended over the roadway with a giant American flag hanging below. The graveyard was full. Where we gathered, there was the smell of fresh dug earth and flowers filled the air. Words were said over him, the bagpipes played Amazing Grace. The music floated over grass and granite and seemed to linger for an extra moment. Then all the radios crackled to life, calling Chief William 'Dad' Hager to last his general alarm. Bill once told me that fire didn't scare him but the call, 'Fireman down' did. He said, 'When my guys are coming out of a smoker, bells ringing and canaries are singing, their tanks empty. Then, when you hear, fireman down, it means that one of my sons is in trouble.' When the pipes play, I hear those words, 'Fireman down.' These are the people and things I remember."

Ryan's eyes filled with tears. Before they could run down his cheeks, he tilted his head up, looking through the salty liquid into the darkness of night, through the Milky Way into eternity and beyond. He hadn't noticed how much time had passed. The constellation Orion, the Archer, denoted how much had passed, as Orion stalked Ursus Major the Great Bear across the sky. Orion now was well past the half-way mark, day light would be here soon. Ryan felt the tiredness coming on, a fatigue that seemed to drain him. He lowered his head, looked at the dying fire, and then back up to his guest. Ryan apologized, saying, "I can't seem to stay awake anymore."

Kami said, "Go ahead and close your eyes, my friend."

Ryan fought sleep for a few more minutes, but as he stared at Kami through the slits of his eyelids just before sleep swallowed him, he clearly saw the human and animal forms that now had completely encircled them. The forms rose and started to dance and walk around them just at the edge of the light. They danced in circles, wrapped in shadow and dying firelight. Ryan asked himself again, is this life, is it death, or is it part of the great circle that Sam talked about?

CHAPTER NINE

RINGS RISING

W hile Ryan dozed, lucid visions walked in and out of his sleeping mind, passing through the ring of dancers. These were friends and family members that had passed away but now they walked up to where Ryan sat. They smiled, said a few words and shook his hand, some even hugged him. Each leaving their footprints across his spirit and on his soul as they passed, like they had on his heart when they left this world. Sam would have called them dream walkers. When the last one passed by, Ryan stood up and started to follow, only to feel a hand on his shoulder, holding him in place. He turned to see who was holding him back but there wasn't anyone there. Just a warm gentle pressure on his shoulder that was slowly leaving. To soon, it would be gone, perhaps it was a passing promise, as were the visitors in his vision.

Then in an instant, Ryan saw a sphere of absolutely clear liquid, a drop like a single angel's tear. He watched the falling drop until it hit the surface of a seemingly endless body of water. The surface deformed, creating a depression until the surface tension broke, allowing the drop to penetrate and mix with the waters below. The depression then rebounded, creating a bulge. From the bulge, another drop broke from the surface to hang in the air for a single moment before falling back to the surface. Rings radiated out from the center, traveling away toward infinity. When the rings passed over Ryan, they sent ripples through him, washing over his spirit, rocking his soul like a baby in its cradle. Ryan felt a reverberation inside him like a drum had been struck or a bow string after the arrows release. It was ten in the morning. Ryan awoke with a start to the sound of wind flowing over feathers as a black shadow passed close overhead. Not more than five feet away, another turkey vulture glided past him. Ryan jumped up from his chair only to fall back into it. His legs had gone to sleep. He looked over to the chair where Kami had sat the night before, but Kami was gone. Ryan stretched out his legs, feeling them tingle as the blood flowed back into them. When he thought his legs could hold him, he stood back up. Then he heard, "Good morning." It was the now familiar voice of Kami, who was walking up the hill behind him. Kami was coming from the ravine where Ryan had fallen asleep on that first day.

Ryan looked up, and in the air above that same ravine the two vultures that sailed over him had joined up with five others. They glided in lazy circles, as if something had died. That's funny, there was nothing there yesterday, Ryan thought. Ryan returned Kami's greeting, then pointed to the vultures. "I wonder what's got their interest. Let's take a walk and see what's up."

Kami looked over at the vultures and back to Ryan. "There's nothing down there, I've just walked up from the road. There's nothing there of interest, anyway." Kami pulled his collar away from his neck, stuck his face into the opening, and inhaled deeply. "Didn't you say that there's a creek around here? I could use a bath. I'm smelling ripe enough that those birds probably think I smell like a blue plate-special. If you feel up to it, would you mind showing me the way to the creek?"

"You're right, there's probably nothing down there and you've got a point, we're both a little ripe. A bath would feel good, even a cold one, but there's a slight problem - soap. I've got soap, but it could be a little hard on the fish that live in creek. We could go back down to Mountain Ranch and see if they have something biodegradable. But first we've got to secure our coals. Let's grab some tin and cover the pit."

While looking for tin at the barn, Ryan found a plastic bucket that looked pretty good. "Here's an idea, since neither of us is much interested in hunting, we could take this bucket to the creek. Using the bucket, we'll wash and rinse ourselves up hill far enough away from the creek that we shouldn't hurt anything."

"That sounds like it should work, but are you sure you don't want to keep hunting?"

"No, I had my chance on the first day. I have this friend, Ron Wilson, who told me once that when he was a youngster, he'd go duck hunting with his grandfather. Sometimes after getting up early and putting out a spread of decoys, they would hunker down in the blind and try to keep the cold away. To keep Ron from getting bored, his grandfather had a fondness and a talent for telling stories. He would tell story after story while waiting for daylight and the birds to arrive. There were days when his granddad would say, "It's a no-shoot day. Let's not shoot today. Let's just watch." Ron said that those days were some of the best." Today we'll just watch and see what we can see." Ryan smiled. Kami looked relieved, "Then it's okay. Let's cover the pit and get going."

They covered the pit, placed the bucket and soap in the cab of the pickup, then the two friends jumped in as well. Ryan started the engine. "We're off and running like a herd of turtles. Forward-Hoooo!" Ryan called out as the wheels of the truck started to roll.

"What does forward-hoooo mean? Turtles don't travel in herds." Kami looked confused. His confusion was also reflected in his voice as he asked these questions.

"Duke, you know John Wayne, Rowdy Yates, Wagon Train, Raw Hide, and Saturday westerns. Come on, I might believe that you haven't seen big-time wrestling on TV, but I know for a fact that Bonanza and all the westerns have been on the tube in your country. You're messing with me again, aren't you?"

Kami just smiled and apologized. "It's been a long time since I've heard that expression."

Ryan accepted this explanation but still gave Kami a cockeyed look. They hadn't hit the property line yet when Ryan said, "The herd-of-turtles thing is something my Uncle Walley would say when we were going somewhere. He was a like a second father to me. He was funny. You'd give him a call and ask how he was doing, the answer was always the same, 'Super' and if you asked him how's Aunt Milly, he'd say, 'Better than nothing.' He was kidding of course. He loved my aunt. He had a great sense of humor. Just an all-around good guy. He and my dad were more than brothers. I'd have to say they were best friends, but they both had a way of having more than one best friend or brother for that matter, if that makes any sense."

"Uncle Walley was a belly gunner or ball gunner in B-17's during World War 11. He was stationed in England and survived fifty missions over Germany. He was everything from a fireman to a master tool and die maker. He worked for Martin Marietta in the late fifties working on the lifting-body aircraft, which was a precursor to the space shuttle. Later he worked on the B-1-B and the B-2 Stealth bomber. These were big projects, but he loved more than anything else to work with a friend, I'll take that back, friend yes, but Andrew Toti was more like a brother. Both have now passed away."

"Would you say that Andrew, and your uncle Walley were also your hero's? For some reason, I feel that they are hero's but for different reasons, I could hear the pride in your voice." Kami was right. "Yes. Andrew was a local businessman and inventor. He's has more than five hundred and fifty patents to his name. When you asked last night about heroes, he was one I forgot to tell you about. His inventions run from the automatic chicken plucker and grape picker. He didn't invent it, but he came up with one design for the May West, or now it's called a horse collar. You know, the flotation device the stewardess shows you how to use when a airplane flies over large bodies of water. You know, like the plane you had to fly on to get here." Kami again nodded his head.

"Well, Andrew made improvements in the original design. Uncle Walley had it around his neck on every flight over the English Channel. Uncle Walley may have had it around his neck, but it helped save the neck of the future President, George Bush. Andrew received a few thousand dollars for his redesign. The thing that makes Andrew a hero in my eyes was the way he took in strays dogs or what ever wandered onto his property. One of these dogs became Andrew's favorite. This dog went every where with Andrew. Andrew bought a membership at a duck hunting club. Since Andrew was going hunting, the dog had to go along too. The dog watched what the real hunting dogs were doing, he must have figured it out, because he just started retrieving ducks from the blind. One day the hunting was slow, not mush happening. Then a single duck flew strait across in front of a bunch of duck blinds. Everybody was shooting at this lone duck; somebody finely put a B.B in the bird. It dropped in front of Andrews blind and Dog retrieved it, Andrew hadn't got a shot off. On the way back to the club house somebody called out 'Hey buddy your dog picked up my bird.' Andrew turned to see a face that looked kinda familiar. Andrew offered to give the duck back to the guy. The guy declined the offer and introduced himself, 'Clark Gable, and then added, do you know that dog is not a hunting dog.' Andrew brought his index finger up to his lip 'shhhh,' looked at the dog and said, 'He doesn't know that.' Andrew had just met a movie star. After introductions and a season of hunting, they became good friends. Andrew introduced Clark Gable to his friends, mostly just regular guys, they'd all get together for hunting and dinners, he became just one of the guys."

"Andrew was one of my hero's not because he was a friend of a movie star, or for all of his inventions that have touched so many lives. It was his ability to find value in what others found worthless and what they had discarded, both in animals and in humans. Andrew kept two wallets one in his back pocket with his money. The other was in his breast pocket over his heart. This held his most valued treasure; it contained small pieces of Kleenex tissue paper that he used to wipe the tears from each of his dogs upon their deaths. The wallet was in his breast pocket when Andrew was laid to rest, there until the end of time. His was a generous spirit."

"Before my father died, he gave me a list of friends to check on every so often for him. Andrew was one of them, so once a month I'd drop by Tropical Awning and see how he was doing. This was for me a privilege." Ryan parked the truck off the road by the old pond. Ryan became somber, with reverenced in his voice he began to talk about Andrew.

"Andrew believed in signs. Like I said, he loved to duck hunt, but in front of is home office across the drive way he had a small pond. The pond was surrounded by a four foot high chicken wire fence, to keep other animals out and the ducks in. One of Andrew's friends came by one day an asked him if it was okay to leave a young hen mallard in the pond with his domestic ducks and geese. Andrew loved the idea, why not. Besides the hens mate had died, she was alone and fit in well with his birds, she was more than welcome. Then one day a wild drake mallard dropped in and won her heart. They matted and raised a family, when it came time to fly north they left, only to return in winter, stayed, and repeated the process. They did this four years in a row. Then for three years, nothing, they didn't return. Andrew knew that with predators or age that this time would come. Andrew's health was deteriorating, knowing his time was near; he shut down his shop, and started working out of his homes office. The home offices windows faced the pond. There, he would watch his birds while working, surrounded in thoughts of how to improve the lives of others. On the week of his death, after a three year absence, the mallards returned, they left the day he died. Andrew would have loved it." Ryan grabbed the bucket and said, "We're going to have to walk from here. I used to be able to drive to the creek, but somebody bought the property up the road. They've chained it off, so we'll have to walk a mile or so down this ravine. I have permission to hunt on this side of the road all the way to the creek."

"Are you sure it's okay to go to the creek?" Kami seemed hesitant. Ryan's answer was to bail off the side of the road into the waste-high horse tail that grew there. Kami jumped over the side and followed. At the bottom of the ravine, they picked up a game trail and followed it as it criss-crossed, winding around obstacles through the bottom of the ravine. At times, the bracken ferns were so high that they had wash-outs, where water had dug out holes big enough to hide a truck. Ryan pointed out these hazards.

Ryan and Kami walked quietly, saying nothing, just pointing out animals and stopping now and then to watch them as they moved through the woods. A pack of coyotes were high up on the hill-side. Ryan saw them first and stopped Kami. He pointed and said, "Coyotes." The coyotes kicked out a group of deer that were bedded down. They deer bounced down the hill toward the two men. When the deer were a couple hundred yards off, Ryan and Kami dropped and hid in the ferns. The deer hadn't seen them and were coming fast; they closed the distance in seconds and passed within a few feet of the men. Only the last doe noticed them, she jumped sideways and stopped for a second before bounding off with the others.

The deer headed up the ravine towards the truck. Ryan and Kami stood up, both were excited. Kami exclaimed, "That was great! Those coyotes were neat. They didn't have a chance to catch any of those deer, they didn't even try. I'd never seen coyotes before. When you pointed to the tracks of the possum and the coyote the other day, I wondered if coyotes looked like dogs, because that's what their tracks looked like. They do look a lot like dogs."

"That was fun all right. Well, now you've seen one. What do you say we keep going and see what other critters we can run across?" quipped Ryan.

"That's good, let's go," said Kami as he patted Ryan on the back.

Still moving as quietly as possible, they watched wild turkeys fly across the canyon, apparently spooked by the same bunch of coyotes. Squirrels were the only animals besides the one doe to see the men, but the squirrels on the other hand wasn't as nice as the doe. They barked their disapproval and announcing that man had invaded the forest. Ryan stopped, "I can't believe it, it's still here!" Ryan ran down to a cedar that had fallen a cross the ravine. It was the same cedar that Ryan used to cross over this ravine when he was a kid. Ryan jumped up onto the dead fall. He stomped his foot and again jumped up and down some more. "This is it, it's still here! I can't tell you how many times I've crossed this log." He raised his arms out to his side, closed his eyes, and started to walk across the log. Ryan looked a bit awkward and unsteady, in one hand he still had the bucket, and it had been years since Ryan had performed this stunt.

"Do you think that's safe?" asked Kami.

"No. You know, some say ignorance is bliss. Do you know what bliss is?" But before Kami could answer, Ryan stopped in the middle of the log, he was fifteen feet off the ground. Then he started jumping up and down, he stopped and said, "Balance is bliss. Balance in all things is bliss."

Kami followed Ryan across. On the other side, Kami asked, "Have you ever fallen?"

Ryan laughed. "Heck, what? Me fall? Sir, I have cat-like reflexes." They had only traveled a short distance from the log when Ryan stepped on some loose shale. Losing his footing, he started to slide down the hill. Kami reached for Ryan but tumbled after him instead. They both ended up rolling and bouncing butt over bucket to the bottom of the ravine into a clump of poison oak. They scrambled to their feet.

Kami had a crooked smile on his face as he quipped, "Cat like reflexes?"

"So much for balance. The law of gravity is still in effect, and I think I bruised my bliss. Let's find the soap and find some mugwort sage because we're going to need it, we're standing poison oak" Ryan said while rubbing his back side. They continued on until they reached the creek. Here's where Ryan knew he could find some mugwort. After picking some mugwort, he took some change from his pocket and tossed it into the patch of mugwort. Kami had a puzzled look on his face. Ryan explained, "When you take something from the earth, you need to give back something of value in return. We need water, would you please get us a bucket full?"

Kami got a bucket of water. Ryan stripped his clothes down to his underwear, as did Kami. Ryan sat down on a rock straddling the bucket and he stripped the mugwort leaves from the stems. He placed the leaves on a rock and ground them into pulp with another rock. He instructed Kami to do the same. When Ryan finished, he rubbed the fragrant pulp over his exposed skin. Kami followed Ryan's example. Ryan then placed the leftover pulp into the bucket, followed by his clothes. He washed his clothes around in the bucket, then placed them in the sun on a rock. He did the same with Kami's clothes.

As Ryan did this, Kami had a questioning look on his face. Ryan saw this and said, "Mugwort- it's something that Sam showed me. Mugwort will keep us from getting blisters from the oil of the poison oak. Our clothes also had the poison oak oil on them so they also needed to be neutralized. Besides, they smelled pretty bad already and the sage could only make them smell better. Come on, cheer up. I'm the one with the bruised bliss." They laughed, then they used the rest of the water in the bucket to soap up and rinse. Ryan got another bucket of water and walked back up to where they washed and they both rinsed off, one more time.

They both walked back down to the creek. Ryan had seen something that he hadn't caught at first. Several rocks that were covered with ladybugs. Looking around, he saw the air was full of them. "Look at that, isn't that beautiful?"

"Yes, yes, there are so many of them. What are they called?"

"Ladybugs. You have got to know about ladybugs. They're probably called something different in your country and they do bite, or at least they like to bite me. I'm probably the only person on the planet that they do this to."

Under a canopy of oaks and dogwoods, they sat on rocks with their feet in the cold water. Up creek was a ledge where the creek narrowed down to around seven feet wide. The ledge was about three feet high, creating a small waterfall. The sound of the falling water was very soothing. Ryan looked up to the top of the fall, this placed Ryan's line of sight at water level. The creek was wider and shallower, above the falls, maybe two feet deep at the most in the deepest holes. There in the flat slow waters above the falls he saw a ring form, he pointed it out to Kami. "Trout. Look at that, it just pulled a ladybug from the surface!" Then another ring formed and another. The trout didn't rise to break the surface and make a splash, they gently pulled the ladybugs from just beneath the surface. The rings reminded Ryan of something. Oh yeah, the dream this morning, he thought.

"Is there a lot of fish in this creek?" asked Kami.

"No, James and I used to fish the creek when Sherry Windsor was alive. We caught a few small ones. What these fish are doing is feeding and filling themselves up for winter, putting on a little fat to get them through the hard times."

Ryan started to think about rings on the water and his dream of this morning. He thought about what he could remember of that first dream on Saturday. Ryan looked into an eddy next to the water fall where dead leaves were floating. The leaves were slowly going in circles, each following the next. Ryan wondered which leaf was the first to be caught in this endless current. He watched as other leaves traveled over the waterfall and floated into the eddy to get caught in the circling waters, while others floated past, following the creek.

"What are you thinking about?" It was Kami again.

Ryan snapped out of his thought-induced coma. "What?" Kami repeated his question.

"I was thinking about things that Sam used to talk to me about. I was watching the leaves there in the eddy. They're caught; they keep going around in the same circle. Sam, one day on the river, pointed to a bunch of leaves doing this same thing and said, 'Look at those, life is like this. Leaves and people are a lot alike. They see a group of people and the group seems to be going somewhere, so they follow. It's because they think that they are going to be part of something, something going somewhere. They're so desperate to be part of something, they question little, just fallow. They're unable to see the end of the circle. So all they're doing is traveling in endless circles, always moving, going nowhere. Humans are desperate to identify with a group or tribe. They don't understand that we are all travelers and need to walk our own lives. Now watch those leaves and remember what I just said. Remember there's something that I didn't say, and that's what you have to figure out for yourself.' I think I understand." There was a look of contentment on Ryan's face. He had a smile that said that a large piece of the puzzle had come together.

"Could you tell me what you mean when you said that you think you understand?"

"I should have said that I now know what Sam meant. We gravitate toward groups or religions in the belief that they're going somewhere. We believe we'll end up arriving at some point in time and at that same place with this group, whatever or wherever that place might be. But a circle is a circle is a circle, life itself is a circle. Even the leaf that isn't caught in the eddy is still traveling on the outside of this ball we call earth, which is, in essence, still a circle. The water is the spirit, the soul is the traveler. The spirit is the wind that fills the sail, the soul is the ship, time is the river. The spirit is the dancer and the soul is the audience witnessing the moment. It's all part of the great circle of waters."

"I watched the trout rising to pick a ladybug from the surface, creating a ring on the surface of the water. The rings briefly travel with the current while still radiating out from their center, connecting the event to everything the ring touches. Then another ring is created. Each announces the death of a bug and says that the trout will live a little longer. The circles of life and death are interconnecting. As a life is lost, another is sustained, this is the way and reason balance is maintained."

"Last night you told me that your friend, Sam, left you with another question, 'What does God need us for?' Did you ever find an answer to his question?" Kami's question made Ryan pause for a moment and think.

"Well, at first I had to think real hard, it seemed like a strange question. I was a born-again, Bible-thumping Christian. I had all the answers. God needed our love and the reward for our love was His love and everlasting life in Heaven. Being fourteen years old at the time, this was my best guess. Later I studied the Bible and listened to different ministers, some liberal, some more fundamental in the way they viewed the Bible. There was a vast difference in the face that they placed on God. I took off my Son glasses and looked into other religions. I found that most religions had similarities in truths and myths, truths and myths that were open to interpretation by these so-called teachers of truth. Each one saying that they had the only truth and the only right answers, yet they all had different truths. Some of these people were so closed minded that only their interpretation was the right one. Listening to them, hearing that theirs was the only right way, and to think otherwise was a sin. They believed that their God was the only God or the biggest God. I had a problem with this." Ryan broke into song, a take off from an old dog food commercial, the old Kennel Ration song. "My God's bigger than your God. My God's bigger than yours. My God's bigger because he is inspiration. My God's bigger than yours. By the time they'd finished with me, I didn't know if God was the boogie man or Santa Clause, who's making a list checking it twice, going to find out who's naughty or nice. Then maybe he was the universe's biggest voyeur who was watching everything, and keeping notes." Ryan paused.

"I don't know if I understand your answer," Kami said as he scratched his head.

"That's because, I haven't given it yet. I was just catching my breath. All that other stuff is the history behind my answer, that is coming in a minute. I looked at the way life teaches us our lessons and noticed that while life creates the questions, it also reveals the answers. When Sam showed me how to use mugwort, he said, 'God doesn't create a poison without leaving the antidote or cure nearby.' So the way I think, right or wrong, God needs not only humans but every living thing, to feel and live life through us, so He's is in all of us. Like Manuel said, 'We should live the life He gave us to its fullest and not waste the gifts He gives us, even if it's just a grape. Death follows us every minute of our lives. Death is like a cat with a ball of twine. Always there toying with us and our love ones. Everyday there are hundreds of close calls that we walk past, oblivious to this fact. Death plays this game until we come to the end of your string, then it loses interest. Live and never miss a chance to tell a friend or family member that you love them. This is all gone too soon.'"

"I feel that we are given everything we need, both the good things and the bad. They're ours before we're born, so our life's experiences will all be different. While we work the problem called life, we create the formula and solve the equation with our last breath. Maybe God waits for our answer and the question is, where is God in all of this? Each lesson is to teach us how to define our lives for ourselves. At some point, hopefully we gain the wisdom and not allow others to define us. I also believe that we can't experience everything in just one lifetime; it takes more than one lifetime. We are books bound to bone wrapped in flesh, a story to be told, a song to be sung. Maybe this is how God experiences life-through us, he lives."

"Very good. That theory sounds as good as any. But what if you're wrong?"

"Well, Christians believe that Jesus was God's only son, others say that Jesus was a man and a prophet. I think we are all God's children and that each of us again has a bit of God in us, God being a parent of quite a large, diversified and somewhat dysfunctional family. He has to have a great sense of humor and hopefully a lot of patience for an inquisitive child, or maybe in my case, just maybe a retarded one."

Kami smiled and nodded his approval at Ryan's answer. "So this is what you believe. How do you pray?"

"The same way I'd talk to my Dad or Mom. I ask a question, and then believe that an answer will show up when I need it. I was told once the difference between praying and meditating. Praying is talking to God and meditating is shutting up long enough to listen to the answer. I can only imagine how much noise God has to put up with all that praying and so little listening. Then there's the chanting and posturing, the traditional chaining and chanting of prayers. If you were standing in front of a telephone waiting to make a call. So lets see, your there waiting behind people. People who believed that they had to jump up and down and all around, or talk in tongues, or chant some endless prayer before picking up the phone and dialing. Wouldn't you decide that you'd either find another phone or give up and forget it all together? Then think of all the things that are done in God's name. Some horrible, terrible things. I think that if God wanted these things to be done he is more than capable of doing them himself with out our help. "

Kami nodded his head and said "Yes."

Ryan smiled. "Yes, that's what I thought-we think a lot alike. We're like children who want to show a parent how high we can jump or how good we can sing or how well we can recite a poem. We demand that we be watched, 'screaming watch me! Watch me.' We're self-serving and self-centered, demanding heaven, and creating hell on earth. If we can't create heaven here, why do we deserve it somewhere else after we die? It must be annoying as hell to have to put up with arrogant children and this never-ending din of noise. I've learned to whisper to God, giving thanks to him for the beauty of the sun rising and setting and the life that falls between those two events. I lie quietly and listen for God to whisper back, with the answer I need. Sometimes it's not the answer that I was hoping for, but it's always the one I need. Sometimes, I guess, I just needed a spanking."

"Yes, I see." Laughing as he said this, Kami then looked at the scars on Ryan's knees and shoulder and asked, "Have you been in war or a battle?"

Ryan looked at the scars and said, "No, football. The knee kept me from entering the service. I tried to enlist, but they told me that I was a liability and they were right-I would have been a liability. The doctors tell me that some day they'll have to replace the knee joint or maybe even amputate my leg all together."

"You didn't really give me an answer about other hero's like your uncle, were they all warriors. "My uncle was a hero not only because he was in World War II but how he lived his life afterwards. So the answer is again yes and no. Everybody who servers their country's needs in war or peace are hero's. I'll tell you about two who served in World War II. They served in the European theater. As a paratrooper Mr. Stedman made all four major jumps behind enemy lines and was the recipient of four purple hearts. Mr. Hideto (Nelson) Tanaka he was an American born Japanese, after Pearl Harbor his family lost all their properties because the government made them to relocate. They lived in this dry dusty camp out in the desert. This didn't stop Mr. Tanaka from joining the army. He was assigned to the all Japanese unit the 442/100th (A) Company. It was one of the most decorated units of the war. Remember when we talked about prejudice. After the war was over Mr. Tanaka was given the job of returning the bodies of fallen comrades, he was limited to returning only minorities solders. It became his duty, and his honor to do so. These two men are hero's not just because they fought in a war, but what they did after the war, was just as important. Mr. Stedman became a fireman and taught his son's the ways of the of outdoors. Mr. Tanaka help build one of the largest sea food markets in the US and raised a fine family. They're both proud to be Americans. There is one irony that separated these men; Mr. Tanaka had family that lived in Japan during the war. If they had gone over the hill to market that day, they would have been at ground zero for the first atomic bomb. Instead they were witness to the bright flash and dust that flew over the hill that protected them. It was like the spirits of all those that died that day were released and traveled within that bright flash light."

"What war would you have been part of, and did you really want to go and why." Kami voice was somber; he shook his head as he said this.

"Viet Nam, and at first I did want to go. You see, I wanted to avenge my cousin, Clifford Green, who died from wounds he received in Viet Nam. He was a door gunner on a Huey. While providing cover fire for troops trying to get out of a hot landing zone. He was hit four times, leaving him paralyzed. They shipped him home, where we watched him die an inch at a time. The gangrene started at his toes. Doctors whittled him down, eventually stopping at his waist, then he died. There was a terrible odor, like something that was rotting. That smell became Viet Nam to me. The veteran's hospital tried to hide the odor with bleach and Pine-sol, but that just made it worse. These are my bad memories of Clifford. I prefer the good ones, like, when Dad first opened the service station; there was an old case of Big Red chewing gum. The stuff was hard and stale, so Dad let us have the whole case. Cliff and I sat down and ate the whole damn case. Our parents were afraid that we'd be so plugged up that they'd have to use a cork screw to get us going again. Clifford was about six years older than me so we didn't do much together but he did play catch with me once in awhile. He also gave me my first baseball mitt. I wish I still had that old mitt. The mitt was an antique. It had super big fingers and a small web, it looked like Mickey Mouse's hand. "

Ryan hadn't noticed it, but while he was talking about the death of his cousin, Kami became lost in his own thoughts. Ryan now noticed that as Kami was no longer following him, then Kami realized the same thing, an appeared to be embarrassed. There was a moment of awkward silence. What was wrong with his guest, wondered Ryan. Maybe he had monopolized the discussion too much or maybe he had said something wrong. Ryan nudged Kami's arm, "What's the matter-you okay?"

Kami stared into the water a moment longer. "It's nothing you said or did, it's something I did once. I need to think. Please forgive me, I need to think." With those words, Kami pushed himself away from the creek's bank and sank deeper into the water. The cold water barely covered Kami's body. He crawled along the bottom until he reached the deeper water at the waterfall. There he sat upright, folded his legs, and let the waterfall run over his head. Ryan had his feet in the water for only fifteen minutes and they were going numb from the cold. He decided to submerge his entire body in the creek and see if he could last as long as Kami. The creek is spring fed and the water seemed colder than it had when he was a kid. Ryan lay there trying to think warm thoughts. He watched an American Water Dipper land nearby. The bird bobbed up and down on the rock where it had landed and then it walked into the creek. Ryan had seen this before, but every time it amazed him. A bird that walks under flowing water on the bottom of creeks, it just seems strange, thought Ryan. He lowered his body until the water was just under his chin. An hour passed, he thought that if Kami could stand this, he could. Time ceased to mean anything; hypothermia was starting to take its toll on him. Then there was silence, he couldn't hear the water flowing past his body anymore. He was almost completely numb. Suddenly there was a muffled thump and then another thump. Was this the last few beats of his heart, Ryan wondered. Before panic set in there was another louder thump, then another sound.

Ryan heard voices, followed by the sound of drums and men locked in battle. He looked down stream and there was the silhouette of a warrior standing in front of what looked like a fog bank. The warrior stood there staring into the mist, as the carnage continued under a blanket of fog. He could see banners flying above the fog looking like shark fins above the waves. Ryan heard warrior's shouts plus the screams of the wounded and moans of the dying. The screams seemed to last forever, in reality, they lasted only a minute or two. Then the warrior slowly turned in Ryan's direction. Ryan saw that it was Kami, fully dressed in ancient Japanese armor. He had a sad look on his face as he walked away from the battle and slowly vanished along with the mist and the noise of battle. Ryan turned his head and looked in Kami's direction. There he still sat, like a stone on the creek's bedrock bottom. This had to be a hallucination caused by the cold. Ryan couldn't take anymore of the cold and pulled his body from the water. He ached all over. He lay himself out on a rock that had been warmed by the sun and watched Kami. He wanted to make sure that Kami didn't drown. A short time later, Kami stood up and walked out of the water. He seemed to be totally unaffected by the cold. Ryan didn't say anything about what he had seen. Besides, he though it was a hallucination from the cold. There was no other explanation.

Ryan said, "Let's put our clothes back on, they should be dry by now." Kami was quiet as they hiked to the truck and drove back to the ranch in silence. Kami wasn't even interested in listening to the radio, he just sat there quietly for the whole ride. Ryan didn't say anything either. Ryan had many things to think about since that first day of hunting. He now had questions that were circling around in his head like those big black birds that were still circling above the ravine.

When Ryan and Kami reached the ranch, they got out of the truck, and Ryan walked over to the pit and removed the tin. What had started in the morning was ending in the late afternoon, with evening closing in fast. Ryan moved the ashes away revealing the hot coals, he placed some kindling on top of the exposed coals. After the kindling caught fire, Ryan put larger pieces in the pit. Kami silently watched while Ryan rebuilt the fire. Something weighing heavily on Kami's mind, Kami took the chair that he had used the night before and carried it over to the edge of the flat. Ryan didn't ask what was wrong. His friend was shaken to the core and sadness draped over him like a shroud. The fire was burning by now and Ryan rummaged around in his dry box to see what he could put together for dinner. The good news was that there were two large cans of baked beans. The bad news, there was only beans not much else. Ryan dug them out and set them on the tailgate. He looked over at his friend and felt bad for Kami but didn't know how to help, so he left him alone to think.

Ryan walked away and headed toward the barn. He walked though the open gate into the pasture and ended up at the base of a big black oak tree. He stood there in quiet respect. There was something here, something that he had thought about every day since the day of the accident, his thoughts focused on a bare patch of dirt beneath the canopy of the oak. Ryan stood there in the shade. Some time had passed before he felt a hand on his shoulder. He turned to see Kami, who had a concerned look on his face. "Are you ok?" Ryan nodded his head. They walked back to the pit, where Ryan opened the beans and placed the cans on the corner of the grill so they wouldn't heat up too fast. While Ryan was doing this, Kami retrieved his chair and placed it back where it was before and both men sat in their chairs. Ryan was the first to speak, he apologized, saying, "This is all we have left for a hot dinner, so it's beans, oranges, and whatever else that's in the dry chest. Tomorrow we'll need to head to town, that's if we decide we want anything besides cold sandwiches. Sandwiches. Yes, we could have a sandwich with our beans."

Kami still had the look of weighted seriousness about him, but he smiled. "You seemed quite concerned this afternoon that we protect the creek and not do it any harm."

"Yes," Ryan replied as he stood to stir the beans.

"You told me stories about growing up along the river. What's the name? Oh, yeah, the Tuolumne River. When you started talking there was a sense of pride in your voice. Then toward the end , the tone of your voice changed as if you were talking about ancient history - as if the river were gone. You started out speaking of magic, and then you tapered off to a whisper. Why?"

"As a kid there was magic along the river, then I grew up. As for the creek, we were on somebody else's property. Invited or uninvited, we needed to respect it and always remember that all of this belongs to the future and we are only the caretakers. I have a need to believe that I'm doing my best not to contribute to the problem. The problem is that the Tuolumne and other rivers have had so much water diverted or impounded that their water flow is much like the creek's. There is so little water flow that they are majorly affected by what would have been a minor problem. When I was a kid, almost any day I could go to the river and catch enough fish for dinner, even if they were just perch, and feed my whole family. A poor person could eat. Sam said, 'Listen to the animals. They'll warn you, let you know when somethings wrong. Listen, always listen, they're rarely wrong.' My daughter Amy was four or five years old, and she loved, and still loves, to fish. I was divorced and needed a way to reconnect with her, so I asked her what she wanted to do. She said she wanted to go fishing. This was something that her sister, Erica, wasn't interested in, but Amy, she wanted to fish. So on a Saturday, Amy and I headed to my secret perch hole. I wanted to show her how fishing was when I was a kid. The river was still there, the rock was still there, but the fish were few, and the ones that we did catch had open sores on them. I was shocked. The river was sick, and I was unaware of what had happened to it. I kept one of the perch and released the rest. On Monday, me and the perch went to a friend of mine at the college where he taught wildlife biology. He looked it over and called me up a couple days later. He said that the perch's sores were caused by flat worms. The reason was warm, slow moving, low oxygenated water. The perch told us that the river was sick and maybe on its last breath. The magic of the river was gone. I guess when you can find everything you need in a store wrapped in plastic, you no longer need to find them in the wild. Unless you can't afford store-bought and need a healthy river to provide for you and your family, that is."

"At one time in Europe, only the royal families had the right to take fish or game. To even own a net or trap, even a hunting dog could mean death of a subject. Dogs that pointed game had there tails cut off so not to give away their use. In America the common folks have had this privilege of being able to harvest fish and game for the table. Since the first human crossed over from Asia some twenty or so thousand years ago, this is the way it has been. Now there are those elite individuals with power, fame, or influence and noble intentions. They wish to stop sportsmen and leave us only what is beneath plastic behind a glass counter in the stores meat section. They've never taken the responsibility that the hunter or fisherman takes when he has harvested game. They have no idea how balance is maintained by hunters and the heritage and tradition behind these activities. They want to keep their children sheltered and completely safe from life. They want their kids never to feel the wind or rain on their faces, a childhood protected into extinction, media raised, is it media's failure or ours? In essence the children will be cocooned in plastic without the skills to live a productive life. A life out in the open, not knowing the chill of the predawn or the thrill of ducks setting their wings over a spread of decoys. These same elitists will fight for the rights, lifestyle and traditions of the native people's in other countries. They embrace these foreign people and their traditions, while shunning hunters and sportsmen in their own country. Denouncing hunters and trying to limit sportsmen rights and traditions that are part of this lifestyle. These are traditions that we are accustomed to and have passed down from one generation to another. There have been so many generations in this country that we are all natives now. Sam said. 'If there's only one drop of blood from the Five Hundred Nations in your blood, you're an Indian.' Believe it or not, most Americans fall into that category. This means that we all have the responsibility of protecting grandmother earth and all her gifts."

"So you blame these elite people or hunters like Charlie for the way people look at today's hunters and fishermen and saying that hunters are the problem, and yet they're not. Because that's what it sounds like to me." There was a sternness in the way Kami said this.

"Again, yes and no. We, and I'm including myself, have a hard time seeing our part in the problem. Some divert their part in the responsibility of what's happening to wildlife and the planet. All they have to do is just point at those like Charlie White Horse and judge all sportsmen by Charlie's example. They will never hear of hunters the likes of Sam Bird. It's the loss of habitat to roads and buildings, plus poor farming practices, that have had the greatest impact on wildlife and our rivers. Then there's the pollution that has damaged the land, air, and water. Need power? Well, build a dam, but you need to provide for the wildlife. We need to learn from our mistakes and correct them. This crazy state we're in sometimes baffles the shit out of me. When the Exxon Valdez went aground in Alaska, Californians drove their cars to the capitol to protest. The oil spill was a disaster for sure, but cars run on oil and gas, and that's the horse that carried those same protesters to the capitol. Even those in Alaska who receive State allotment money from the pipeline are part of the problem. They are as much at fault as everybody who uses petroleum or its bi-products. We've become a country of consumers and non-producers. We use words like 'interactive' to sale computers and electronic games. The world outside is interactive, life is interactive. We need to fix our problems and balance our needs with the needs of the environment. If it comes to driving or walking, you bet I'm driving. It reminds me of the time that I had my nephews, Michael who was two and a half years old at the time, and Timothy who was six. They were in the back seat of my car. I had just picked them up at my sister-in-law's in the town of Patterson. They were coming to my house for a sleep-over with my kids. I bought them hamburgers and was headed out of Patterson. We had just crossed over the railroad when it happened-a blood-curdling scream. I pulled over, and looked in the back seat. There Michael sat with his mouth wide open and tears welled up in his eyes. He was glaring straight at Timothy, slowly micro-waving him with his glare. There was more than an accusing look on Michael's face. Timothy, on the other hand, was shocked and looked as confused as I was. Michael now was caught in that place where a kid can't really cry or scream but just take in small short breaths. I looked Michael over, maybe a bee had came in the open window and stung him. Nothing. I finally got him to settle down enough to tell me what was wrong. He pointed to Tim and said, 'Somebody bit my tongue.' He had bitten his own tongue when we went over the railroad tracks and he couldn't accept the blame or the fact that what happened was an accident, or his part in his own pain. Some people never seem to grow out of the terrible two's. Homes and roads, whole cities pave over and cover habitat. Yes, I'm also guilty as charged, but I understand balance. Then there are those who are verbal and loud, they've been slighted by life and want government intervention. It's always somebody else's fault, that's why they're screwed up and the world is screwed up. They take no responsibility for their own actions. They ask our government to pass laws like the twenty thousand plus gun laws to protect us from ourselves and solve all the problems we've have created. Hunters have raised more than fifteen billion dollars for habitat. Habitat that is used by hunters and non-hunters alike. For the most part, hunters are quiet, saying little, asking little. These sportsmen and women are cleaning up and reclaiming wildlife habitants. They're taking responsibility for themselves and other hunters, all this, while being beaten about the head and shoulders by those who will not or can not understand the importance that hunting plays in wildlife management. I'm up on my soapbox again and have given you a long-winded answer; I'll try to shorten them up a bit. Anyway, the beans are warm. Let's eat." There was passion in Ryan's voice. The men were hungrier than they thought and dinner was short but sweet. Ryan was still hungry and said, "Let's make a couple sandwiches. Oh, I forgot, we still have a little soda left to go with the sandwiches, if that's okay with you."

Before Ryan could get out of his chair, Kami said, "Sit, I'd like to have some tea."

"Well, I wish I could help you there, but all we have is half a bottle of soda. I guess I could go up to the house and see if there's any tea there."

"That's not necessary; I think you need a little magic." With that Kami reached into his shirt and brought out what appeared to be a folded piece of black fabric. "Do you know what this is?"

"A napkin, or a table cloth for a very small table. It doesn't look like a tea pot. I give up."

"Well, let's see." With those words, Kami pulled at the fabric, folding it into the shape of a bird, then a butterfly and a horse. Before Ryan could say anything, Kami unfolded the cloth. It now appeared to be a rather large black sack. Kami reached into the sack and came out with a Japanese tea bowls, then the tea and a ceramic pot to boil water. This was followed by all that was necessary for a traditional tea ceremony. There was a beautifully glazed bottle filled with water. Kami even produced a short stool that he placed near the fire. Ryan's mind went into tilt, this couldn't be real. Kami sat next to the stool. He placed everything on the stool, which was really a table of sorts and prepared to make the tea. Kami explained the significance of each movement he made. Then he presented the tea bowl to Ryan and instructed him how to accept the bowl and how to turn it one hundred eighty degrees before taking a sip. After sipping the tea, Ryan tried to get a good look at the tea bowl, even by fire light it was still impressive for its texture and glaze.

"This was a surprise, not just the magic show, but these bowls. They appear to be very old. How did you do this, anyway?" asked Ryan.

"Magic, like I said. I'm still a little hungry." Kami reached into the sack and produced many different foods. Some were wrapped in bamboo leaves while others were in small bowls. He placed some items on the ground and others on the cold end of the grill. Ryan could only watch in amazement. Kami rolled and turned the different foods on the grill and then handed Ryan something wrapped in bamboo leaves. Ryan unwrapped it, inside was fish and rice and a sweet sauce. After he had finished, another was placed in his hand. This time there was some sort of meat like beef and bamboo shoots and ginger. Then the other dishes were presented, and to finish it off, some sort of lightly sweetened dessert. "Is there anything else that you would care for?"

Ryan rubbed his belly. "Nope, I think I'd explode if I tried to eat one more thing." Kami placed the leaves in the fire and gathered up the bowls, placing them in his bag. Kami shook out the bag again like one would shake out a table cloth. The bag now appeared empty. "That's some trick."

"Trick? Is your belly not full?"

"Yes, but it has to be a trick." Ryan seemed firm until Kami invited him over to inspect the bag and the ground around him. Nothing was there-just an empty bag and dirt under Kami's feet. Now Ryan wasn't sure and things that he held to be solid didn't feel so solid anymore. Yet somehow this fell in with everything that had happened up to this point. Ryan sat back down. He sat there quietly for a moment and then said, "At the creek, I saw something, something that I passed off as a hallucination caused by the cold water. I heard drums and men locked in battle. I saw banners in the mist and the sounds of men dying. Hell, I even for a moment thought I could smell it. Then I saw you standing there watching, wearing armor with two swords in your hands. You watched for a few minutes and then you turned and walked away. What the heck was that?"

"Yes, I'll answer your question and any other that you might think of, but first answer a question for me. The first day that I met you, when you awoke, could you still smell the fragrance of the tree and hear the sound of the blossoms in the breeze?" This visibly shook Ryan. How could Kami know of his dream?

In a low voice from a place deep within him, Ryan could hear his voice. It sounded as if it were somewhere else. Somewhere in the distance came an answer. "Yes, I could. How do you know this? It was a dream."

"Dream? Maybe, maybe not. How about an answer or maybe it was a gift? Haven't you been remembering what happen? Didn't you think that maybe this is what happens in death, or maybe even heaven for that matter?" There was a gentleness in the way Kami asked his questions.

"Yes, those were some of my concerns and questions. But how could you know this?"

"I followed you. I like you. I once found myself there and also left my patch of flowers. I sat beneath that same tree and asked why I had been given this gift and who had left this tree? I was questioning all, waiting for answers, and then you showed up."

"How could you follow me? It was a dream." Ryan's expression was that of disbelief. Every so often Ryan's rational mind kicked in and somehow rationalize that one abstract event was real and the other was a dream, without substance.

"Well, what I have to believe is that most of your life, you seemed to have done the right things and asked the right questions. You have chosen good heroes. You were open to even questioning God and his needs. So, I guess you were given a gift, a gift that allowed you to see what lies at a different level and reality. It's a reality that's very different from the one we presently believe we're in right now. Perhaps we exist in multi, or even parallel, realties. All I know is that one day I ended up where you did, and instead of leaving and going back as you did, I stayed. I had no choice. I wasn't in the best of shape when I arrived. I needed to learn and to heal. This is my first time back to this place, this reality. Somehow I believe that in some way, part of my healing is connected to you."

"You say that heaven is a multi-level, or perhaps, an alternate reality. Heaven might be infinitely large and infinitely small at the same time - one in space, the other in time. Maybe it's as some people believe, sub-atomic not a solid, without mass, yet weighable, pure potential. A place where light photons collect like sand at the bottom of a hourglass. Or like snow flakes, photons pile up into drifts against heaven's walls, to be picked up on a gentle breeze and float suspended on the membrane of a bubble. There they move along with the particles that have the ability to pass through the universe and not touch anything, and yet are connected to everything, creating new relationships. A place where there isn't anything to indicate the passage of time and everything stands at one edge of infinity. It's like infinity starts at the end of my nose and goes straight out away from me. Then it curves and the other end of infinity is meeting the back of my head at the same time, and if I could spin around fast enough, I could fold time and see infinity coming toward me. What do you think?" There was excitement in Ryan's voice.

"Did I say all that? Sounds a bit complected. Well, I don't understand what you just said, but I think it's simpler than all of that. All I know is that the place where I ended up is a place to learn, like a school. You were right when you said that we are all students and teachers. It seemed that I was there to learn and at times to teach. Then you showed up, and somehow I ended up here with you and in this time. This makes me think that you're right about the time thing, because much has changed since I was here last. Many years must have passed-maybe hundreds, I don't know. When I was there, there seemed to be no concept of time. It seems that I could understand and speak your language, or maybe you're speaking mine, I don't know. All I know is that after I shook your hand and touched other items, pictures started appearing in my mind. As for my dress and the things that I came with, it's like when you said you get what you need. This is what I apparently needed to be here."

"What about the bag and dinner, that was real? How did you do that?"

"That's something I learned from one of my teachers. All things are possible if you believe. It's kinda like your grandmother's mustard seed. My teacher pulled that sack out and asked what scared me the most. When he asked me this question, the sack lay flat on the ground. The sack started to move as if there was something alive in it, alive and mad as hell. It was the thing that most scared me. He instructed me to reach in and face my fear. I did as instructed and nothing was there except a flower. I wasn't afraid of flowers. The exercise was to confront my fears, not to hold what I feared but to release what I was afraid of, the unseen, the unknown. Reaching in the sack accomplished the reason for the lesson and to learn that our fears are limits. They're limits we accept, holding us back. We travel at the limits of our fears. Later he taught me to release the limitations. It was limitations that chained my body and soul to a thought and my spirit to a stone. Then he taught me to focus my thoughts without thinking, just knowing that what I had thought already happened. He taught me to create matter or things at will by focusing without thought, believing that what I willed was within that same sack. After I learned this, he gave me the sack. That's when he gave the sack a name, the sack of self. From that time on, every time I reached into the sack with fear or doubt, I'd pull something other than what I wanted. Sometimes it was something awful, even gruesome, something to remind me of my past, something I chose to hide. Today at the creek, when you started talking about your cousin's death, and described the smell of dying, I found myself thinking thoughts of events and things that I thought were gone and perhaps even forgiven." There was a sadness in Kami's voice.

"So, you say there is an afterlife, and that afterlife is like a school? That doesn't sound like heaven to most people, especially to any kid in school.

Where are the angels and clouds, the ethereal music, where eternal bliss is the order of the day? The extended vacation?" Kami looked a little annoyed "Hey, man, I'm messing with you. It might not be traditional, but what you described sounds good to me. I have to wonder that, if we are on different levels of consciousness and, let's say, different levels of enlightenment here, after we pass, there are different levels of enlightenment in heaven also? How do we meet our friends and relatives there if we're in different levels in life?" Ryan's questions still seemed a bit baited.

"You said heaven, I said school. Heaven maybe? Yes, you'll see those who have connected to you, or their essence, anyway. It's like you said about the rings on the water. The rings travel, connect, and relate to each other even after the event that created the rings have long past. Rings are circles within circles and, again, as you said, infinity is still a circle." There was the tone of assuredness in Kami's voice. This calmed the fear that had been churning in the pit of Ryan's stomach.

"What did you mean when you said that the essence of those who have passed would meet you? Last night I saw something out of the corner of my eye, something like people watching us. Then when I fell asleep and later woke up, I remembered seeing friends and relatives who had passed come up where I sat, greet me, and then walked away. I wanted to follow, but something held me back. Did that really happen? Why had they come here?" I said, "it's like a school. We are there to learn and that first lesson is that when we are alive, we learn life lessons. When we sleep we dream of spiritual lessons. What we need to learn on one of the other planes. So, in essence, your sleeping mind is walking and living a moment on that other plane, while your body is on this one. On the other plane, we're shown how to be on more than one plane at a time. The idea that God is everywhere at the same time and spirits watch over us, in a way, is right. As you said, I believe that God's in everyone and everything, even the rocks. Then even when we pass, his essence goes with us and travels within our spirit or soul. He is the connector that binds the rings. When you pray or think or tell a story about a loved one, they often are there with you, to listen, observe, and learn. Sometimes it's like they're watching TV, like when you told me about your grandmother was watching wrestling and yelling at the TV. In some cases, if you're in danger or doing something wrong, you hear a voice warning you. Or you become aware that something is wrong with a family member or friend and at that instant, they call you. Or for some unexplainable reason, you turn and go another direction, then to later hear about some accident in the direction that you decided not to go. The answer that seems to come from nowhere, just out of the blue, often as gentle as a breeze, in most cases it is them yelling at the screen. Only there isn't any screen, and you react to what you perceive. It's the love that connects us, and God is love. I'm sure that you've heard that before. So, if your there to learn, would this be considered a homework assignment or extra credit? Don't get me wrong, I want to believe. You say that this might be a gift, or that maybe I asked the right questions. It's like an alien landing and contacting some farmer, the alien giving the farmer all the answers to all of mankind's problems. But after the alien leaves, the farmer will remember only fragments of the encounter and pieces of the answer. Of course people have been waiting for God or aliens or science to show up and save us from our governments or maybe just ourselves. Then there are those who stand on street corners, crying out that the end is near. I believe that those who are waiting for help will be disappointed. It's said that God helps those who help themselves. Again, we need to make our heaven where we are and not wait for someone to bring it to us. As for the guy on the corner, he's right, the world will end someday. What a hollow victory that would be. He stood there and let life walk right on by without even living it or, for that matter, seeing it." There still was a bit of skepticism in Ryan's voice.

"You're right. On this level, it sounds a bit outlandish and alien, as you stated, but, again, it's not all about you. I'm here to learn something for me. Maybe if I tell you about me, we might figure out what it is. I was born in the time of the Tokugawa period in Nipon. My mother died when I was young. I started life being called Ben No Suke, this was my first name. Later they would give me many names. I chose part of one of those names to introduce myself to you. When I was old enough, my uncle enrolled me in a school of Kendo. I learned to bind or fold Zen and Shintoism together along with other philosophies. When I say fold together, I mean in the way that a master sword smith folds and pounds metals to create a great sword. It's hardened on the outside and soft in the middle. If it's too brittle, it breaks, and if it's too soft it won't hold its edge. Then there's the word master. I was called master; I learned everything about techniques and the strategies of war. To be a strategist is to see patterns in the chaos of battle against single or multiple opponents or armies. I learned everything to be a samurai, to kill in an honorable way. I learned everything except that, that which you wish to master will soon enslave you, bending you to its will. I killed my first man when I was thirteen, after I crossed that line, it became too easy. I killed as I was taught, without fear or thought of killing or even dying. Learning to fight as a dead man without fear and allowed my training to do my fighting. 'Ai Uchi'-to cut an opponent as he cuts you. When he attacks he is open to attack, it's all timing and lack of anger. Then you attain spontaneous knowledge of every situation. There are no surprises-you know ahead of time. To do this, you shed your arrogance and pretense of knowing anything. This is the first step into enlightenment, to understand that you know nothing; this allows the universe to pour into the void. This can happen in the blink of an eye or, in my case, one day during battle, I became aware that it was all pointless. What honor was gained? Then I heard a bird singing. Its song seemed louder than the noise of the battle. I looked around and located the bird. It was sitting there on the ground with the battle waging all around it. I went to pick it up, but it flew a few feet away and continued to sing. Then it started do what only could be called a dance, spreading its tail feathers like a fan and strutting and singing. I followed as it continued to move through the battle. I felt invisible, no one challenged my travel."

Ryan thought of the first sparrow he'd killed on that Sunday so long ago and the hundreds that followed and of the night when the mocking bird sang.

Kami continued, "I followed the bird past the field of battle onto a little knoll that overlooked the fighting. At that point, I turned for one last look. The bird continued to move away, I followed it to a cave not far from here we started. This would become my home. It was close enough to the battle field that I could smell the decay that follows death. The sounds of the dying and the smell filled the cave, lingering there like ghosts. At night their spirits moved around, rustling the leaves outside the cave. For years their spirits called to me from the darkness, taunting me and challenging me to come out and fight. There was madness to the life I was living, as there was to the life I had left. The bird's songs held me back and focused my momentary madness. I shared my rice with the bird and it was my only company. He lived a long life for a bird. When the bird passed, another took his place, like the changing of the guard, and I, a willing prisoner. To earn some money, I wrote a book about strategy and my way of fighting. This was a bad move because others came to test me. I had long since given up steel swords. The very swords that, at one time I thought contained my spirit, in reality contained only my ego. I now use wooden swords or sticks to defeat those who came to challenge me. At times I still had to kill, when there was more than one opponent attacked at a time. Then one day, I decided that I would kill no more. It was at this point that I put to use my other training. I wrote poetry, painted, and created sculpture. I practiced the art of art, being involved in the process of creation. I was trying to forget the process of killing and destruction. I now participated in creation, which was infinitely more rewarding, filling an empty place inside and healing some of my wounds. When you talked about your cousin, I remembered the smell. I again smelled the decay of rotting flesh that once permeated my soul." Kami's voice went from pride to shame as he talked, but for only a brief moment.

"So, do you believe that all war is bad?"

"No, it's not necessarily good or bad. There are bad reasons to wage war, like you said. God can do His own warring, He doesn't need our help. Remember, when war has to be fought, heroes are made on each side. Heroes should be honored by both sides as worthily opponents, who deserve respect. But to take life for meaningless things, like with gangs you mentioned, and turf wars, killing over property they don't even own or for lapse of etiquette, are all senseless reasons to take or to lose life. Governments at times are as guilty as individuals for bad reasons to go to war. I, for all these years, have had lessons to learn to heal my spirit and soul from all my sins. Instead of coming back to live other lives, I waited until the healing was almost complete. It was only after I saw you under the tree that I knew that the last piece of the puzzle had something to do with you."

Still thinking of the sparrow Ryan looked into the ambers that remained of the fire. He heard what Kami had been saying. He raised his head to speak, but all he could do is stammer out fragments of words. Shame held his tongue and muted his voice.

"Is there something you need to say? Please speak." There was an understanding tone in Kami's voice.

"No, there was something I was thinking of, but it's not important. But remember when you said that we're connected by a question and an answer? Have you figured out what they are?"

"Yes, but now you have to figure it out." Kami picked up the sack and raised it up to hide his face. He held it there for a second and then tossed the sack into the air. Ryan watched it as it rose and began to fall toward the fire pit. He jumped to catch it, but before he could touch it, it had disappeared into nothing, like the smoke of the fire. It was gone as was Kami. All that remained was an empty chair. Only the feeling of abandonment was left. Ryan was left with the same feeling he had at the end of the dream on that first day of the season.

Ryan slept an uneasy sleep, waking now and then to stare at the empty chair in front of him. For all this, it remained a empty chair. Not long after daylight, Ryan started to break camp. He moved the ashes around in the pit and poured the water from the ice chest over the coals and covered them with dirt. He placed everything in the back of the pickup, but when he went to the tree where his bow hung, to his surprise, the bow that Kami had was still there. He broke down his bow and placed it and the arrows into the truck, leaving Kami's bow where it hung. He opened the truck door and climbed in behind the wheel. Before he put the key into the ignition, he looked up into the air above the ravine and saw that the vultures were still there. He had been lost in thought and hadn't remembered them. Curiosity got the better of him. Getting out of the truck, he wondered off down into the ravine. Before he reached the patch of mountain misery someone shouted, "Hey! What the hell do you think you're doing?" Ryan spun around, there stood Kami. "Talked to your friend Sam. You're right, he is a good teacher, with many students, and the beliefs that he held as sacred are a lot like the beliefs of my culture. Again, like you said, truth is truth." Kami walked past Ryan.

Ryan stood still, almost afraid to ask the question that had been on his mind since the vultures arrived. "Kami, did you come back here for me or for your bow? What or who are they here for? Am, I still on that hillside?" He pointed to the black birds circling overhead.

"No, I came back for him." Kami pointed around a bush that hid where Ryan had fallen asleep on Saturday.

Who's him? thought Ryan. Ryan walked over to Kami and looked around the bush to see what appeared to be the buck that he saw with Kami in the ravine on the second day. The buck lay motionless, its head to one side, he was dead.

"How or why did he die?"

"It was just his time, and, who knows? Maybe before he died, he asked the question, where do humans go when they fall asleep and dream?"

"I have a problem. Is it okay to hunt and take game? I now find myself conflicted, and I'd like some help with an answer."

"Do you think lions or eagles contemplate the right or wrong of a decision to take a life to maintain life? It's necessary to maintain balance. Just do it as Sam taught you and you'll be okay." Kami smiled and raised his arm to shoulder height. He whistled, and a falcon flew down and landed on his arm. "Is that Care-if-val?" Ryan was captured again in the falcon's gaze. He was held there as he had been on that first day he had seen her.

"Yes, she wanted to see you, but there's another one that wanted to see you even more." Ryan hadn't noticed the sack draped over Kami's other outstretched arm. Kami lowered this arm to reveal a dog.

"K.C.! God I miss you!" All Ryan could do was hug the dog and cry. K.C. was with Ryan when he wrecked his other truck five years before. Ryan came close to dying, K.C. did. K.C. now sleeps with a stuffed toy animal beneath the black oak in the pasture. He was alive after the accident and had tried to protect Ryan from the firemen who were trying to remove Ryan from the wreckage. Ryan gave K.C. the command to leave the truck. Ryan felt guilty because he lived and K.C. died. It was like he had left a buddy behind. Ryan looked up at Kami and asked, "Can I go with you?"

"No, that's not possible. You have a lot to learn. Your lessons are just starting to get interesting, aren't they? Besides, there's something that you have to do, you need to face your fears."

"Which fears are you talking about?" There was confusion and fear within Ryan, and it reflected on his face.

"For one, you need to write about your dream and those wonderful stories and adventures. At least do it for your grandchildren and other family members. This isn't a choice; this is something that you have to do. You were chosen. Tell of the heroes, help heal the river, find the magic. If it's too hard to find, create it. Believe that all that's promised on the arch is possible and will come to pass. Perhaps wealth is really only subjective. You, yourself, said that in the stories of family, and that of the elderly were treasures. This is were you said that you had found to be real wealth. This is treasure that needs to be shared with those who will listen. It's a treasure that can be given away, without dwindling away, like a smile given without thought of loss and received without thought of owing. It's returned as good as it was received."

"I can read, but I can't write. That's something that I absolutely can't do," Ryan said as he stared at the ground. He had a look of shame on his face and agitation in his voice.

"It's an absolute fool who believes in absolutes. These are just limits that you accept. Believe me, you can. Don't be worried, there will be a time when we'll meet again. There are those who only know a life of substance and are poor. Then there are those who know the substance of light and obtain wealth of a different kind. The question that you have wondered about so many times, does the sparrow matter? The answer is, the sparrow does matter as do all things. Nothing and no one is insignificant." Kami's answer was so simple, so uncomplicated. Then Kami reached into his pocket and brought out a small sculpture of a sparrow and handed it to Ryan, saying, "Take it, it's yours." Ryan held the sculpture, tears streaking his cheeks. Wiping them away he asked Kami, "Kami, what answers did you get?"

Kami smiled and said, "You have given me a great gift, you shared your family with me. I never had the love of family. I now know what it is to be part of a family, and I now know that we are all family. I understand what I was missing - love. Thank you my friend. Now may I call you brother?"

"Yes," was all that Ryan said.

Kami again smiled, then he turn and walked away. He shimmered for a second, then he, K.C. and Care-if-val disappeared.

Ryan headed back up the hill. He walked past the truck, past the barn to the garden and the crypt that held the remains of his parents. There Ryan placed the sparrow into the open palms of the kneeling angel that sits atop the crypt. It must have been a trick of light and shadow - the sad angel seemed to smile. On the way back to the truck, Ryan went over to Kami's bow and removed it from the tree limb. Something caught his eye, and there on the ground it was a tea bowl. Ryan picked it up. This time it didn't startle him and he didn't even turn around when he heard Kami's voice say, "They are gifts. Oh, yeah, remember one man's miracle is another man's magic, and wisdom is a fruit slow to ripen. Then, in the end, ask yourself this question. Were you loved, and how well did you love?" Then Kami started laughing. "Who's this Minnie Pearl you thought I looked like that first day? Never mind, it was a joke, wasn't it?"

Ryan laughed along with the familiar voice but only said one word, "Thanks."

Later that year, during rifle season, Ryan harvested a nice buck. He did all that Sam had taught him. He said a prayer to the spirit of the buck, telling the spirit how unworthy yet proud he was. He said how privileged that such a buck would allow him the honor of offering his flesh to feed his family and friends. Ryan then offered the buck a ceremonial gift of food and water. He promised the buck that because his flesh would feed Ryan's friends and family, Ryan would bring hay to feed the buck's kin through the winter. Ryan shared the venison and stories with his remaining friends who had given to him the gift for the love of the outdoors. It was the gift of showing him the way of the sportsman and of the responsible hunter. The ones that shared their experiences, enriching him and all who stayed and listened to their stories.

One day less than a year later, pencil met paper. Fear began to rise which quickly turned to terror. Ryan could read but writing still terrified him. Then, in an unsure hand, he began filling the paper with words. It was four thirty in the afternoon. The checklist was complete; everything was accounted for and loaded into the truck. Ryan paused a moment and took a deep breath. When his pencil next touched the paper his fear was gone. Ryan thought to himself. Someday we'll see each other again in the tall grass beneath a tree of blossoms. When we meet I'll have a story to tell.

This was the start of a new journey down a long road. Many more stories and new heroes were to be added and circles continued to make infinite connections. Ryan learned to keep it simple. He never forgot to make a little magic every day. He smiled often and reveled in the wonder of a bird in flight across stained glass skies.

BONUS
SHORT STORY

NEVER TRUST A DOG THAT WINKS

There we lay staring into each other's faces, eye to eye, first one to blink loses. After about ten minutes, it happened; his left eyelid slid down over his eye, then opened back up. Did this count as a blink, did I win? Was my will the greater, or did he just wink at me? To test this last question, I winked at him with my right eye. He then repeated what he had just done before. Yes, he was winking at me. I gave myself a pat on the back. I hadn't lost my touch. I had picked out a smart pup, one that was quick to learn. But then again he might have been the one doing the picking. After all, he was the first of his litter to come forward and wrestle with my shoe strings and pant cuffs. Since we were lying on the carpet and making such great progress, an idea struck me that maybe I'd try to see if he'd roll over if I did. Well, I rolled over to the left, then to the right and back again. When I had stopped rolling, I looked back at the pup. With his tongue hanging out the side of his mouth, he had what could only be described as a puppy smile on that hairy mug of his. He seemed quite pleased with himself. Then he winked at me again. I tried to show him one more time. He just sat there looking kinda smug. He then stretched out his paw and kind of patted me on the hand as if he was saying, "good boy." It was as though he was thinking how good a trainer he was, after all, it was less than twenty minutes and he already had me winking and rolling over. This was our beginning. I ended up naming this pup K.C.

He was my first dog in fifteen years. Since there was a lot of traffic where I lived, he would also be the first dog that I ever let stay indoors most of the time, when I was home. At first he stayed in the laundry room, but within two months he had weaseled his way into the bedroom. We had gotten past that awkward housebreaking phase of the training in record time. He was really a fast learner, but then again, I've always found that most Labrador's had this same trait. One day, when I was taking the dirty clothes to the laundry room, I dropped a sock and the pup picked it up and followed me to the hamper. The next day, this chore became his job. He performed this duty with great gusto, making many trips bringing a mouth full of laundry each time. I would wait in the laundry room, and he would do the rest. When he finished, I'd give him a treat.

I didn't know how devious a critter this pup was until one day when he had finished doing his chores. I knew that was all the clothes, but I asked him to double check anyway and see if he had missed anything. He shot out of the laundry room and headed to the bedroom to take another look. His dog tags were clanking all the way, or so I believed. When he returned empty handed, or more precisely empty mouthed, I asked him to have another look. He took off again, dog tags clanking. We played this game every morning. One morning, when he was sent back to check if there was anything left, he was caught red-handed. He had stopped short of the bedroom and was just around the corner out of my sight. There he was, kinda jogging in place, shaking his head and making a lot of noise with the tin hanging from his collar. He was busted. K.C. looked at me, gave me that puppy smile, and I'll be darn if he didn't wink at me. How could you ever be mad at a dog like this? What a performance!

K.C. also made a game out of stealing and hiding things of mine or things belonging to my girlfriends. When we would ask him where he had hid these items, he would cock his head from side to side and gave us that, "who me?" look. He would make a huge production of looking for these things, the big show off. He'd go looking all over the house, eventually finding what he had hid, right where he had hidden it. Now, on the other hand, if you asked him if he wanted to go for a walk and then asked him to find his leash, he would be standing next to you in two seconds flat, holding his leash and ready to go. His tail would be wagging back and forth so hard you'd swear he was leaving bruises on your legs where it hit you.

K.C. was just nine months old the first time we went pheasant hunting. Once again, he showed me how fast he could catch on. The birds were different from the dummies that he had trained with. The real birds were a lot more fun. K.C. was born for this; it was in his every fiber. This moment would defined K.C and my relationship from that point on. Connecting us to the ancient spirits, of the first dog and human to have formed this special bond. Non-hunters wouldn't understand this feeling, or when I say, it's like taking your child to the one place on this planet and witnessing the one thing that triggers the first moment of self-awareness and purpose and reason. This feeling would be repeated every time that we were in the field or out of it for that matter. Like watching his eyes as he tracked birds that crossed the sky even while we relaxed in the backyard. There are few words to describe the feeling you get when you see a pup getting birdie for the first time.

The first bird he found was flushed from the deep cover out of the tules that grow on the levees next to the rice stubble we where hunting. The bird busted cover and went almost straight up. As it flatten out and started flying away from us, I shot, knocking him down near a telephone pole. I saw where the rooster fell and headed in that direction, K.C. following close behind. Because this was his first bird, I didn't expect him to run in and retrieve it, but I did expect him to stay with me. When I got to the spot, I knew the rooster had to be there. After all, I had seen it hit and then there was all these feathers on the ground where I stood. This had to be the spot all right. I looked around for K.C. He had stopped twenty or so feet behind me. I knew the bird was where I was and I tried to call K.C. over, but he wouldn't budge. I called him again, trying to get him excited and all worked up- it worked. He was really excited. He was wagging his tail so hard that, it was more like a whole body wag. He still wouldn't come to where I knew the bird had to be. I kept calling him and saying, "dead bird, seek find, lets go boy, find the dead bird, come on boy." He only became more excited but he was steadfast, solidly anchored in place. He finely stopped waging his tail, looked me in the eye and then looked down at his paw and then back at me. He kinda shook his head from side to side, as if he was disappointed. Like he couldn't believe that I was so slow to catch on, maybe even a little stupid. I walked over to him, fully intending to take him by the collar over to where I knew the bird was. I started to pull him, but he wouldn't budge. Then something moved in the tall grass beneath his paw. The bird was completely hidden and he was only wounded. K.C. was holding it down with his paw. Not long after this, he must have thought it would just be easier to bring the birds to me since I wasn't bright enough to learn this trick myself. By the third season, he pretty much had me trained.

K.C. loved to ride in the truck or the boat. On one occasion, we were on the Delta fishing. We had been there since sunrise and it was late in the day when K.C. made it known that nature was calling and he needed to go to shore. He pawed my arm, pulling at me and looking at me in the face and then looking over to the trees at the water's edge. It seemed as if every time we were ready to pull anchor and head to the bank, the fish would start biting again. I walked to the forward end of the boat. K.C. followed me. I looked down and saw the drain hole that lets any water that comes over the bow to run back out of the boat and into the river. I half jokingly told him, "If you need to go, use the drain hole." You should have seen the look on my fishing buddies faces when he did just that.

Later that year, during pheasant season, we were waiting for the fog to raise off the hunting club. I told the boat story to one of the old timers, Windy was his nick name, short for Wendell. There might have been some other reason for this nick name? Anyway, he'd had heard it all and seen it all; all of these hunters had the smartest dogs in the field and would tell you so. So he politely listened, occasionally yawning and stretching. Windy then asked me if K.C. was a male or female? I answered, male but neutered.

Then he added, "Does he always squat to pee?" I was taken aback by his question and asked him when he had seen K.C. pee. He kinda chuckled and pointed towards my left foot. I had been holding K.C. on a short leash and he had just squatted and peed in the dirt close to my shoe. I looked down at K.C. and kiddingly scolded him, saying that I could have stepped in it. K.C. put his head down and began to push some dirt up with his nose to cover the round wet spot at my foot. After he had pushed about an inch of dirt over the spot, he tamped the dirt with his nose. The old man hadn't spoke a word, just stood there slack jawed, while all this was happening. When K.C. had finished, Windy dropped to one knee and with his gloved hand wiped the dirt off K.C.'s nose, telling him what a good boy he was.

Windy looked up at me and said, "You know, I didn't believe you about the boat, but now I have to. The sad part is that I'll be telling your story and adding to it what I have just seen and nobody's going to believe me either."

K.C. and I went everywhere together and since I was working swing shift, there were many opportunity's for him to ride with me, like when I was out paying bills and such. I kept a small stuffed toy animal on my dashboard and often when I was out of the truck K.C., would take it down and play with it. Sometimes I'd see him tossing the toy into the air and catching it; he was gentle with it and never damaged it in any way. Other times he would hide it. When I'd ask him where it was, he'd turn his head as though he didn't hear me, or he'd wink and give me that, "Who me look?" that I was so used to seeing. Then, he'd dive under the seat or the dash and retrieve it from where he had hidden it.

One day, my oldest daughter asked me if I'd take K.C. to the school where she was helping teach. These kids at one time were called problem children. They were the under privileged or were born drug addicted children, all of them had some kind of behavioral problem. My daughter wanted to see how the children would interact with K.C. I gave the kids a short lecture about hunting and hunting dogs. The kids seemed to be more interested in K.C than they were about anything I had to say. Some of them had, had bad experiences with dogs and were a bit scared of them, but K.C's gentle nature won even these kids over. He was a big hit. Oh, yeah, did I mention that K.C. was a bit of a ham, the big show off. I had become the straight man for a smart ass dog, he stole the show. Every child had a chance that day to throw the dummy for K.C. he'd retrieve each and every one of their tosses. The kids loved him.

When my father was in a convalescent hospital, I would take K.C. along to visit. K.C. made friends fast and he was loved on and by the old folks. He happily returned their love with interest.

There doesn't seem to be a family in this country that is untouched by this problem. The problem was drugs, and my mother was having trouble with a niece that she'd taken in. My niece had fallen in with a bad crowd; she was drinking heavily and into drugs. She was giving my mom huge attitude and creating even bigger problems. One day mom needed me to help her with some things around the ranch; I left K.C. with mom for a while. Before I left to do these chores, I told him to "Take care of mom and protect her, don't let anybody bother her or mistreat her." He laid down at Mom's feet and every time my abusive niece acted out K.C put her in check. He seemed to know what needed to be done and did it. I wish that I could have taken credit for this but it wasn't anything that I trained him to do. I wouldn't even know how to start training him for this, but somehow he just knew?

It was starting to get a little scary. At times I would test how close we were by thinking of things for him to do. Sometimes he would do what I was thinking before I asked him to. Unbelievable, yes, but true.

Because he almost always rode in the cab with me, it was only natural for him to be beside me that day, a day when things went bad. We were headed up to the ranch to visit with Mom. There was a forest fire running several miles away, in some of the hollows there was a light haze of smoke. I reacted to something in the smoke. My eyes had watered up and I was coughing so hard that it seemed I couldn't get enough air. The truck left the road and I tried to hold K.C. with my right hand and keep him from hitting the dash. I watched the windshield turn opaque and the side window shatter. I saw and heard K.C. hit the dash, I couldn't hold him back. This was the first time that I had ever heard K.C. give out yelp in pain. The truck was resting at the bottom of an oak tree. It had flown fifty feet off the road and had hit the tree ten feet up the tree's trunk. K.C and I were both awake, and stayed conscious, but the pain was intense. I later learned that I had six broken ribs on one side and six on the other. I had lots of blunt force trauma, all my internal organs were involved, everything was badly bruised. The greatest concern was my heart, liver, lungs and spleen. I was a mess and I was the one wearing a seatbelt. How much damage had been done to K.C.?, because when help arrived at the seen of the accident K.C. started growling trying to protect me from these strangers. I was close to becoming unconscious, everything was kinda fuzzy. The firemen said that they needed K.C. to leave the truck before they would even try to get me out. I gave K.C. the order to leave the truck and he shot out of the open door. K.C. stayed at the edge of the woods watching the firemen extract me from the wreckage. I asked them to catch him for me and please hold him until my mom could pick him up. A helicopter had been called in from U.C. Davis and it was waiting for me at the hospital when we arrived, but it would leave without me. The E.R doctors thought that I wouldn't survive the ride. I signed the donor's card and went into surgery. When I woke up my first question was, "Did anyone find my pup?"

K.C. stayed around the crash site. When anybody tried to catch him, he would run into the woods. K.C. might have been waiting for me to return, it was any body's guess. I was held captive, lying there with i.v.'s running into me. Lying there kicking myself in the ass for not having the presence of mind to ask one of the firemen to hand me the leash from the truck bed. I could have hooked it to K.C. Then one of the firemen could have held him for me. Damn it, if I just had asked that one favor! What I needed was to get out of there and find my pup. It was like leaving a friend in the field, I felt that as if I had deserted a buddy. K.C. had always slept in our bedroom, and now he was in a strange dark place, as was I. There wasn't anything I could do, what would he eat?

As soon as I was released from the hospital and with the help of my mom, I returned to the crash site to try and find my pup. I didn't have to call him; K.C. was at the base of the oak tree. He'd curled up around something that must have reminded him of home. The stuffed toy had somehow fallen out of the truck. They were together and will forever remain so. They now sleep in the shade of a black oak at the ranch not far from where Mom and Dad now rest.

NEVER TRUST A DOG THAT WINKS, HE'LL STEAL YOUR HEART.

GIVE YOUR PET A HUG.

THIS BOOK IS DEDICATED TO THE HEROS. THOSE THAT HAVE SERVED THE BETTER GOOD OF THEIR FELLOW MAN AS WELL AS THAT OF THE FEATHERED, FURRED AND FINNED. THEY HAVE PROTECTED WHAT THEY HELD DEAREST, COUNTRY, FAMILY, FRIENDS, WHILE PASSING DOWN TRADITIONS. THEY HAVE LIFTED SPIRITS, CREATED HOPE, AND FOFILLED DREAMS. PRESERVED LIFE WHILE TEACHING US THAT EVERY BREATH IS A GIFT. TO THEY THAT GAVE THEIR VOICE FOR THOSE THAT COULD NOT SPEAK.

SHOW THEM THAT THEY HAVE MADE A DIFFERENCE. HONOR YOUR HEROS AND MENTORS BY WRITING DOWN THEIR NAMES IN THIS BOOK. TELL THEM HOW THEY HAVE TAUGHT YOU LIFE LESSONS. GIVE THEM A COPY OF THIS BOOK EVEN IF IT'S ANONYMOUSLY. WRITE THEIR NAME BENEATH HERO IN THE FRONT OF THIS BOOK. THE REST OF THIS STORY IS IN YOUR HANDS FILL IN THE LINES BELOW, FINISH THE STORY, PASS IT ON. LET THE HEALING BEGIN.

WHO KNOWS, MAYBE THOSE THAT ARE IN THE PUBLIC SURVICE WILL BE REMINDED THAT THEY ARE IN THE PUBLIC EYE, AND ON NOTICE. IT'S NOT JUST THE PUBLIC BUT THEIR OWN CHILDREN AND FAMILY'S THAT'S WATCHING. SO THEY CAN RISE TO BE THE HEROS THAT THEY SHOULD BE.

_____

_____

_____

_____

_____

This is where I let you in on a secret; you are now part of the hero's of this story. Hero's, because a good portion of the money raised through sales of will go to scholarships and other education programs. Also, programs making outdoor dreams come true for some vary sick kids. Scholarships for students entering fields of studies connected to wildlife management and habitat. With emphasis on the global environmental issues concerning to natural resources, in all areas of earth sciences. They with our help will receive the tools to help us make better decisions about our country and world. For the greater good of the one place in the universe that we know life exist, planet earth. While keeping the next seven generations in mind.

I'm just a regular guy, I work for Post Cereal, who knows, I might have made your breakfast today. There is one thing that I believe in, if enough regular people get together, great, no extraordinary things can happen. Plato in his book (The Republic) he said, we are all artist, artist by which we do best. I believe that art provokes thought, good art provokes emotions, great art provokes change. This book was written so simple that smart people could understand it, and some of the smartest have. But the very smartest have past it along.

Thank you.

KIM

www.ingramcontent.com/pod-product-compliance
Lightning Source LLC
Chambersburg PA
CBHW030312290526
45785CB00001B/314